Exploring Victorian Travel Literature

Edinburgh Critical Studies in Victorian Culture

Series Editor: Julian Wolfreys

Volumes available in the series:

Visit the Edinburgh Critical Studies in Victorian Culture web page at www.euppublishing.
com/series/ecve

Also Available:
Victoriographies – A Journal of Nineteenth-Century Writing, 1790–1914, edited by Julian
Wolfreys.
ISSN: 2044-2416
www.eupjournals.com/vic

Exploring Victorian Travel Literature

Disease, Race and Climate

Jessica Howell

EDINBURGH
University Press

Edinburgh University Press Ltd
The Tun, Holyrood Road,
12 (2f) Jackson's Entry,
Edinburgh EH8 8PJ
www.euppublishing.com

Typeset in 10.5/13 Sabon by
Servis Filmsetting Ltd, Stockport, Cheshire,
printed and bound in Great Britain by
CPI Group (UK) Ltd, Croydon CR0 4YY

A CIP record for this book is available from the British Library

ISBN 978 0 7486 9295 8 (hardback)
ISBN 978 0 7486 9296 5 (webready PDF)

Contents

Series Editor's Preface

'Victorian' is a term, at once indicative of a strongly determined concept and an often notoriously vague notion, emptied of all meaningful content by the many journalistic misconceptions that persist about the inhabitants and cultures of the British Isles and Victoria's Empire in the nineteenth century. As such, it has become a by-word for the assumption of various, often contradictory habits of thought, belief, behaviour and perceptions. Victorian studies and studies in nineteenth-century literature and culture have, from their institutional inception, questioned narrowness of presumption, pushed at the limits of the nominal definition, and have sought to question the very grounds on which the unreflective perception of the so-called Victorian has been built; and so they continue to do. Victorian and nineteenth-century studies of literature and culture maintain a breadth and diversity of interest, of focus and inquiry, in an interrogative and intellectually open-minded and challenging manner, which are equal to the exploration and inquisitiveness of its subjects. Many of the questions asked by scholars and researchers of the innumerable productions of nineteenth-century society actively put into suspension the clichés and stereotypes of 'Victorianism', whether the approach has been sustained by historical, scientific, philosophical, empirical, ideological or theoretical concerns; indeed, it would be incorrect to assume that each of these approaches to the idea of the Victorian has been, or has remained, in the main exclusive, sealed off from the interests and engagements of other approaches. A vital interdisciplinarity has been pursued and embraced, for the most part, even as there has been contest and debate amongst Victorianists, pursued with as much fervour as the affirmative exploration between different disciplines and differing epistemologies put to work in the service of reading the nineteenth century.

Edinburgh Critical Studies in Victorian Culture aims to take up both the debates and the inventive approaches and departures from convention that studies in the nineteenth century have witnessed for the last half century at least. Aiming to maintain a 'Victorian' (in the most positive sense of that motif) spirit of inquiry, the series' purpose is to continue and augment the cross-fertilisation of interdisciplinary approaches, and to offer, in addition, a number of timely and untimely revisions of Victorian literature, culture, history and identity. At the same time, the series will ask questions concerning what has been missed or improperly received, misread, or not read at all, in order to present a multi-faceted and heterogeneous kaleidoscope of representations. Drawing on the most provocative, thoughtful and original research, the series will seek to prod at the notion of the 'Victorian', and in so doing, principally through theoretically and epistemologically sophisticated close readings of the historicity of literature and culture in the nineteenth century, to offer the reader provocative insights into a world that is at once overly familiar, and irreducibly different, other and strange. Working from original sources, primary documents and recent inter-disciplinary theoretical models, Edinburgh Critical Studies in Victorian Culture seeks not simply to push at the boundaries of research in the nineteenth century, but also to inaugurate the persistent erasure and provisional, strategic redrawing of those borders.

Julian Wolfreys

Acknowledgements

This book has travelled with me across continents, and so thanks are due to an international network of friends and colleagues. It began as a doctoral thesis at the University of California, Davis, where it benefited from the valuable input of Catherine Robson, Bishnupriya Ghosh, Mike Ziser, Faith Fitzgerald and Liz Constable. Thank you to Mandy Dawn Kuntz, Julie Wilhelm, Jenni Halpin and Darcy Irvin for their friendship. I also appreciate the UC Davis English Department's support, in the form of writing and research grants, which allowed me to visit archives in Britain.

As Research Fellow at the Centre for the Humanities and Health, King's College London, I have been privileged to work with Anne Marie Rafferty, Anna Snaith and Rosemary Wall. Thank you to Rosie for introducing me to the Centre's work, and to Anne Marie and Anna for their stellar mentorship. At various key junctures, Athena Vrettos, Catherine Belling, Johanna Shapiro, Martha Stoddard Holmes and Josephine McDonagh have all been generous readers of my work, and I thank them.

It has been my pleasure to work with the editors at Edinburgh University Press, including Jackie Jones, Jen Daly and the series editor, Julian Wolfreys. Thank you also to the anonymous Edinburgh University Press readers, whose comments were both constructive and insightful. The archivists at the British Library, the Royal Geographical Society, the University of Birmingham and the Huntington Library in Pasadena have provided excellent assistance. Special thanks belong to Lucy McCann, head archivist at the Bodleian Library, Rhodes House, and to Courtney Hopf. Earlier versions of Chapter 1, on Mary Seacole, and Chapter 5, on Joseph Conrad, appeared in *Victorian Literature and Culture* and *Literature and Medicine*, respectively. I thank both journals for their permission to include this material.

I am grateful to my mother, Janet Howell, for her unwavering support and confidence. I thank my sister Katryn Howell and my nieces and nephew – Steffanie, Deanna, Amber and Brandon Bowerman – for much shared laughter. Thank you to Xinning Zhang Paulot, Lianne Zwenger and Diane Chandès VanDulken for their friendship and understanding. I am lucky to share life's adventures with my husband Anatol Bologan. While living in London, we have welcomed Mira, our daughter of the world. This book is dedicated to her.

Introduction

The 'Contact Zones' of Climate

> Fatal Africa! One after another, travellers drop away. It is such a huge conti-
> nent, and each of its secrets is environed by so many difficulties, – the torrid
> heat, the miasma exhaled from the soil, the noisome vapors enveloping every
> path, the giant cane-grass suffocating the wayfarer, the rabid fury of the
> native guarding every entry and exit, the unspeakable misery of life within
> the wild continent, the utter absence of every comfort, the bitterness which
> each day heaps upon the poor white man's head, in that land of blackness,
> the sombrous solemnity pervading every feature of it, and the little – too
> little – promise of success one feels on entering it. But never mind, I will try
> it! (Stanley 1909: 296–7)

Henry Morton Stanley sought to restore his honour by revisiting Africa
in 1874, after doubts arose about his discovery of the 'lost' David
Livingstone. The foregoing meditation on 'Fatal Africa!', inspired by
Livingstone's death, concludes with Stanley's renewed commitment
to carry on the great 'work' of African exploration. The passage illustrates Stanley's bravery in endeavouring to 'enter' Africa and discover
its 'secrets'. The furious native is only one of the many challenges
Stanley expects to face – all the rest stem from the African environment.
According to the theory that influences of the environment can lead
to disease, the 'torrid heat', 'miasma exhaled from the soil', 'noisome
vapors' and 'giant cane-grass' are not only annoying but threatening and
potentially fatal to the intrepid explorer. If one's body was predisposed
to illness due to intemperance, anxiety or constitutional weakness,
Stanley and many of his contemporaries believed that any subsequent
challenge of climate could cause heatstroke, malaria or other 'tropical' diseases. Stanley's characterisation of climate may be paraphrased
thus: 'the African environment is fatal for many whites, but I am man
enough to make the attempt'. This passage is a retrospective addition

to his autobiography. In the original narrative of his 1874 travels, *Through the Dark Continent* (1878), Stanley simply states that the news of Livingstone death 'fire[s]' him with 'resolution' to complete Livingstone's 'work' and to be, 'if God willed it, the next martyr to geographical science' (1878: 1). In 1878 Stanley clearly seeks to associate his own explorations with the perceived selflessness and humanitarianism of missionary Livingstone's travels. When Stanley later expands upon this justification in his autobiography (published posthumously in 1909), he includes more sensory detail regarding the 'fatal' African climate: this detail makes martyrdom to 'geographical science' come alive for his readers and thereby enhances Stanley's own heroic persona.

While initially it may seem an unusual pairing, I would like to offer Dr Henry Ford's earlier medical advice tract as a counterpoint to Stanley's imperialist bluster. Ford lived in what is now Gabon for four years from 1851 to 1855 and wrote *Observations on the Fevers of the Western Coast of Africa* (1856) as a guide for white travellers to the region. Throughout his book, Ford explains the symptoms of illness from 'fever'.[1] He says, 'For a length of time (perhaps days) before the access of fever, the patient notices a loss of appetite, restlessness or sleeplessness, an unpleasant taste in the mouth, particularly on rising.' The subject demonstrates 'susceptibility to cold' and disturbance of 'the mental faculties'. There is 'an incapacity for close thought, and the patient is soon wearied by study, occasional moroseness and peevishness, or perhaps timidity, and an indefinable apprehension of coming dangers'. These preliminary symptoms may be brought on from 'exposure to the direct rays of the sun; severe and long continued exertion; sitting in wet clothes after a rain. Great mental excitement produces a chill, [such] as joy, sorrow or fear.' During what is termed the 'invasion' stage, the patient tries to 'shield himself from the wind, or put on additional clothing', or 'lying down covers himself with blankets'. The sensation of cold starts in his hands and feet, but then 'passes to the spine, and creeps over the whole body' (1856: 5–6).

The connections between Stanley's and Ford's excerpts are historical and ideological as well as structural and stylistic. Many famous colonial explorers, including Richard Burton, knew and respected Ford's text, carrying either this tract or others like it abroad with them as a guide to understanding their own symptoms. They then embedded reports of their own illness in their published travelogues or memoirs. These reports follow a similar progression to Ford's case study. In other words, minute observation, sequential sensory description and hypothesised causation all become hallmarks of explorers' colonial illness narratives. Further, the two genres – colonial travel literature and medical treatise

– often share a common purpose: to understand tropical illness and its impact on colonial expansion. Ford wrote a health guide for West Africa; explorers contributed personal observations of their own illnesses and those of their companions. It sounds deceptively neutral to say that they 'contributed observations', however. As this book will show, illness narrative in the colonial context is neither selfless nor unbiased. A sustained focus on individual writers' experiences of illness also sheds light on the biopolitical ramifications of making those experiences public.

Both of the foregoing excerpts may be productively read as examples of imperial 'contact'. In *Imperial Eyes*, Mary Louise Pratt defines the term 'contact zone' as the 'space of colonial encounters, the space in which peoples geographically and historically separated come into contact with each other and establish ongoing relations, usually involving conditions of coercion, radical inequality, and intractable conflict' (1992: 6). Alan Bewell suggests in *Romanticism and Colonial Disease* that Pratt's notion of contact zones be 'reconceptualized' to include biomedical as well as cultural contact (1999: 3). He argues for more research into how those individuals living in the 'contact zones' perceived these 'radically new disease environments' (9). One may be tempted to read 'radically new disease environments' as the effects on the body of disease endemic to specific locales, and 'biomedical contact zones' as between contagious carriers of disease. However, this does not fully capture the lived experience of nineteenth-century subjects.

In *Picturing Tropical Nature*, Nancy Leys Stepan notes that the German explorer and naturalist Alexander von Humboldt (1769–1859) used 'isothermal lines' to present the 'world encircled by climatic bands', which divided the globe into 'climatic zones': 'in doing this, he separated visually and conceptually the northern climatic bands [in the Americas] from the tropical southern ones' (2001: 39). I suggest that, following Humboldt's visualisation, many nineteenth-century travellers envisioned their world in terms of contact zones of climate. The body of Ford's fever patient is disordered by contact with the tropical sun and wind, while Stanley summarises the frustrations and dangers of contact with miasma, local plants and extreme heat. Victorian travel writers perceived themselves not only as in conflict or in negotiation with foreign peoples and cultures but with the 'space of colonial encounter' itself – the tropical environment.

To understand how travellers perceived disease environments, one must consider their views on the environmental causation of disease. Writers during the mid-to-late nineteenth century often perceived climate as affecting their health, whether for good or ill. Therefore, the ways in which they characterise the weather and topography of a location are linked to the effects on their physical bodies of these aspects of the colonial geography. *Exploring Victorian Travel Literature: Disease, Race and Climate* suggests that we read 'contact zones' not just between peoples and peoples or cultures and cultures, or even between disease carriers and disease carriers, but between bodies and weather, bodies and plants, bodies and landscape. By paying close attention to writers' unsettling portrayals of tropical climates, this book draws out the political and social repercussions of linking environment with disease. It seeks to better understand the human ecologies of the colonies, conceiving of 'environment' not in terms of the bucolic but also in terms of climatic contact zones.

In order to pursue this mode of enquiry, it becomes necessary to redefine the commonly identified beginning point of illness narrative, placing it well before 1900. Chapter 5, for example, argues that because illness provided a dominant lens through which many nineteenth-century subjects saw the world, it is productive to trace the early threads of what Anne Hunsaker Hawkins (1993) has defined as the genre of pathography back through earlier texts. In his 1880 essay 'Fiction – Fair and Foul', John Ruskin contended that the Victorian novel was characterised by 'detailed, clinical depictions of disease and death' (qtd in Judd 1998: 7). The nineteenth-century literary emphasis on disease could have stemmed from several factors: a 'myopic squint of realism' reflecting the 'century's surfeit of afflictions'; an obsession with 'that which they could not master'; or a substitution of the 'medical realm' for the 'clerical realm' as the source of authority, which then became a 'momentous, if insidious, channel of power'. In this sense, Ford belongs to an elite group of 'therapeutic clergy'. Medical advice tracts such as his helped 'spread the gospel of public health' (Judd 1998: 18–20), while also perpetuating specific worldviews. By closely examining these worldviews, this book suggests that disease narration is often fraught with racial and political ideologies.

Postcolonial critics such as Edward Said, in *Orientalism* (1978) and *Culture and Imperialism* (1993), and Mary Louise Pratt in *Imperial Eyes* (1992), have examined the myriad power structures used by European explorers to justify and perpetuate colonial expansion. Europeans not only practised physical methods of oppression, such as violence, exploitation and enslavement, in order to control and subdue 'native' populations, but also employed the rhetoric of religion, science and aesthetics in order to depict their own culture and race as vigorous and strong and to cast native peoples as weak, inferior and in need of colonial protection. While acknowledging the importance of studies that expose such tools of racism, this project questions the extent to which 'conviction of imperial inevitability' was pervasive among nineteenth-century explorers (Franey 2003: 62).

The travel writing of empire often worked to reinforce binary divisions between coloniser and colonised, civilised and savage, viewer and observed. Consequently, much scholarship of travel writing has analysed its ordering function – how authors grapple with and lay to rest uncertainty and the unexpected. However, by focusing on narration of disease in the colonial environment, this book analyses what Brian Musgrove calls 'the neurotic unknowingness of the travelling euro-subject' (1999: 31). It therefore joins studies such as Johannes Fabian's *Out of Our Minds: Reason and Madness in the Exploration of Central Africa* (2000), which take up the disorientating effects of colonial travel, specifically by studying illness narration in the context of empire.

Medical rhetoric within mid-to-late Victorian travel literature reflected a great deal of ambivalence, both regarding the biological viability as well as the morality of imperialism. The authors under study in this project – Mary Seacole, Richard Burton, Africanus Horton, Mary Kingsley and Joseph Conrad – use climate in multivalent and sometimes conflicting ways, to encourage or discourage imperial expansion, to emphasise or undercut a sense of their own heroism. However, they all depict the causes of illness as de-centred; they all draw on a foreboding characterisation of the colonial natural environment and weather; and they all stratify and separate racialised bodies according to locality and elevation. To figure one's own race as biologically as well as culturally superior is a common colonial strategy; however, climate also can indicate white constitutional weakness, a subtext to which Victorian readers were very well attuned.

This project makes a case for studying the narratives of sensation and illness within colonial travel writing. Though Carl Thompson identifies the 'sensational, sentimental and scientific' as several common modes of travel writing (2011: 148), these discourses are often interlinked within Victorian literature. Jenny Bourne Taylor, Laurie Garrison (2011) and Jill Matus (2009) have shown that, in a domestic context, Victorian sensation novels were in dialogue with and influenced by scientific theories of psychological trauma as well as physiological reactivity, both of which are also relevant to colonial literature. In fact, as Warwick Anderson observes in *The Cultivation of Whiteness*, for much of the nineteenth century colonists used 'their own bodily sensations, their feelings of comfort or unease, to judge whether the land they coveted was a properly British territory' (2006: 11).

Each chapter of this book considers an explorer's own contact with and sensory input from colonial environments, and how he or she interpreted these experiences for a reading public, as well as discussing how harrowing stories of colonial illness may have affected opinions regarding colonialism on both an individual and national level. Domestic sensation fiction was often depicted as having pathological effects on the individual reader, usually gendered female, as well as on broader society, due to its shocking plot devices and resulting overstimulation of the reader's senses (Flint 2012: 231). In contrast, within the traditionally 'masculine' genre of travel and adventure, explorers wrote about their first-hand experiences of the shocks, frustrations and challenges of colonial travel in order to shore up their narrative authority. My analysis considers how each author's gender and race identity affects his or her writing of colonial illness. For example, both Mary Seacole and Mary Kingsley studiously avoid demonstrating narrative hyper-reactivity and susceptibility to illness, taking a matter-of-fact and practical approach to the challenges of travel, while Africanus Horton assiduously documents his own medical knowledge, rationality and powers of observation.

By placing fictional texts in dialogue with lesser-known nonfictional texts such as travel memoirs, treatises, speeches and diaries, I am able to trace how narratives of tropical illness function across genres. In addition, ephemeral texts highlight colonial health anxieties through their often blatant rhetorical functions. Elaine Freedgood describes such texts as 'on the verge of breaking into a serious rhetorical sweat': they 'circulate the modern cosmologies at the margins of culture ... giving them a flexibility and agility they would not otherwise enjoy' (2000: 3). Rather than functioning as an exhaustive study of the science of sensation and colonial illness, this book engages the flexibility and agility of climatism – its shifting values and persistence within different forms of empire literature.

The Persistence of Climate

In order to understand the psychological as well as the political appeal of climatism, let us turn to Charles Darwin's 1871 study *The Descent of Man*. Darwin asserts, 'When civilised nations come into contact with barbarians the struggle is short, except where a deadly climate gives its aid to the native race' (1981: 238). Darwin counts himself a member of a civilised nation, and he labels the natives of European colonial holdings 'barbarians'. He uses New Zealand and Africa as examples of each extreme – the native New Zealander may 'compare his future fate with that of the native rat almost exterminated by the European rat' (240), whereas black Africans 'escape to a large extent the fatal fevers . . . of the shores of Africa . . . which annually cause one-fifth of the white settlers to die, and another fifth to return home invalided' (242). In these examples, each race's disease resistance helps to determine the outcome of the struggle over colonial control. The race that proves more physically fit perseveres, while others do not have the strength to resist.

As an evolutionist who believed that only members of a biologically superior race survive to reproduce, Darwin understandably wished to delimit the situations in which whites would die more readily.[2] He portrays the colonial struggle as favouring 'civilised' subjects, except in those places, such as Africa, where colonists commonly die from tropical diseases. Those exceptional instances he attributes to the foreign lands' 'deadly climates', personified as an ally of 'the native race'. If tropical diseases are quantifiable and explicable, then Europeans' intellectual superiority should compensate for their physical vulnerability, allowing them to develop fail-safe preventative and curative measures. As 'climate' cannot be changed, however, Darwin's schema functions as an excuse for the 'civilised' nations' biological susceptibility. Colonial Europeans were well practised in attributing the mass death of racial others to white superiority: imported disease had decimated the native peoples of North America since contact with Europeans in the late 1500s; the Maori of New Zealand also suffered enormous loss of life. However, situations in which 'the exchange of diseases favored [non-white] populations' demanded 'different colonial structures' (Bewell 1999: 8–9). This project studies the literary expression of these 'different colonial structures', one of which is the medical rhetoric of climate.

However, using climate as an excuse for white mortality was a double-edged sword: it also introduced concerns that European colonisation was biologically untenable in 'the tropics'. As Mark Harrison (1999) has demonstrated, the establishment of hill sanitaria in India was motivated by the belief that Europeans could not thrive in hot climates for long without degenerating. Those who most strongly believed in Britons' right to colonial dominance were often polygenist, and justified the exploitation of 'dusky races' by arguing that 'natives' were a different species than Europeans. However, if different races had originated spontaneously in different regions and were thus suited only for the climate of their own region, then colonisation became 'a practical impossibility' (Harrison 1999: 17). The writers under study here attempt to fortify, revise or resist this conceptual short circuit.

The search for the healthiest locations within unhealthy climates was pursued through such practices as medical topography and medical cartography, which were used to make recommendations for sanitary reforms, including drainage, hygiene and the relocation of whites to higher elevations. Harrison argues that these measures were 'akin to restoring health to a diseased and decaying body' (1999: 146), and peaked during times when colonists felt especially under threat. He claims that 'the division of India into medico-geographic zones was a consequence of imperial crisis', and that these 'confident expressions of European superiority' often 'masked a sense of insecurity' (113). These insecurities were brought into stark relief during conflicts such as the so-called Indian Mutiny (1857), when colonists speculated that the Mutiny was 'deliberately timed to coincide with the hot season, when Europeans were at their most vulnerable' (147). Dane Kennedy observes in *The Magic Mountains: Hill Stations and the British Raj* that there were 'social purposes that underlay the desire to invest the highlands with therapeutic value' (1996: 30). Though relocation to higher elevations may have decreased the incidence of diseases made worse by overcrowding, such as cholera, and, depending on location, lowered malarial risk from the anopheles mosquito, it also functioned to keep the masters physically and culturally separate from their subjects.

Exploring Victorian Travel Literature builds on such studies of geography and medicine by Harrison, Kennedy and David Arnold, as well the work of David N. Livingstone (2004). While the social history and values associated with Indian colonial medicine are relevant to discussions of African and Caribbean contexts, this research examines the different, geographically specific motivations for racial separatism in the latter regions. For example, analysis of Richard Burton's and Mary Kingsley's work takes into account their relationship with African trade in the wake of abolition, and how scientific evidence for African racial difference was often articulated in terms defined by the debates about slavery.

Europeans' emotional responses to the challenges they faced abroad included fear of illness and resentment of local populations' apparent immunity from disease. As Harrison observes, colonisers reacted to this fear by reinforcing concepts of environmental determinism and race science. However, none of the aforementioned scholars have made a sustained analysis of the literary expression of these emotions, which I argue are especially evident within narratives of illness. For example, Harrison quotes J. M'Cosh's 1834 description of an outbreak of cholera in the Almora region, but it is outside the scope of his study to analyse the complexity of M'Cosh's representation of 'savage inhabitants'. Indian 'natives' are described as looking on 'composedly from the skirts of the woods, as if they anticipated our extermination without there being occasion for any efforts from themselves' (Harrison 1999: 183).

Although, in this instance, many Indians were also struck down by illness, the speaker's emotions of anguish and anger are especially evident when anticipating his own race's 'extermination'. The word 'extermination', also used by Darwin, is associated with the utter destruction of 'species, races and populations' (*Oxford English Dictionary* online). It is the language of biological warfare, which seems to require an actor and an acted upon. However, the statue-like 'savages' of this passage are all the more threatening because they need not participate, but can merely stand back and observe the destruction as it unfolds. They are, however, complicit with their environment, which, as Darwin claims, 'gives' them 'its aid' (1981: 238). M'Cosh paints local subjects on the 'skirts of the woods' – naturalised bodies, finding acceptance from the same surroundings that reject European interlopers. Even by the 1870s, when it was acknowledged in Europe that cholera is waterborne, India's Sanitary Department continued to express the official position that it spread through 'monsoonal air currents' (Harrison 1999: 206). Similarly, writers such as Richard Burton and Mary Kingsley continued to focus on environmental pathology and its effect on different races well into the mid-to-late Victorian era.

By analysing travel writing and scientific tracts in conjunction, this project follows Felix Driver's suggestion that more focus be given to 'the unsettled frontier' between 'discourses of adventurous travel and scientific exploration' (2005: 2). After all, scientists and doctors not only 'reported on the tropics' but also 'invented them', cataloguing distinctive characteristics of their 'flora and fauna, climates, soils and vegetation,' with 'a scientific precision and a pathological potency' that distinguished the tropics from temperate zones (Arnold 1996: 9). Hence, the previously cited excerpts from Henry Morton Stanley's literature of exploration and Henry Ford's medical treatise are productively read together because they also both contribute to a growing discourse of tropical fatality and foreboding.

Such an approach is complementary to studies that explicitly take up the imaginative construction of the tropics in both visual and written texts, such as the previously cited work of Nancy Leys Stepan (2001). Following Patrick Brantlinger's insight that 'the harsh facts of disease and death themselves contributed to the darkening of the Dark Continent' (1988: 174), Stepan explores a variety of nineteenth- and twentieth-century representations of Western 'dismay at tropical excess' (2001: 48). Specifically, she claims that tropical nature's abundance was pathologised, seen as both symptom and cause of corruption and death. She cites 'environmentalist' understandings of disease as contributing to the belief, by the late nineteenth century, that 'plague, malaria, leprosy, and yellow fever' were 'fundamentally tropical diseases', and that 'India, Africa, and the New World tropics' came to represent 'all that was pathogenic' (158).

More recently, there has been a move to analyse non-European depictions of the tropics, where such sources are available, as well as colonial subjects' depictions of the metropole (see Snaith 2014; Innes 2008). Volumes such as *Postcolonial Travel Writing* (2011) and Tabish Khair's *Other Routes: 1500 Years of African and Asian Travel Writing* (2006) argue for further consideration of 'textual and cartographic evidence of vast parts of the world being navigated and traversed by Asians and Africans before, during and after Europeans set out on their post-Enlightenment voyages' (Khair 2006: 12). This book takes up this challenge, considering how Jamaican Creole author Mary Seacole and Sierra Leonean James Africanus Beale Horton draw upon metaphors of climate and racial constitutionalism in order to subvert dominant understandings of white superiority.

This book thereby contributes to studies concerned with colonial and postcolonial subjects' self-representation, including Bart Moore-Gilbert's *Postcolonial Life-Writing* (2009), by considering the discourses of racialised disease resistance that colonial subjects had available to them in crafting their own identities. It also shares with recent work such as Deborah Shapple Spillman's *British Colonial Realism in Africa* (2012) a focus on points of opposition by colonised subjects, but instead of locating these points around the circulation of material objects, it focuses on colonial subjects who rewrite the discourses of their own biological inferiority. For example, Seacole and Horton both privilege their own indigenous knowledge of the curative properties of African and Caribbean plants, respectively. One may argue that, by so doing, this 'doctress' and doctor seek to make themselves useful to the project of protecting the Anglo body from the insidious effects of tropical climates. However, as the first and third chapters demonstrate, Seacole and Horton imply that their very best remedies are not enough to counteract whites' weakness under foreign climates.

While studies of the 'tropics' in the colonial imagination may group together India, Africa and the New World, this book is mainly concerned with travel writing about Africa and the Caribbean between 1857 and 1899. The environments of nineteenth-century Africa and the Caribbean are linked together both in terms of their epidemiological profiles, as well as their resulting reputations as fatal destinations for white colonists. This book analyses writers' sensory depictions of health threats, which they perceive as emanating from tropical nature. Whether they portray themselves as susceptible to these threats or largely immune, the work of these five writers in Africa and the Caribbean demonstrates especially acute perceptions of tropical danger.

During this period, Britain held as either colonies, annexes, protectorates or dominions parts of Canada, Asia, Central and South America, Antarctica and Africa; islands in the Pacific, Atlantic, Caribbean and Indian oceans; as well as most of the Indian subcontinent. Some British colonies, such as Australia and New Zealand, were perceived as healthy and were supposed to have salubrious effects on white subjects, many of whom left behind them the overcrowding, meagre nourishment and poor air quality of Britain's industrial cities; however, other colonies, such as those in Africa, the West Indies and the Indian subcontinent, were commonly regarded as disease-ridden and dangerous to the Anglo-British constitution. The military gathered factual information regarding instances of illness, often in the form of soldiers' vital statistics. Especially influential was a series of studies entitled 'Statistical Reports on Sickness, Invaliding and Mortality among Troops' published in 1838, 1839, 1840 and 1842 to document the death rates in various British colonies. In *Death by Migration*, Philip D. Curtin outlines the group's findings: that mortality for whites in India varied greatly according to location; the 'Jamaican death rate was exceptionally high' due to yellow fever epidemics; and 'tropical West Africa [fell] into a category all its own, with the highest mortality and morbidity rates for outsiders found anywhere in the world' (1989: 18).

Victorian travellers to Africa and the Caribbean had a long tradition from which to draw alarming depictions of these unhealthy environments. As David Arnold observes in his introduction to *Warm Climates and Western Medicine* (1996), by the middle of the seventeenth century the 'exotic representation of the tropics was becoming relatively common in medical literature, especially in relation to West Africa and the West Indies'. Writers 'repeatedly stressed the fierce malevolence of the tropics' – the 'sudden hurricanes and devastating storms', the 'tigers onshore' and 'predatory sharks by sea', and, 'by extension or by analogy, the extreme violence of tropical diseases compared to those of Europe'. Each chapter of this book studies an author's manipulation of '[t]he heat, humidity and rapid temperature changes of the tropics', the 'abundant and tiresome insects', 'rapid . . . putrefaction and decay' and the 'offensive smells of swamps and rotting vegetation' which contribute to an 'acute, indeed palpable, sense of tropical danger' (Arnold 1996: 7).

In order to better understand Victorian ambivalence regarding the biological superiority of whites, this project examines books set in some of the most reputedly 'fatal' of Victorian British colonies. Four of the authors – Burton, Horton, Kingsley and Conrad – write about

Africa, while Mary Seacole draws upon her experience in Jamaica to provide examples of racialised disease resistance.[3] These writers privilege imagery of illness from climate rather than infection, though each was individually familiar with alternative theories: for example, Mary Seacole suspects 'a steamer from New Orleans' was 'the means of introducing' cholera to Jamaica in 1850 (Seacole 1857: 9); Burton mocks quarantine as ineffectual (1863); Kingsley amusedly claims that scientists have recently attempted to isolate 'the peculiar microbes of everything from measles to miracles' (1897a: 515); and, in his other fiction such as *The Nigger of the Narcissus* (1897), Conrad uses quarantine to good plot effect (Bock 2006).

However, in the works chosen for this study, each author analyses how suited his or her racial constitution is for the tropical environment, thereby claiming or disclaiming affiliation with certain colonial spaces. For example, when depicting her own mixed-race constitution as better suited than her vulnerable white patients to Jamaica's climate, Mary Seacole undermines conventional Anglo-colonial discourse that depicts Jamaica as 'a hot place and belonging to Us' (Winifred James, qtd in O'Callaghan 2004: 62).[4] However, Richard Burton attempts to counteract and contain the negative affects of climate as a means by which to conquer the land and its peoples. In both of these cases, surviving the climate of an exotic location can symbolically prove ownership, or the right of association with that place.

I only treat briefly texts written about British colonial India for two reasons: first, white subjects' health in India was viewed with gradually decreasing urgency by the second half of the nineteenth century. As Timothy L. Alborn states in his article 'Age and Empire in the Indian Census, 1871–1931', mid-century 'pension-fund reports ... revealed that the white man's burden in India (measured in terms of alarmingly high mortality rates) was growing lighter' (1999: 68). As this book is mainly concerned with instances of uncertainty and doubt regarding imperial viability and how these manifest through images of climate, India's well-established nineteenth-century 'Imperial framework' provides a less appropriate test case (Bewell 1999: 22). For example, Britain's Indian Medical Service traces its origins from 1714; a similar institution in Africa, the Colonial Medical Service, did not begin operation until 1927 (Macleod 1988: 3). Further reason for studying the literature of travel to Africa and the West Indies is the fact that explorers to these regions often followed the same trade routes used to transport black bodies less than a hundred years before. This study directly engages five authors' investment in the 'legitimate' trade that replaced slave trading, as all sought a livelihood through colonial travel.

By the late nineteenth century, much progress had been made towards defining disease sources and proving that many 'tropical diseases' did not have environmental but infectious origins. However, metaphors drawn from climate continued to circulate in colonial discourse. Mark Harrison observes that 'The longevity of the climatic paradigm cannot be ascribed solely to its political utility' (1999: 206). Even after scientists pinpointed the organisms thought to cause certain diseases in the 1880s, the discoveries were only 'slowly accepted by the medical profession in India', and medical wisdom 'continued to stress the importance of meteorological conditions' (206). In his review of Harrison's book, Warwick Anderson underscores and broadens this claim, suggesting that 'environmental pathologies', persisted 'in the colonial world', 'long after their disappearance in Europe' (2002).

What could be the reasons for the persistence of 'environmental pathologies' in the colonial imagination? It might at first seem natural, given the 'conceptual inadequacies of Western medical theory' and the 'discomforts' associated with the tropics, that Europeans would link illness to climate (Kennedy 1990: 119). However, neither the concepts of contagion nor of vector-borne diseases were foreign to nineteenth-century travellers, who were familiar with the progression of illnesses such as syphilis, leprosy and rabies. Syphilis has been understood as a sexually transmitted disease since the Middle Ages. Rabies was commonly thought to be transmitted through rabid animals, though it was not until 1885 that Louis Pasteur and Emile Roux gave the first rabies vaccine to nine-year-old Joseph Meister after a rabid dog mauled him. Leprosy was in fact supposed to be even more contagious than it is, with leper colonies formed to quarantine sufferers.

During the mid-nineteenth century, Margaret Pelling argues, 'between the two fixed poles of smallpox' (understood as contagious) and 'intermittent fever' (understood as not contagious) there was a spectrum of illnesses with 'ambivalent or undetermined' etiology, including yellow fever, 'typhus' and the 'other continued fevers' and 'Asiatic cholera' (1978: 16). Medical practitioners, as well as writers and social theorists, attempted to decide disease causation based on their own study, experience and beliefs. However, as the century progressed, more and more evidence emerged in support of germ theory. John Snow identified the Broad Street pump as the source of the 1854 cholera outbreak in London. Louis Pasteur's 1860s experiments with fermentation demonstrated that micro-organisms only develop in environments where they are introduced. In the 1870s Robert Koch developed his Postulates working with the Anthrax bacillus. By 1878 Patrick Manson had reported the first insect vector of a human disease: he determined that elephantiasis microfilariae were carried in mosquitoes (Bynum 2006: 103).

If it was widely acknowledged that certain diseases are spread through contact with infected hosts (both animal and human), then it was possible for mid-to-late nineteenth-century writers to draw upon contagionist and vector-borne explanatory theories in their writing. Thus, it becomes even more notable when writers emphasise climate as the cause of disease. Well known are the ways in which contagionism can be used to support racist ends, especially when applied to specific, delimited groups of racial others who are perceived as threatening (see Arnold ed. 1998; Davidson and Hall eds 2001; Bashford and Hooker eds 2001; Bashford 2004). However, despite the alternative modes of understanding and rhetorical tools available to them, certain authors favoured instead images, tropes and metaphors influenced by the earlier disease theories. The authors under study in this book all portray the tropical environment as threatening. They engage with the appropriateness of foreign climates for the British constitution by using atmospheric disease images of sun, heat, 'miasmatic' fog or mist, tropical plants and impure water.

The concept of 'miasma' is an example of a particularly rhetorically flexible element of climate.[5] During the nineteenth century, it was commonly believed that exposure to noxious gases, exhalations from decomposing organic matter or damp night air could cause disease. These airborne factors were often labelled 'miasma', from the Greek *miainein*, meaning 'to pollute'; miasma in turn was thought to cause the disease 'malaria', from the Italian *mala aria*, or 'bad air'.[6] Of course, to label the night air of a certain place as inherently miasmatic has very different rhetorical implications than to identify as unhealthy only specific kinds of mist, such as those that occur below a certain elevation. For example, Mary Kingsley portrays African miasma as insidious, implying that for most visiting Europeans, illness is inevitable; Richard Burton depicts miasma as characteristic of only certain locations or elevations in Africa, and then encourages whites to relocate their settlements in order to avoid disease. Each redefines miasma in a way that suits his or her personal and political needs. Further, Joseph Conrad's fiction emphasises tropical heat and the ways in which it causes internal humoral imbalance within the white body.[7] His work demonstrates that living at higher elevations does not protect one from the malignant quality of heat and light; Conrad's daunting imagery of the tropical sun augments his critique of colonial exploitation in Africa.

As observed by Allan Christensen in *Nineteenth-Century Narratives of Contagion* (2005), Victorian novelists such as Charles Dickens in *Bleak House* (1852) suggest contagion through the spectre of venereal disease and physical degeneration. However, I propose that Seacole, Burton, Horton, Kingsley and Conrad choose to use imagery drawn from theories of environmental disease because of the unique rhetorical opportunities this fading system affords them. Factors of climate are ill-defined and uncontrollable and therefore such imagery can be manipulated to support different, even contradictory conclusions regarding disease causation and resistance. For instance, by focusing on discrete measures, such as changing settlement location and hygiene, authors can encourage their readers to perceive the tropical environment as remediable. Conversely, they can throw the colonial project's feasibility into doubt by emphasising the omnipresence of miasmatic mist and harsh tropical sunshine. Contagionism and vector-borne disease theories may not offer as much rhetorical subtlety, as their chief recommendations usually consist of eliminating or avoiding infected hosts.

It is significant that none of these five authors locates disease in the bodies of racial others. This is not to say that they avoid racism – for example, Richard Burton relegates inferior black bodies to unhealthy climate zones, which he argues suit them best. However, not even Burton attempts to argue that Africans are the cause of the environmental factors that make whites ill, whereas 'pollution' stemming from the lower classes' living conditions was a real fear for sanitary reformers in Victorian Britain.[8] Therefore, the medical rhetoric used in colonial locales is arguably different from that used by the sanitarians of Britain, who focused on cleaning up England's slums. Such sanitarians included Edwin Chadwick and late-century social reformers such as William Booth of the Salvation Army, who believed that the cause of disease was overcrowding and filth, which gave rise to disease-carrying miasmas. More fundamentally, however, these sanitarians held that illness could spread beyond the confines of the most poverty-stricken areas and affect the upper classes, which added strength to their fervour for hygiene reform. If smell and pollution indicated disease, then sanitation measures were instituted to counteract what Alain Corbin calls 'the heavy scents of the masses with their disturbing messages of intimate life' (1986: 143).

Miasma proves particularly flexible in domestic fiction, as well, as a multivalent symbol for death, decay and degeneration. Miasma can be invoked to blame the lower classes for disease, and racial others as well. For example, the narrator of *Shirley* (1849) claims that 'the yellow taint of pestilence, covering white Western isles with the poisoned exhalations of the East, dim[s] the lattices of English homes with the breath of Indian plague' (qtd in Glen 2002: 178). This depiction of miasma was doubtless informed by the repeated cholera epidemics which swept England during the 1840s. It was at this time still termed 'Asiatic' cholera, as the first reported epidemics had been in China and India: thus, cholera 'miasma' was often identified with the East.

After what is sometimes termed the Second Industrial Revolution (1865), which increased the mass production of consumer goods, miasma was often used to symbolise degeneration from the excesses of industrialism (as in Hardy's 1866 *Mayor of Casterbridge*, for example). By the end of the century, reports of colonial abuses filtering back to Britain caused whites a certain amount of guilt-inspired fear of retribution. Miasma evoked the dreaded degenerative effects of reverse colonisation in Bram Stoker's *Dracula*: when the Doctor and Jonathan enter the Count's house in England, '[t]here was an earthy smell, as of some dry miasma, which came through the fouler air' (1897: 291).

As demonstrated by Darwin's assertions in *Descent of Man*, climatism may also hold appeal because it does not implicate whites' biological inferiority as directly as contagionism. While contagionism and germ theories may be of rhetorical use when a biomedical contact zone favours whites, they may hold less attraction when the situation is reversed. The message 'we are giving them virulent, European diseases and decimating their numbers' would potentially harmonise better for subjects who believe in their own racial superiority than the opposite message: 'they are giving us virulent, native diseases and decimating our numbers'. In the latter circumstance, pinpointing disease in the environment may be more ideologically appealing.

Authors also often have large-scale designs uniquely suited by climatism: to convince their readers that colonies such as Africa and Jamaica are either irrevocably off limits or innately promising for exploration on a national scale. Therefore, they must arouse emotional responses about an entire landscape, not just its people. Climatic theory provides them with this necessary elasticity. Authors may characterise elements of the tropical climate as insidious or malicious, use de-familiarising environmental imagery, and depict white subjects as vulnerable to environmental disease either as a result of a flaw in their constitutions or their own bad judgement.

The nineteenth-century rhetoric of climate not only implied that a certain environment was or was not appropriate for one racialised body, but for all members of that race. It did so by drawing upon the belief that each race shares a definable mental and physical nature or constitution. Many false but unfortunately still influential racial stereotypes have their roots in constitutionalism: for example, the idea that Europeans are cerebral and rational, as well as physically hardy; or that blacks are impetuous and childlike, as well as sexually virile. Such characteristics were thought to have developed in tandem with the race's climate of origin: in other words, northern Europeans' vigour arose from the cold, bracing climate, whereas black Africans' laziness developed because of the tropical heat. By writing environment in a way that delimits racial groups within specific geographical and characterological boundaries, authors may use climate to include certain subjects in the project of travel and colonial exploration and exclude others.

Illness, Environment and Authority

In *The Wounded Storyteller*, Arthur Frank claims that the genre of illness narrative arose in response to the strictures of twentieth-century 'modern' medicine. He says, 'The *modern* experience of illness begins when experience is overtaken by technical expertise' (1995: 5). Drawing upon evidence from diagnostic tests, physicians recount to patients the story of their patients' own illness, and 'the story told by the physician becomes the one against which others are ultimately judged true or false, useful or not' (5). Frank calls this process the patient's '*narrative surrender*' (6). In contrast, '[t]he *postmodern* experience of illness begins when ill people recognize that more is involved in their illness than the medical story can tell' and 'reclaim' their 'capacity for telling' their own stories (7).

Knowledge regarding infectious disease has indeed shifted the focus of medicine towards laboratory data and diagnosis and away from the patient's own experience as evidence; however, earlier disease systems conferred much more authority to the patient's story than a focus solely on 'postmodern' narratives of illness allows. In *The Cultivation of Whiteness*, Warwick Anderson observes that, during the nineteenth century, '[t]o explain the basis of health, and the causes and expressions of disease, medical doctors and lay people alike drew on a language of place and circumstance' (2006: 12). It was believed that '[a]n individual's constitution was always responding dynamically to fluctuations of local conditions' and 'the body was an amazingly sensitive system of intake and excretion, of give and take with its changing environment' (12).

Although a doctor made his own observations in order to form his diagnosis based on factors such as the patient's temperature, the appearance of skin and eyes, demeanour and apparent temperament, during the nineteenth century the instrument of proof was the patient's body itself, not the laboratory results derived from it. Concepts of environmental pathology dictated that the doctor consider the patient's own story, in order to reconstruct events and circumstances relevant to the disease. What is now called the patient 'history' and relegated to a small corner of the medical chart was integral in the nineteenth century to the medical encounter.

As Anderson observes, colonial medicine began to take germ theories of disease more seriously in the 1880s and 1890s, when doctors no longer focused as exclusively on 'airs, waters, and places as causes of disease' (2006: 12). However, this change was far from uniform in literature: later nineteenth-century writers such as Mary Kingsley and Joseph Conrad continue to use imagery that links disease with the environment. This makes sense, not just because environmental imagery is evocative, or for the political and social reasons previously outlined, but also because narratives of illness from environment give the narrator's own observations more authority. The patient who experiences tropical heat stroke, or prostration, for example, might tell the doctor 'I travelled by foot to a certain outpost, during which time I was exposed to the midday sun, the constant smell of putrefying vegetation, and received the shock of my companion's death.' This evidence cannot be verified or disproven and must be taken into account when considering the patient's current state.

Explorers such as Richard Burton or Mary Kingsley did not often have direct access to a doctor while tramping through the jungle, however. Instead, they retrospectively craft stories of illness for their readers, drawing authority from personal experience as well as scientific knowledge and then forming their own conclusions, not only regarding what a disease was and how it happened but also what it meant. They claimed the right to such authority through the extent of their own experiences abroad and their personal encounters with illness. For example, when Henry Morton Stanley gives his stamp of approval to Thomas Heale Parke's 1893 *Guide to Health in Africa*, he says in the Preface 'I am something of a "doctor" myself in regard to fevers and intestinal complaints – at least, I ought to be by this – and I feel assured that the advice given [here] in regard to them is particularly wise and sound' (Parke and Stanley 1893: vi). The writers under study here also use such authority in order to predict what may befall their hapless readers, if the readers should go to a certain place or behave in a certain way. All five authors augment the impact of their colonial illness narratives through sensory description, threatening environmental metaphors and medico-geographical 'mapping'.

This process shares much with Michel Foucault's description in *The Birth of the Clinic* (1973) of how individuals create and reinforce knowledge regarding epidemic diseases. For example, those travellers who suffered tropical 'fever' in Africa or the Caribbean might well have had malaria or yellow fever. These are both endemic diseases, with regular epidemic spikes when climate shifts and mosquito vectors reach previously uninfected populations. Therefore, late Victorian travellers who described their experiences with 'fever' were participating in the mapping of both endemic and epidemic disease, whether or not they all knew the difference.

Foucault asserts that, by reporting their own personal experiences, those who witness or suffer epidemics contribute to a group consciousness of what causes the disease and how it progresses. He claims, 'Whether contagious or not, an epidemic has a sort of historical individuality, hence the need to employ a complex method of observation when dealing with it. Being a collective phenomenon, it requires a multiple gaze' (1973: 25). The goal of reporting on an epidemic is to circumscribe and make sense of the event: 'it finds its own range only in the cross-checking of viewpoints, in repeated, corrected information, which finally circumscribes, where gazes meet, the individual, unique nucleus of these collective phenomena' (25). Foucault pinpoints 'the drawing up of a "map"' as 'the fundamental act of medical knowledge' in the eighteenth century, whereby 'a symptom was situated within a disease, a disease in a specific ensemble, and this *ensemble* in a general plan of the pathological world' (29).

As the following chapters demonstrate, colonial travellers continued to create these maps of tropical pathology throughout the nineteenth century, drawing upon their own first-hand encounters with illness. However, the maps that these authors create also allow for ambiguity and suspense regarding the source of disease, which implies that the literary manipulation of illness narrative highlights its malleability and aesthetic as well as political functions. By linking the diseases they observe with their environment, travellers are also often mapping the survival of one race over another. This is based on the assumption Foucault highlights, that '[t]he race is a living being that one can see degenerating' (1973: 35).

According to Foucault, after the end of the eighteenth century diagnosis most often depends on the medical 'gaze', whereby the doctor considers the patient's body in order to connect the symptoms (visual evidence) with what they signify:

> Doctor and patient are caught up in an ever-greater proximity, bound together, the doctor by an ever-more attentive, more insistent, more penetrating gaze, the patient by all the silent, irreplaceable qualities that, in him, betray – that is, reveal and conceal – the clearly ordered forms of the disease. (1973: 15–16)

In the absence of a doctor or clinical setting, however, travellers are often the most qualified medical authorities present. They must turn the medical gaze both on the landscape and on their own body or the bodies of their companions, in order to detect the probable cause of disease. As previously mentioned, in interpreting and reporting their findings and experiences, the writers structure their narratives to reflect reputable models, such a medical guides. They also draw upon the commonly detailed environmental descriptions of the travelogue. This book is interested in the moments when these two modes, description of illness and description of environment, are interlinked: when the gaze of the coloniser is the gaze of the medical geographer. Parke's *Guide to Health in Africa*, previously cited, demonstrates that these two gazes are often one. Parke says, 'The hitherto dark interior of the African continent is now being gradually opened up to the scrutinizing gaze of the civilized nations of the earth.' The 'observations collected' illuminate 'the important question of the probable survival of the white man in Africa' (1893: 1–2).

Both Arthur Frank and Michel Foucault attribute authorised description and medical analogy to the purview of the doctor, from after the French Revolution (Foucault) until the mid-twentieth century (Frank). However, nineteenth-century colonial travellers adopt both these functions within their own writing. First, Foucault observes, 'It is description, or, rather, the implicit labour of language in description, that authorizes the transformation of symptom into sign and the passage from patient to disease and from the individual to the conceptual' (1973: 140). Doctors borrow from the patterns of natural history, he says, to 'describe' and 'order' disease 'manifestations', attempting to follow 'the intelligible sequence of their genesis' (140). While Foucault focuses on the power of seeing and sight, colonial travellers draw upon all their senses, including smell and touch, when describing their encounters with tropical illness. Rather than using language to 'master the visible' (140), writers such as Seacole, Kingsley and Conrad imply that there are disease-causing factors that are felt rather than seen, and make good dramatic use of the pervasiveness and ambiguity of tropical illness.

Secondly, all five of the authors under study mobilise the rhetoric of medical analogy, but use it to different ends. As a doctor might say that the individual typifies disease manifestations in other bodies, so too the travel writer may imply 'as it happened to my (racialised) body, so might it happen to other (racialised) bodies'. However, writers also exempt certain bodies from the model they set out – their own body, those of their friends, native Africans, or mixed-race subjects are painted as immune to specific diseases. It is the rare writer, such as Joseph Conrad, who dwells on the possibility that not only he, but all those like him, are likely to perish 'under the midday sun'.

During the nineteenth century, narrators' desire to bolster their own 'eye-witness status' and 'credibility' 'precipitated more autobiographical and inward-looking strains of travel writing' (Thompson 2011: 98). Description of illness from climate was hard to refute, and lent the writer authority through his or her claim to scientific precision and detailed observation. It is no wonder, then, that the writing of 'environmental pathologies' continued well into the heyday of germ theory. However, as previously mentioned, the rhetoric of illness from environment also can reflect much ambivalence. As a result of the links between the medicine of environment and race science in the nineteenth century, to write of a threatening climate could also be to write one's own vulnerability. Examining literary works from this perspective allows us to better understand not only how each author crafts his or her narrative persona, but also how illness influenced both the content as well as the form and structures of Victorian travel writing.

As I have outlined the resonance between the literature of colonial medicine and the literature of colonial travel, so too each of the following primary works performs multiple functions and resists simple genre categorisation. Mary Seacole's *Wonderful Adventures of Mrs Seacole in Many Lands* (1857) is an autobiographical memoir that also functioned as a petition for financial support; Richard Burton's *Wanderings in West Africa* (1863) and Mary Kingsley's *Travels in West Africa* (1897) may both be considered informative travel guides, but were also used to advance the authors' political opinions and goals; the works of Africanus Horton were often ostensibly meant to educate and inform readers regarding West African diseases, but use disease to further the author's objective of African independence; Joseph Conrad's 'An Outpost of Progress' (1897) and *Heart of Darkness* (1899) are fictional tales of travel, but were based on Conrad's own encounters with colonial illness and corruption, as recorded in his *Congo Diary* and 'Up-river Book' (1890).

These five writers were selected because a common thread links their writing together, over a significant historical span: each author includes in his or her longer works stories of whites becoming ill from the tropical environment. While they each inhabited very different subject positions and roles within British society – those of female hotelier and nurse of mixed-race; risqué male explorer; African nationalist doctor; spinster ethnographer; and expatriate Polish novelist – they all circulated on the margins of British society. Their race and gender identities necessarily affect each author's relationship with colonial environments. For example, Mary Seacole and Mary Kingsley deploy common Victorian concepts of female vulnerability in order to emphasise their own superior strength. In addition, the first and fourth chapters posit that these two authors both depict themselves as unusually resistant to climatic challenges, thereby creating new visions of female healthfulness.

Seacole, Burton and Kingsley make good rhetorical use of their autobiographical personæ in writing about colonial environments. For example, Mary Seacole represents herself as a hybrid subject – not only in terms of race and culture, as she draws upon black and white, Jamaican and British identities, but also in terms of constitution. She implies that her mixed race imparts greater disease resistance and physical and emotional hardiness than is possessed by the white Britons she nurses. Chapter 1 explains how Seacole's *Adventures* played on the insecurities of her white readership, already heightened by recent disease epidemics and mid-Victorian discourses of white British 'enervation'.

Seacole calls upon common sense, folk wisdom, maternal instincts and real-life nursing experience to lend authority to her remarks. In contrast, Africanus Horton, Mary Kingsley and Richard Burton invoke scientific knowledge, drawn from their studies of anthropology, medical climatology, ethnology, botany, natural history, hygienic science and geography, and combine this knowledge with exhaustive detail to give their works an aura of authenticity. They intersperse first-person narrative with mini-lectures: Burton digresses to outline the ancestry of an African tribe or Kingsley explains the concept of fetish. These passages, while seemingly trying to be objective, are shot through with fearful climatic imagery that leads to policy recommendations or reflects underlying race biases. For example, while most criticism has focused only on Africanus Horton's later, explicitly political work, Chapter 3 argues that one may see the development towards political activism nascent in Horton's *Physical and Medical Climate, and Meteorology of the West Coast of Africa* (1867), wherein he depicts West Africa as full of danger for white subjects. My analysis compares how Seacole and Horton, both subjects of colour, use their first-hand knowledge of local conditions and local remedies as a source of authority and as a means to write white vulnerability.

Finally, Joseph Conrad takes advantage of the creative possibilities provided by fiction, using his short story and novella in order to explore the conflicting emotions of white characters in the Belgian Congo. Unlike Seacole, Burton and Kingsley, who project an aura of certainty, Conrad's narrators repeatedly discover that the facts of which they were previously convinced are not true. His characters feel especially acute insecurity about their own health status. For this reason, Chapter

5 suggests that one may use concepts drawn from the study of pathography to analyse both texts.[9] White characters' ominous 'impressions' of Africa's atmosphere may imply to Conrad's readers that they too are not suited for tropical climates. While Franz Fanon famously observed in *Black Skin, White Masks* (1967) that white women are often portrayed as susceptible to sexually predatory 'natives', this book asks what other rhetorical methods come into play when the threat to white health is not perceived to be the natives themselves but their environment. For example, this chapter demonstrates that Conrad's fictional narrators often perceive Africans who are at home in the tropical climate as sinister, at least in part because of their immunity to tropical disease.

Although much work has been done to excavate the ways in which writers attempt to justify their country's domination of other races, by focusing on literary representations of climate one may observe that nineteenth-century discourses of racial science could also throw into question and undermine the imperial impulse. Through the analysis of illness narratives embedded in Victorian travel writing, this project seeks to open new areas of enquiry in nineteenth-century studies by bridging the disciplinary boundaries between travel and race theories and the analysis of illness narrative.

In his *Society Must be Defended: Lectures at the College de France, 1975–6*, Foucault argues that a sovereign nation enforces its right to 'make live and let die', using both regulatory and disciplinary techniques in order to separate groups of people into racialised bodies. This 'biopolitics of the human race' 'is not individualizing but . . . massifying; that is, not directed at man-as-body but man-as-species' (2004: 241–3). Racism may be considered the practice of dividing the human species into biological hierarchies whereby the dominant force determines 'what must live and what must die' (254) – not only through physical domination or exploitation, but through the deployment of discourses of medicine, which often portrays subjects of privilege as more disease-resistant and hardy. *Exploring Victorian Travel Literature* examines the ways in which individual Victorian travel writers wielded biopower by manipulating climatic imagery and metaphors of disease. Although I have found that some authors chose to emphasise their own race's biological weakness rather than strength, either positioning is based in power. These authors play upon their readers' fears of tropical disease, claiming for themselves narrative authority through the aesthetic and political manipulation of illness narrative. Although they themselves crossed boundaries of geography and convention, by implying that tropical environments cause disease, these authors divided the rest of 'man-as-species' into discrete, geographically delimited factions.

Notes

1. For further discussion of 'fever', see Chapter 4.
2. Though a monogenist who believed that the different races evolved 'from a single primitive stock', Darwin is willing to entertain the idea that the races may have diverged so far as to now be classifiable as different species (1981: 229). He believes the designation is open to debate, as no adequately precise differentiation between 'species', 'race' and 'subspecies' has yet been developed. However, he casts the outcome from struggles between races as 'survival of the fittest', with whites most often the victors. 'Genocide decimated the American Indians, Tasmanians, Maoris and Australians, but Darwin believed they would have withered on the vine anyway – the less fit races vanishing as the more fit advanced' (Brantlinger 2004: 67).
3. Africa and the West Indies both had sinister reputations within Victorian medical discourse. This may have been because many of the diseases which struck white settlers and explorers were the same in both locations. As Bewell explains, Britain had originally imported blacks from Africa to work the slave plantations of Jamaica, 'ostensibly because blacks could withstand diseases that regularly kill white people'. Ironically, 'since the African slaves brought with them the same sicknesses and helminthic infections that the Europeans were seeking to avoid . . . the epidemiology of the West Indies ultimately became like that of Africa, so Europeans were largely back where they started' (Bewell 1999: 8–9).
4. O'Callaghan (2004) presents a variety in nineteenth-century women writers' descriptions of the West Indies: some depicted sublime or Arcadian scenes, some attributed healing qualities to the region, while still others characterised it as a disease-ridden swamp.
5. This term's many forms re-emerge throughout this book and thus deserve brief explanation here. 'Miasma', when referred to in nineteenth-century texts, most often means disease-causing mist, fog or stench. Victorian authors further use the adjective 'miasmatic' to describe unhealthy places or unhealthy air. The theory which outlines sources and effects of miasma is called 'miasmatism'. Sanitarians and hygienic scientists, who focused on cleaning up the sources of stench, were often proponents of miasmatism. Contemporary critics and disease historians often use 'miasmatism' as a catch-all term meant to indicate any historical anti-contagionist theory positing that disease arises from environmental or climatic influences. Instead, I have chosen to use 'climatism' or 'climatic theory' here, in order to more clearly indicate that my chosen authors focus on a variety of climatic elements, including but not limited to 'bad air'.
6. During the mid-century 'outbreaks of malaria, cholera and fevers in general' were most commonly attributed to 'miasma from open sewers, slaughterhouse offal, dumps, graveyards, and . . . stench-filled areas' (Guillemin 2001: 2). Edwin Chadwick, the most famous proponent of miasmatic theory, went so far as to tell a parliamentary committee in 1846 'All smell is, if it be intense, immediate acute disease; and eventually we may say that, by depressing the system and rendering it susceptible to the action of other causes, all smell is disease' (qtd in Halliday 2001: 1469). Smell was not nec-

essarily disembodied and invisible: mists, creeping vapours, smoke and other fumes also qualified as 'miasma'. Further, malaria is defined not only as 'bad air' but also 'a pervasive influence or atmosphere that tends to deplete or corrupt' (*OED* online).

7. Humoral theory was articulated by Galen of Pergamon, who associated the four cardinal humours (blood, phlegm, black bile and yellow bile) with four elements – earth, air, fire and water. When one humour was dominant in a patient, Galen determined, 'illness would follow' (Lane 2001: 2). As Philip J. Curtin explains in *Disease and Empire*, humoral theory allows 'some measure of human control' in that an individual can attempt to avoid illness 'by manipulating the basic qualities – hot and cold, wet and dry – that affected the humors' (1998: 12). Therefore, travellers could abide by the elaborate humoral 'hygiene' rules for self-protection outlined by practitioners, hygienists, by trying to carefully moderate and regulate perspiration, diet, liquid intake, heat and cold.

8. As Judith Walkowitz observes in *City of Dreadful Delight*, Victorian 'literature of urban exploration' mimicked the 'privileged gaze of anthropology in constituting the poor as a race apart' (1992: 19). One may see this dynamic at work in texts such as *London Labour and the London Poor* by Henry Mayhew (1851), *How the Poor Live* by George Sims (1883) and *In Darkest England* (1890) by William Booth. Walkowitz claims, 'The opposition of East and West increasingly took on imperial and racial dimensions, as the two parts of London imaginatively doubled for England and its Empire' (1992: 26). In Booth one sees the analogy made explicit: 'The Equatorial Forest traversed by Stanley resembles that Darkest England of which I have to speak, alike in its vast extent – both stretch, in Stanley's phrase, "As far as from Plymouth to Peterhead"; its monotonous darkness, its malaria and its gloom, its dwarfish, de-humanized inhabitants, the slavery to which they are subjected, their privations and their misery' (1890: 12).

9. Pathographies can either document the past sources of a subject's pathology or narrate his or her current illness. See Anne Hunsaker Hawkins' *Reconstructing Illness: Studies in Pathography* (1999).

Chapter 1

Mrs Seacole Prescribes Hybridity: Climate and the Victorian Mixed-race Subject

In an 1857 *Saturday Review* article about the novel *Two Years Ago*, T. C. Sanders characterises Charles Kingsley's ideal man: he 'fears God and can walk a thousand miles in a thousand hours – [he] breathes God's free air on God's rich earth, and at the same time can hit a woodcock, doctor a horse, and twist a poker around his fingers' (qtd in Haley 1978: 108). Tom Thurnall, the fearless, constitutionally robust, well-travelled doctor and hero of *Two Years Ago* (1857), fits these requirements. His physical strength also manifests as a charmed immunity to illness: during a cholera epidemic in the fictional Cornish town Aberalva, '[Tom] thought nothing about death and danger at all . . . Sleep he got when he could, and food as often as he could; into the sea he leapt, morning and night, and came out fresher each time' (1857: 288).

For the majority of Aberalva's fictional inhabitants, not blessed with Tom's iron constitution, disease is a particularly terrifying foe, omnipresent but invisible:

> All men moved about the streets slowly, fearfully; conscious of some awful unseen presence . . . some dreadful inevitable spell, which lay upon them like a nightmare weight; [they] walked to and fro warily, looking anxiously into each other's faces, not to ask 'How are you?' but 'How am I?' 'Do I look as if – ?' (1857: 284)

Disease is retributive in Charles Kingsley's schema, punishing those who choose to live in close, cramped quarters and who refuse the vigorous physical activity that God intended. The men's terror in this excerpt stems not just from disease's invisibility, but also from the sense that they could be already carrying cholera with themselves unawares. They must ask an acquaintance to read their own death sentence imprinted upon their features. Thus, the vulnerability felt in the face of disease is compounded by dependence on one's neighbour. Both reliance and gratitude are even more acute when the neighbour has some medical training or ability. The inhabitants of Aberalva express pathetic regret that they did not listen to Tom's exhortations to space themselves out and become more active before the cholera arrived. They now turn to him with frantic appeals to save them from their fate.

A sanitary reformer in the mould of Edwin Chadwick and Florence Nightingale, Kingsley felt that disease arose from crowding, filth and poisonous vapours.[1] Kingsley's contemporaries named his perspective 'muscular Christianity', recognising that the author strong-arms his readers by inspiring in them fear and uncertainty about their own health practices and then shows them the way, with examples like Tom Thurnall, to an active, devout lifestyle. Kingsley's muscular Christianity, however appealing it may have been to some English subjects, was not uncontested in its bid to define the ideal British subject. *Wonderful Adventures of Mrs Seacole in Many Lands* by Jamaican Creole nurse and hotelier Mary Seacole, also published in 1857, presents an alternative vision. During this fraught time, British soldiers and colonists were suffering strikingly high death tolls abroad. Mary Seacole's status within British society could not have been more different from Charles Kingsley's, and yet both imbue their narratives with medical authority in order to inspire doubt and fear in their white readers regarding white vigour. Although Kingsley is writing fiction and Seacole autobiography, both depict characters who protect England's national interests by healing white Anglo bodies during peacetime and in the Crimean War.

How does a mixed-race woman wield authority through first-hand narration of illness in distinctive ways from her white counterparts? The majority of Kingsley's stories are set within the boundaries of Britain, and he demonstrates that the weakening of the Anglo-British constitution can be reversed through exercise and better sanitation. In contrast, Seacole uses the language of climates and constitutions in order to stress white British subjects' incompatibility with the tropics and to valorise racially mixed subjects, who survive different disease environments. She is content to leave her readers disoriented, their concerns unresolved. While Tom Thurnall provides a model of good health to which many white Britons can aspire, Mrs Seacole's model – namely, herself – cannot be copied.[2]

Since its original publication, Mary Seacole's book has received critical praise for its straightforward, sincere tone. Readers have been encouraged to experience her words as strikingly honest, beginning with W. H. Russell's original 1857 introduction. As a famous Crimean war correspondent known for exposing military and medical disorganisation, Russell's commendation lends credibility to Seacole as war witness and as caregiver. Russell also stimulates readers' sympathies by emphasising Seacole's personal sacrifices and depicting her as much more vulnerable than she ever would have depicted herself. More recent analyses of *Wonderful Adventures* have begun to acknowledge, however, that a sincere tone often can be considered rather than spontaneous, and that Seacole's 'confessional strategy' 'entices readers to accept [her] assertions at face value' (Fluhr 2006: 107). Her transparent narrative persona no doubt enhanced the book's primary function – to garner money to reimburse her nursing efforts abroad. One can think of the text as a kind of retrospective résumé: Seacole wishes to be paid now for a job she performed in the past. A mysterious and opaque text would be ineffective.

This chapter reads Seacole's strategies of self-portrayal as intentional and powerful, rather than as a plea for racialised acceptance. By emphasising her own superior constitution, Seacole does not align herself with her white readership but rather claims their respect and acceptance on her own terms. Frantz Fanon, in *Black Skin, White Masks*, argues that 'Ontology does not permit us to understand the being of the black man. For . . . he must be black in relation to the white man (1967: 109). Unfortunately, the 'white world, the only honorable one, bar[s] [him] from participation' (14). Several contemporary critics and biographers have tended to read Seacole in the Fanonian tradition (see Robinson 2005; Killingray 2003; Innes 2008). They believe rejections from British society dampened Seacole's spirit and that one of her primary motivations was to find acceptance within white British culture. In *Maps of Englishness*, Simon Gikandi argues that '[Seacole] assumes that it is only within the dominant codes of Victorian England that she can inscribe herself as a subject' (1996: 131). It is important here to distinguish between the 'dominant code' of racist hierarchies and the 'dominant code' of national pride. Indeed, Seacole may feel a loyalty towards Britain as nation that she does not feel towards the Britons as race. One need not read Seacole's memoir as motivated by the same 'shame and self-contempt' that Fanon believes people of colour develop when confronted with their own otherness (1967: 116). Rather than inscribing herself within the 'dominant codes' of British society, Seacole manipulates elements of several discourses to script an alternative identity. She maintains the integrity of the disparate strains of her ancestry, rather than subsuming one into another to gain entry into a dominant group.[3]

Rather than manipulating scientific discourse in order to allay her readers' worries as to their biological supremacy, as might a colonial apologist, Seacole chooses to reinforce those worries and establish herself as a palliative for British ills. However, she implies that she can only help Britons to survive temporarily in inimical climates: they never will be 'adopted' permanently by colonial environments. While biographers, literary critics and historians have highlighted the self-authorising function of Seacole's narrative as well as taking note of her claims to medical knowledge, none have fully explored how racialised narratives of illness form the very foundation for her autobiographical authority.

Amy Robinson rightly suggests that *Wonderful Adventures* be read as 'a public manual of self-authorization as well as an entertaining and profitable account of a "life"' (1994: 537). She notes the important precedent set by Seacole's public performance of identity, arguing that in 'claiming public image as identity, and claiming that identity as authentic' (549), Seacole both 'rejects the distinction between private and public which has so often relegated women (as wives, mothers, domestic workers) to the "private" domestic sphere' and 'satirizes the ontological model which would make her the inferior copy of the true British subject' (554). Self-authorisation often involves demonstrating superior knowledge, strength or ability to those around one. As Sandra Gunning observes, Seacole 'negotiates the politics of white crisis very deliberately, making use of the ideological fissures that inevitably come into being to achieve her own economic and social success' (2001: 953). C. L. Innes notes that Seacole 'frequently affirms her superiority to European doctors and scientists in her understanding of the causes and cures for particular diseases' (2008: 128), but neither Gunning nor Innes explains how Seacole puts her scientific knowledge into play when 'negotiating the politics of white crisis' (Gunning 2001: 953).

This chapter bridges these two approaches, analysing Seacole's self-authorisation more clearly in terms of her medical narratives. By focusing on Seacole's depiction of suffering white colonists as well as her claim to superior medical knowledge and skills, one may observe how she exploits the fissures within the ideology of white constitutional superiority created by Britons' experiences with tropical disease. Seacole presents herself as the ideal, mixed-race subject, whose strong constitution allows her to travel between disease environments, curing colonisers of what ails them. Some might argue that this only proves that she ingratiates herself by inspiring guilt and fear in her readers rather than pity. On the contrary, Seacole cannily borrows, subverts and appropriates rhetorical elements from the overlapping mid-Victorian discourses of racial hybridity and constitutional medicine to suit her own goals. She proves her legitimacy as a hybrid Briton, while undermining scientifically justified racism, and by implication, Imperial ideology.

Climate and Hybridity

Seacole opens her book by presenting her own mixed-race pedigree. She was born to a Creole mother and a Scottish father in Kingston, Jamaica in 1805. Though she invokes her father's background first, perhaps in order to establish a common ground with her reader, equal emphasis is placed on both her positive Scottish and Creole inheritances: 'I am a Creole, and have good Scotch blood coursing in my veins . . . My father was a soldier, of an old Scotch family . . . my mother . . . was, like very many of the Creole women, an admirable doctress' (1857: 1–2). During Seacole's time, 'Creole' could indicate a person of either 'European or African Negro race' who was 'born or naturalized in the West Indies' (*OED* online). However, both the book's original cover illustration and Seacole's repeated references within the text to her skin colour demonstrate that she is frank about her African heritage.

Seacole had almost certainly encountered racial prejudice in Jamaica, where slavery was alive until 1834, and where her mother catered to the needs of guests who probably displayed varying degrees of respectfulness. In Jamaica, mixed-race individuals were ranked into hierarchies 'like sugar or coffee' based on the relative darkness or lightness of their skin, labelled 'sambo, mulatto, quadroon' and so on (Robinson 2005: 6). However, this taxonomy may have arisen partly to articulate the differences between subjects of mixed race, because there were so many in Jamaica. Fluhr states that 'interracial liaisons were commonplace' (2006: 108) in the West Indies; Gunning suggests that miscegenation was 'widely practiced and openly sanctioned' (2001: 957). It was not uncommon for a European soldier to take a native mistress, later establishing her as the head of a hotel or boarding house in order to give her and her children financial and social security. Part of Seacole's later self-confidence and pride may have stemmed from her early life: she grew up in an environment where, although whites might attempt to impose stratifications and guidelines of racial purity, subjects of mixed race and mixed heritage abounded, many of whom were in positions of social power.

In telling contrast to Joseph Conrad, Mary Kingsley and other Victorian travel writers who plot the unknown, 'dark' regions of Africa on maps before venturing there themselves, Seacole grew up tracing with her finger the route to Britain. She believed Britain could be another home to her, as it was her 'fatherland' twice over – the point of origin of her father, and also Jamaica's colonial parent: 'I was never weary of tracing upon an old map the route to England; and never followed with my gaze the stately ships homeward bound without longing to be in them, and see the blue hills of Jamaica fade in the distance' (4).[4] When she first visited England in 1821, she found that mixed-race subjects were not nearly as common or accepted in England as in the colonial context: 'some of the most vivid of my recollections are the efforts of the London street-boys to poke fun at my and my companion's complexion ...' (4). Such treatment would discourage many people, but Mary Seacole regards this episode less as a racial abjection than a miscomprehension of her value as vigorous, hybrid subject.

It is useful to outline briefly the circulating mid-century definitions of the term 'hybrid', in order to establish the discourse into which Seacole implicitly enters. Published in 1857, her book emerged at a time rife with debate about race and racial mixing. Although the furore regarding hybridity in books, magazines, journals and professional societies reached a high pitch in 1864, the rumblings of active discussion had been taking place since the 1840s. As outlined by the editors of the three-volume history *Race, Hybridity and Miscegenation* (2005), James Prichard (*The Natural History of Man*, 1855) was the 'leading race theorist' through the 1840s. He had theretofore 'largely won the day' with his arguments for monogenism.[5] However, American scientist J. C. Nott began a flood of articles and tracts against monogenism in the late 1840s and 1850s, which 'transformed the way racial mixing was seen' (Bernasconi and Dotson eds 2005: vii). His most famous book, *Types of Mankind* (1854), was a bestseller.

At the centre of the dispute was the issue of species distinction: were different races descended from one parent species, or were they discrete? The term 'hybridity' played a crucial part in this debate, because distinct species had historically not been thought capable of productive interbreeding (in other words, black and white mates should not be able to produce viable offspring, or the offspring should not themselves be fertile). Nott suggested that the age-old 'fertility' test was not accurate (Bernasconi and Dotson eds 2005: 9). He held that mixed-race human subjects are indeed 'hybrid' – according to his definition, the progeny of two distinct species – whose fertility does not cease at once but decreases through subsequent generations. By his definition, then, 'mulattoes' – the descendants of one black and one white parent – are less fertile and biologically weaker than 'purebreds' of either race. In his 1846 article attempting to disprove the 'Unity of the Human Race', Nott uses Jamaican mulattoes as an example – he says the progeny of a white and an African interbreeding are 'faulty stock' and the 'shortest-lived of any class of human' (qtd in Bernasconi and Dotson eds 2005: 52). Against Nott there arose a small but vocal contingent of theorists who argued that mixed-race individuals were in fact 'hardier'. The term 'miscegenation' was coined by a tract of that title, which propounded the argument that all races would be stronger through eventual mixture. This tract sparked a series of 1864 debates on the topic of hybridity.[6]

An anonymous review of the 'miscegenation' tract was published in the May 1864 issue of *The Anthropological Review*. The author of this review disagrees vehemently with the original text's assertion that 'The intermarriage of divers races is indispensable to a progressive human-ity', stating with overwhelming precision that 'This is totally false, and . . . rests on no scientific data, and is contradicted by many well-known facts' (Anonymous 1864: 117).[7] F. W. Farrar published 'On Hybridity' in the 1864 edition of the *Journal of the Anthropological Society of London*. His claim echoes Nott's: 'Mixture of types in *most* cases, if not all, leads to an "abrutissement" and degradation. Mulattoes, as is well known to practical physicians, have a special tendency to consumption and other diseases' (Farrar 1864: ccxxv).[8]

These excerpts from Victorian scientific discourse on race and disease demonstrate two things: first, that Mary Seacole tapped in to a very germane and contentious topic and, secondly, that the scientific com-munity was far from decided regarding the 'hardiness' of mixed-race subjects, and had mostly only anecdotal data with which to argue either side. Thus, for Seacole to imply that her own personal experience had demonstrated that white 'purebred' constitutions were inferior to her own was a canny move. Because of the limited sources pertaining to Seacole's life, it would be difficult to prove that she had read or heard of Nott's theories. However, by portraying herself as physically hardier and more emotionally resilient than 'purebred' subjects, she directly, if not explicitly, contradicts the strain of thought propounded by Nott and his followers, who contended that mixed-race subjects were biologi-cally inferior. Further, she rejects the historical definition of a 'hybrid' as being the product of two species, implying repeatedly throughout her book that mixed-race subjects are not only 'natural' but also in fact 'fitter' to survive myriad environments.

Such a celebration of mixed-race subjectivity tends to be associ-ated with a more contemporary definition of hybridity, such as that established by Homi Bhaba in *The Location of Culture* (1994). Many assume, with Robert Young (1995), that the 'old' definitions were only oppressive and polygenic. One may then conclude that the term invariably brings up spectres of scientifically justified racial separatism. However, the Victorian concept of hybridity was not merely under the purview of bigots. Applying the term 'hybrid' to Seacole's mixed-race status, which she repeatedly figures as positive, does not minimise the racial prejudice of the 1800s. It does suggest, however, that key terms and concepts regarding race and disease were in flux and under continual formation.

The book's structure is as hybrid as its narrator. As previously noted, Seacole rewrites the conventions of women's autobiography by stressing her profitable profession and public identity; she affects but undercuts a sense of her own modesty by including excerpts from testimonials. Bart Moore-Gilbert has noted that Seacole's text actively resists or inverts certain travel conventions (2009: 84). This formal hybridity may be related to Seacole's status as a Jamaican Creole, since Evelyn O'Callaghan claims that texts written about the West Indies often 'elude categorization' and 'call into question the usefulness of traditional generic boundaries in approaching the material' – this 'need to problematize categories' also applies 'to the writers themselves' (2004: 10). C. L. Innes observes this tendency to be especially acute in black and Asian writers engaging with a British audience: she says that such writers emphasise 'possibility and potentiality rather than fixed definitions' as well as 'inventiveness' in both their stories' content and the 'forms and genres which they combine or devise' (2008: 2).

If we acknowledge that there existed in the nineteenth century many forms of institutionalised racism, how did this Creole author muster the confidence to subvert both structural as well as thematic conventions? As will be demonstrated later through analysis of her book's reception, Seacole's British readership was amenable to her unique perspective and insights. In addition, Seacole's background and upbringing may have imbued her with a good deal of self-assurance. She had been raised to be skilled and independent. She was able to heal where others had failed, travel worldwide and retain her health, and bounce back from myriad crises with apparently undiminished strength. She was discouraged from foreign service by men and women physically weaker, less capable or less experienced than she, who claimed for themselves a superiority they did not earn but were rather born with. Instead of becoming a colonial apologist whose main goal was to ingratiate herself with these same men and women, Seacole might instead have learned the skill that fictional character Tom Thurnall mastered in his travels:

> He had watched human nature under every disguise, from the pomp of the ambassador, to the war paint of the savage, and formed his own clear, hard, practical estimate thereof. He did not wish to live on men, but live by them he must; and for that purpose he must study them, and especially their weaknesses . . . It was hard work; but necessary for a man who stood alone and self-poised in the middle of the universe. (Kingsley 1857: 35)

In spite of the obvious dissimilarities between Thurnall and Seacole, it is a similar image that I suggest one holds in mind when examining her text – strong, sure of her own abilities and able to inspire in others those emotions that best serve her ends. Although Seacole's rhetorical choices in *Wonderful Adventures* necessarily reflect her liminal status as a female of colour, just as importantly they reflect her powerful personality and undeniable physical resilience.

Disease and Degeneration: Mid-century Worries

One of the human mother's definitive traits is her indispensability. Mary Seacole's presence is vital, she argues, because her hardy constitution makes her exceptionally well suited for the job of nursing British subjects abroad. If whites are determined to colonise foreign lands, exposing themselves to hostile climates, Seacole implies that they will need surrogate mothers of mixed race who can survive different disease environments in order to nurse them back to health. Although her mothering functions to sustain the project of colonialism, it does not follow that Seacole supports or condones the colonial impulse. Rather, her primary goal is to insure for herself a vocation comprised of the elements she most values: personal freedom, entrepreneurship, adventure and exploration.

It was particularly easy to activate white British subjects' fear of disease in the middle of the nineteenth century. Britain of the 1850s was still reeling from the 'massive waves of contagious disease' of the 1830s and 1840s: two influenza epidemics and the first cholera epidemic occurred between 1831 and 1833; 1836–42 saw 'major epidemics of influenza, typhus, smallpox and scarlet fever'; and 1846–49 'felt the reverberations of typhus, typhoid and cholera epidemics' (Haley 1978: 6). The 1850s came after the adoption of the smallpox vaccine (discovered in the early nineteenth century and made mandatory in various countries up through the 1840s), but before the general acceptance of germ theory (refined during the 1870s): the 'causes and patterns of disease' were then still 'very much matters of speculation' (Haley 1978: 11). Undermined by the reported high death tolls abroad in certain tropical colonies, confidence levels about subjects as diverse as medical treatment options and the 'future of the race' were by no means high. As historian Simon Schama explains, 'The omnipresence of death seemed disproportionately chastening to a generation breezy with not entirely undeserved confidence that they had done more than any of their predecessors to master their physical environment' (2000: 223). In the 'tantalizingly slight gap between knowledge and mastery, mortality entered to mock the Victorian sense of control over life' (223).

Mid-century fictions such as *Two Years Ago* reflect such concerns. The experience of Tom Thurnall – a brave and physically rechargeable healthy male English subject, impervious to the lack of life's basic necessities – contrasted with how many individuals fared under nineteenth-century disease outbreaks and their aftermaths. Charles Kingsley's British readership would have been painfully aware that young men cannot rejuvenate themselves with bracing dips in the sea, after having foregone food, water and dry clothes. If Tom Thurnall represented one author's wishful imagining of perfect disease resistance, Mary Seacole was ready to correct this idealisation with a strong dose of bleak reality.

Her readers' awareness of their vulnerability to disease may have been reinforced by reports of the Crimean War, in which poor distribution of medical supplies and government mismanagement caused peaks in soldier mortality. Deaths from disease and malnutrition are now conservatively estimated to have been three times those from battle (Keller 2001: 19). The Crimean War spanned the years 1854–56. It arose from disputes over the control of the Christian holy places, the Danubian principalities and Mediterranean trade routes. The two sides – Imperial Russia versus the allied forces of France, the United Kingdom, the Kingdom of Sardinia and the Ottoman Empire – fought mostly on the Crimean peninsula in the Black Sea, but also in the regions of western Turkey, the Baltic Sea and the Pacific Ocean (Royle 1999: Prologue and chapter 1).

For the British, the Crimean War was militarily inconclusive and unsatisfying. Britain's own organisational and tactical failures were partly to blame for the lack of decisive victory. Supplies and medicine desperately needed by British troops were lost at sea before they reached their intended beneficiaries, or left to rot at the port with no one assigned to distribute them; bad preparation and health practices left troops vulnerable to cholera epidemics and exposure in winter; and military mismanagement led to debacles such as the Charge of the Light Brigade, in which six hundred soldiers were given orders to advance unprotected, with more than half falling to enemy fire. All these blunders have given the Crimean War the reputation of being 'one of history's bad jokes' (Royle 1999: ix).

This military draw had a profound psychological impact on those who directly experienced the war and also on those who observed it from home. Florence Nightingale fought first-hand against such failures in organisation when serving at the military hospital of Scutari. In March 1855, at the same time Mary Seacole was arriving at the front and trying to set up her 'British Hotel', Nightingale wrote despairingly, in a letter addressed to Baron Sidney Herbert,

> A great deal has been said of our 'self-sacrifice', 'heroism', so forth. The real humiliation, the real hardship of this place . . . is that we have to do with men who are neither gentlemen, nor men of education, nor men of feeling, whose only object is to keep themselves out of blame, who will neither make use of others, nor can be made use of. (Nightingale 1997: 107)

As someone who observed the war's mismanagement closely, the Duke of Wellington supported these views in his 1855 pamphlet 'Some Observations on the War in the Crimea'. He stated: 'From ignorance, and want of attention to a proper arrangement, the medical department has been defective in every point', in spite of the 'unwearied and meritorious exertions of the medical officers in the field, in the hospitals, and on board of crowded, unprovided and infectious transports' (Wellesley 1973: 6). For a representative of government, to whom the people looked for guidance, to claim that a significant portion of his army's forces had been inept, or 'defective in every point', shows how seriously Britain viewed its Crimean failures.

Seacole was able to activate a deeper concern circulating during the time of the Crimean War: that military failures might indicate a weakening of the British constitution. The *Oxford English Dictionary* gives 'constitution' a two-part definition: 'a. physical nature or character of the body in regard to healthiness, strength, vitality, etc.' and 'b. nature, character, or condition of mind; mind, disposition, temperament, temper' (*OED* online). These meanings have been in common use since the sixteenth century and certainly were current during the Victorian era. 'Constitution' as a concept is nevertheless slippery: much of one's constitutional make-up was thought to be determined by heredity (as in the sense of coming from 'good stock'), but environmental factors such as climate and lifestyle factors such as physical activity and diet were also thought to play a part. To what extent was not clear, as the theory of evolution was yet to be popularised by Darwin's 1859 *Origin of Species*. In other words, the line between adaptive and innate traits was even less defined than it is today. The two parts of a constitution – mental and physical strength – also bled together, as previously suggested by the analysis of Charles Kingsley's text: one's perspective and 'moral fibre' was thought to influence one's susceptibility to disease. Recurrent illness also eroded one's bravery and mental stability, thus leaving one (and by extension, one's descendants) further open to illness.

Charles Kingsley elaborates more explicitly on his worries regarding the fate of his nation and race in *Sanitary and Social Essays*, which were not published until 1880 but are clearly relevant to these mid-century fears: 'We talk of our hardy forefathers; and rightly. But they were . . .

of the strongest constitutions . . . a hard, valiant, and enterprising race' (Kingsley 1880: 22). English hardiness has declined, he argues, because industrialisation and technological breakthroughs have allowed weaklings to survive, and because most people have lost their appreciation of exercise and manual labour. Thus, constitutional strength is measured in terms of 'hardiness' – resistance to disease, 'valour' or bravery, upward mobility – and 'hardness', perhaps of emotion and will.

Kingsley spoke in the tradition of eighteenth-century physicians such as Thomas Beddoes and Thomas Trotter, who condemned the growing effects of 'modern' comfort on the English character: the English malady was a 'disease of civilization', they said, 'resulting from the consumption of too many luxuries'. This disease of civilisation resulted in British subjects' 'susceptibility to hysteria and a host of related nervous conditions, variously called hypochondria, spleen, vapours, lowness of spirits, melancholia, bile, excess sensibility, or, simply, nerves' (Logan 1997: 1). Although these nervous ailments had been heretofore idealised maladies of the aristocracy, the increase in wealth and luxury made possible by industrialism caused theorists such as Kingsley, Carlyle and Spenser to worry that the middle class was also becoming afflicted and national production would therefore decrease.

If the white British race was suffering a heightening of sensibility brought on by a lack of physical vigour and a slowly decreasing constitutional resistance to disease, this also caused medical theorists to be worried about the viability of colonial expansion. The second edition of Sir James Ranald Martin's *The Influence of Tropical Climates on European Constitutions*, published in 1855, states that the most important predisposing causes of yellow fever are '[a]dult age, the male sex, constitutional peculiarities, mental emotions' (588). There is little in this list that is under an individual's control, except perhaps 'mental emotions'. Those of Martin's readers most likely to be travelling to foreign lands and coming into contact with yellow fever – namely, young or middle-aged white men – could only hope they were free from 'constitutional peculiarities' and able to avoid the emotional extremes thought to leave one open to disease.

Therefore, Mary Seacole, who primarily nursed ailing white soldiers and imperialists, had open to her the possibility that mixed race might give her a physically hardier constitution than that of purebred whites. Further, armed with the belief that 'fear is [disease's] powerful auxiliary', she, as bedside companion, had every opportunity to form her own opinions about whether her patients' display of fear indicated that her own constitution was also hardier emotionally (Seacole 1857: 26). Seacole does not hesitate to display to her readers her conclusions on both of these subjects: conclusions that clearly display her own constitutional superiority.

'That yellow woman with the cholera medicine': Nursing the Sick White Body

Wonderful Adventures of Mrs Seacole in Many Lands documents the heroine's travels in the 'many lands' of Panama, Jamaica and the Crimea; her adventures in each of these locales centre on offering comfort and medical aid to those who are suffering. Her patients were mostly young men who served the British Empire abroad. Through her efforts, Mrs Seacole made many grateful friends among these men and their anxious families back in England. When the end of the Crimean War left her destitute, it was therefore natural that she should write a book pitched towards two main audiences: military men and their doting families. In order to discuss how Seacole perceived and constructed her own mixed-race identity, one must remain aware of this two-part intended audience. Like Charles Kingsley, Seacole strong-arms her readers by inspiring in them both fear of disease and gratitude towards the one protecting them from it. However, whereas Kingsley equates faith and healthful habits with the muscular Christian's superior health, Seacole implies that her racial hybridity is the source of her superior disease resistance.

Although Mary Seacole travelled among strangers in strange lands for much of her life, there was an eight-year interlude in this independent existence during which she married and established a household with Edwin Horatio Hamilton Seacole, a white British merchant about whom very little is known. Seacole's narration of her marriage is as de-sexualised as her later nursing narratives. It sets the tone for how Seacole relates to the men of empire she encounters. Mr Seacole's distinguishing characteristics, within his widow's account, are timidity, tractability and ill health. She uses active, dominating verbs when describing him: 'I married him . . . I took him down to Black River . . . I undertook the charge of him . . . I kept him alive as long as I could.' The only actions attributed to Mr Seacole during their marriage are proposing, becoming ill and dying: 'at last *he grew* so ill . . . Within a month of our arrival [in Kingston] *he died*. This was *my* first great trouble' (1857: 5–6, my emphasis).

Although there are people who Seacole encounters on her travels with whom she does not see eye to eye, such as Lola Montes, rude, young British children, and American men, they are introduced in the

Wonderful Adventures only to be dispensed with, serving as examples for her supposedly more enlightened readers of inappropriate behaviour (41, 4, 48). Seacole consistently exercises medical authority and maternal power over the white British men she nurses abroad. Much like Mr Seacole, these men are vulnerable and dependent on Seacole's abilities, and she is willing and able to minister to them. In the British male patients whose stories she narrates, Seacole commonly inspires acceptance, gratitude and loyalty.

Seacole positions herself throughout the text as surrogate mother to these blue-eyed, blond, young, white male subjects, whom she idealises and infantilises. A clear example can be found in her narration of the death of a surgeon who fell ill in Jamaica. She describes him, in health, as 'busy, light-hearted, and joyous as a good man should be'. When he fell ill, she says,

> they brought him to my house, where I nursed him, and grew fond of him – almost as fond as the poor lady his mother in England far away . . . I think he had some fondness for me . . .; for I used to call him 'My son – my dear child.'

As the young man is dying, he asks Seacole 'let me lay my head upon your breast . . . I miss my mother.' After he dies, Seacole says she wears 'a little gold brooch with his hair in it' (61–3). While lending comfort to this dying young man, Seacole also appropriates for herself the role of his mother, complete with the physical intimacies associated with mother–child relationships. Though she leaves no doubt she is a stand-in for 'the poor lady his mother' whom he misses so much, Seacole still claims for herself the rights of a mother to witness her child's life stages, just as she claims the right to carry a piece of the young man's body with her after he dies.

In order not to alienate the second faction of her audience, likely to have included British mothers, Seacole explains that the man's real mother sent Seacole the brooch after his death and thereby validated her as 'stand-in'. This scene simultaneously portrays Seacole as indispensable to and enmeshed with British society while distinguishing her from the position of charity case. However, she leaves no room for doubt that the Anglo-British mothers she substitutes could not survive, were they to travel to Jamaica or the Crimea. As Sandra Gunning observes, 'the sickly English pale in comparison to Seacole and her ability to survive physical challenges the world over, whether she resides in Jamaica, Panama, the Crimea, or England' (2001: 962). As hybrid nurse and hotelier, then, Mary Seacole recreates home wherever she goes. She subverts the 'Angel in the House' ideal, implying that a white woman locked by disease vulnerability within her own nation cannot truly mother the sons of Empire. Only Seacole, who carries home to wherever it is needed, can truly provide for her 'sons'.

Seacole's maternalism forms an interesting contrast with Mary Kingsley's relationship to domestic roles. Kingsley clearly states that she can go to West Africa only because she has no children or husband to look after, thus excusing herself from ideals of British Victorian mothering. In contrast, Seacole posits herself as more capable of mothering young British men abroad than their own delicate Anglo mothers, who must stay at home. Both simultaneously free themselves from the British domestic sphere while trapping other women within it. Further, both Seacole and Kingsley balance fear-inspiring rhetoric with 'concern' for their British readers. Both portray the loss of life abroad as an unnecessary waste which could be prevented by less foreign intervention. However, Kingsley's concern, for the wives of missionaries or colonial officers, for example, is more sisterly than motherly in tone.

When she serves in the Crimea, Seacole continues to mother as well as to nurse boyish young men. These passages echo earlier ones in terms of diction ('a man's spirit,' 'like a fond mother') and nostalgic tone:

> There was one poor boy in the Artillery, with blue eyes and light golden hair, whom I nursed through a long and weary sickness, borne with all a man's spirit, and whom I grew to love like a fond old-fashioned mother. (153)

It is not just individual men she comes to love, but all those who pass through her care: 'I used to think it was like having a large family of children ill with fever' (152). With this phrase, Seacole uses tropes of motherhood to claim for herself space at the centre rather than at the margins of British society. By 'mothering' the youth of England, Seacole repaints the figure of Mother England as a self-portrait.

As implied by the name of her Crimean business, the British Hotel, Seacole does not merely attempt to replicate certain characteristics of Britain to give the soldiers 'a taste of home'. She play-acts Queen Victoria at the war front, and later presents herself as a representative English woman: 'very much delighted seemed the Russians to see an English woman. I wonder if they thought they all had my complexion' (188). Seacole demonstrates her ability to inhabit the image of the British subject, remaking it to look like her. Thus, her narrative anticipates a project that will be taken up by postcolonial subjects for years to come: to prove that the marginal is already central, hybridity is fait accompli, and the only thing left is for colonisers or former colonisers to realise this.

These repeated invocations of mothering inspire a question: how can Seacole mother white boys without invoking cultural worries of miscegenation? As Robert Young (1995) argues, Victorians often conflated hybridity with miscegenation. After all, Seacole herself exists only through the procreation of a white man and a woman of colour, a fact not likely to be missed by her white audience. William Daverell Cattell, an assistant surgeon in the British army, called Seacole 'an elderly mulatto from Jamaica' (qtd in Fluhr 2006: 104). As previously stated, a mulatto is by definition a cross between one black and one white partner. In her own mind, Seacole might be 'Creole', 'yellow' or even 'Jamaican'. To whites, she was mulatto. Seacole side-steps the explosive issue of miscegenation by carefully portraying herself as a de-sexualised, maternal figure: she becomes a 'nonsexual "aunty" in Panama' and '"mother" at the Crimean war front' (Fish 2004: 68). She does not recommend the creation of new hybrid subjects so much as the embracing of those already in existence. Further, she evades linking herself with any white man, or any man at all, while she is travelling in the capacity of healer and businesswoman, but rather skips over procreation straight to mothering.

Seacole de-emphasises her own sexuality by explaining her choice to stay unmarried – 'it was from a confidence in my own powers, and not at all from necessity, that I remained an unprotected female' – while making it clear that she is not attracted to white men (8). During a farewell speech in her honour, an American man in Cruces says that he wishes he could 'bleach' Mrs Seacole to make her white (and, by implication, thereby be able to court or marry her and bring her into white society). He is soundly rebuffed:

> as to his offer of bleaching me, I should, even if it were practicable, decline it without any thanks. As to the [American] society which the process might gain me admission into . . . judging from the specimens I have met here and elsewhere, I don't think I shall lose much by being excluded from it. (48)

With regard to her 'physical nature or character', Seacole has scientific precedent for thinking her disease resistance superior to that of whites; specifically, the constitutional disease rubric acknowledges that members of a race which have evolved in a certain climatic environment may have innate resistance to the diseases found in that environment.[9] During the 1850s, when she was travelling and writing, this possibility still met with much resistance in the scientific community. By 1871, when he published *The Descent of Man*, Darwin and his contemporaries had begun more often to acknowledge blacks' enhanced resistance to specific diseases: 'That negroes, and even mulattoes, are almost completely exempt from the yellow-fever ... has long been known. They likewise escape to a long extent the fatal intermittent fevers that prevail along at least 2600 miles of the shores of Africa' (Darwin 1981: 238). This 'immunity in the negro seems to be partly inherent,' Darwin opines, 'depending on some unknown peculiarity of the constitution, and partly the result of acclimatization' (243).[10]

As well as calling into question the strength of her patients' physical constitutions, Seacole uses her memoir as a medium through which to assess their 'nature, character, or condition of mind'. Drawing upon her extensive experience observing sickbed and deathbed scenes, Mary Seacole reaches the following conclusion: 'Death is always terrible – no one need be ashamed to fear it. How we bear it depends much upon our constitutions' (61). Feeling fear in the face of one's imminent mortality is natural: how one copes with that fear is determined by the relative strength or weakness of one's constitution. She reads these reactions, in turn, as indicating the subject's moral fibre. Seacole continues: 'I have seen some brave men, who have smiled at the cruellest amputation, die trembling like children; while others, whose lives have been spent in avoidance of the least danger or trouble, have drawn their last painful breath like heroes' (61). In other words, no matter what his socially prescribed role, each man's natural, underlying constitutional tendency asserts itself in times of extreme strain. In both cases, Seacole is not only comforter but also attentive audience to and experienced evaluator of the men's last moments. Although she does not specify whether she was one of many or few people present at their deaths, her description claims for herself the authority of witness, not just observer. Seacole measures both men in the foregoing comparison by their bravery in the face of pain. More importantly, she proves to her readers that she wields the power to publicly evaluate men's deaths in writing. She may depend on her readers for financial support, but they depend on her to protect their loved ones' reputations.

Although she clearly mourns her patients' passing, Seacole's sadness does not compromise her own health. In fact, while attending hundreds of sickbeds through the course of her lifetime, she only once mentions becoming ill: that instance, when she suffers briefly from cholera during a Panamanian outbreak, she attributes to exhaustion brought on by a surfeit of nursing others. One is meant to infer from her continued good health that she has a strong emotional constitution: she never succumbs to habitual or paralysing fear of disease, which was thought to bring on disease itself.[11] She describes herself as emotionally resilient, feeling deeply and then recovering quickly, which she attributes to her Creole heritage:

I do not think that we hot-blooded Creoles sorrow less for showing it impetuously; but I do think that the sharp edge of our grief wears down sooner than those who preserve an outward demeanor of calmness, and nurse their woe secretly in their hearts. (6)

Critics who read Seacole as driven to assimilate to white British culture think this passage's 'line in the sand' function anomalous. However, for Seacole to distinguish her own emotional (simultaneously racialised) constitution from that of her readers could be quite consistent with her underlying goal: to prove herself different through enhanced resistance to disease.

To demonstrate that her hybrid constitution makes her stronger than purebreds of either race, Seacole must form a contrast between her physical and emotional hardiness and the weakness of those whom she encounters. In order to achieve what I infer to be her goal – to prove mixed-race subjects indispensable members of society – Seacole not only portrays herself as healthy, hardy and willing to work, but she also navigates fraught rhetorical waters in order to present both whites and natives of the lands she visits as constitutionally inferior to her. She demonstrates that she has something more than either group, not just in terms of her unique cultural heritage and skills, but in terms of her innate disease resistance.

Seacole is even-handed in her constitutional condemnations of non-hybrid subjects. Although she is inclined to believe Creole Jamaicans, her 'people', constitutionally resistant to yellow fever, she is not so flattering towards the Panamanians. During the cholera outbreak in Panama, Seacole is quick to distinguish herself from natives who are more often afflicted with the disease. She says, 'the Cruces people bowed down before the plague in slavish despair . . . the natives, constitutionally cowardly, made not the feeblest show of resistance' (26). She characterises both whites and natives of foreign countries as weak – 'slavish', in fact – thereby implying that the hybrid is the only subject with a constitution sturdy enough to brave myriad disease environments. Thus, the colonising country should embrace individuals such as her, who are suited to the dangerous work of travelling abroad.

Seacole reinforces a common colonial concept of disease when she represents the natives who die from cholera as 'constitutionally cowardly'; however, such a move has an unavoidable double edge: if death rates from disease epidemics reflect cultural inferiority, what is the explanation for white British subjects dying in droves?[12] She cannot invoke 'constitutional' weakness without implicating all races that have been decimated by cholera, including the British. Like a hardy weed, however, she is quick to point out that she, a 'yellow' or mixed-race woman, is the one left standing: 'I think their chief reliance was on "the yellow woman from Jamaica with the cholera medicine"' (27). At the moment when Seacole manipulates circulating discourses of race and science in order to argue for her own independence and value, she inevitably enters into and changes the current racial discourses. What is especially remarkable is that she deftly inserts herself at the centre of British society without causing her Victorian readers to balk at having been painted as emotionally and physically delicate in the process.

Given Seacole's implication of English constitutional weakness, her remark that 'the yellow fever never made a more determined effort to exterminate the English in Jamaica than it did in that dreadful year' is quite telling (59). It not only personifies disease, but attributes intention to the disease, namely the extermination of English subjects. By pinpointing the English as particular victims, by using the word 'exterminate', common to writings that describe the fatality of tropical climates, and by therefore implying that disease 'cleaned up' the colonies, Seacole accomplishes two goals: she reinforces English colonisers' anxiety regarding the effects of the colonial project on their health and well-being, while also presenting herself as the diligent force combatting disease on their behalf.

These passages (1857: 59–60) are some of the most overtly sceptical regarding the viability of British colonialism to be found in the *Wonderful Adventures*, and Seacole gives force to her critique almost exclusively through medical narrative. She uses constitutionalism in spite of the fact that she clearly suspects some diseases to be contagious rather than spontaneously generative, as demonstrated by her comments during the yellow fever outbreak on Jamaica: 'Our idea – perhaps unfounded – was that a steamer from New Orleans was the means of introducing it into the island' (9). This seems to indicate that she wishes to draw her readers' attention, not to steamers from America, but to their own incompatibility with the foreign climate. Such overtones are made even more explicit in her later description of nursing in Jamaica, most likely because of the identification she feels with her home. 'It was a terrible thing,' she says, 'to see [white] young people in the youth and bloom of life suddenly stricken down, not in battle with an enemy that threatened their country, but in vain contest with a climate that refused to adopt them' (60). The word 'vain' here serves a critical function, by implying that the British case in Jamaica is a hopeless one, as the local climate will always wreak havoc with their health.

As Evelyn O'Callaghan has observed, the climate of the West Indies was often depicted in nineteenth-century cultural discourse as disease-ridden and dangerous; in contrast, certain pro-colonial, white women writers 'vindicated the land from concepts of unhealthiness' by waxing lyrical about the 'natural beauty of the Caribbean' or comparing its weather to the 'bracing English climate' (2004: 73–4). Such narrative strategies serve to neutralise environmental danger and can thereby function as rhetorical acts, both to establish belonging and also thereby to claim ownership and possession. A speaker's belief that his or her body is suited to the land implies that he or she is capable of conquering it. In contrast, by saying that the Jamaican climate 'refuses' to adopt whites, Seacole is employing the language of environmental determinism to imply that they will never become acclimatised to her native land because their constitutions are not suited for it. In this paragraph's concluding sentence, Seacole reinforces her critique: 'Indeed, the mother country pays a dear price for the possession of her colonies' (1857: 60). This statement seems to be underpinned by questions left unspoken, such as 'For what purpose? To what end?'

In addition to establishing her patients' urgent need for her skills, Seacole also documents those skills by narrating her confident application of remedies and medicines, many of which come from indigenous plants. Both Seacole and Africanus Horton, the subject of Chapter 3, imply that they have local subjects' knowledge of remedies as a result of their familiarity with the environments of Jamaica and West Africa, respectively. While Horton takes pains to document his medical knowledge according to the most stringent standards of Western science, Seacole is confident enough to blend both scientific curiosity as well as folk wisdom in her treatment of disease. Her arsenal of remedies includes both classic Western medicines such as calomel, but also mustard plasters, cinnamon water to drink, and massage with warm oil, camphor and 'spirits of wine' (31). Seacole underscores the folk wisdom behind her treatment of whites during the yellow fever epidemic in Jamaica. She says that Creoles practise the 'healing art' by

> seek[ing] out the simple remedies which are available for the terrible diseases by which foreigners are attacked, and which are found growing under the same circumstances which produce the ills they minister to. So true is it that beside the nettle ever grows the cure for its sting. (60)

Though Seacole claims that locals search for remedies out of 'affection' and 'anxiety' for 'English people', this passage underscores that both the diseases and their cures are local, and that the interloping English understand neither.

'Self-poised in the middle of the universe': Mrs Seacole's Reception

As has been demonstrated, in the *Wonderful Adventures* Seacole point-edly calls into question both the physical and emotional superiority of the white British constitution. One might reasonably expect, then, given the established debates regarding hybridity, some objections fol-lowing the memoir's publication – some hue and cry over whether her book was moral, proper or even accurate. It would seem likely that the picture Seacole paints within her book – a world of ailing white colonial-ists nursed by surrogate, mixed-race mothers – would appear to racist men such as J. C. Nott and their contemporaries as a terrible fate for Britain. Even if not perspicacious enough to pinpoint the specific impli-cations of Seacole's references to 'constitutions' and her appropriation of medical authority, one might predict that racially prejudiced readers would take issue with her confident and self-aggrandising tone.

Perhaps surprisingly, the only people who appear to have been biased against Seacole seemed to react more to her personality than to her race, and complained about her actions rather than her book. Florence Nightingale's interactions with Seacole epitomised such a bias: she thwarted Seacole's desire to serve as nurse in the Crimea, motivated by what seems to have been her overarching philosophy that people should keep to their 'places' in society. When asked by her brother-in-law whether she thought he should accept Mrs Seacole's petition to nurse the wounded in the 1870 Franco-Prussian War, Nightingale's reply is unequivocally negative:

> She kept – I will not call it a 'bad house' but something not very unlike it – in the Crimean War . . . I had the greatest difficulty in repelling Mrs Seacole's advances, & in preventing association between her & my nurses (absolutely out of the question). (qtd in Robinson 2005: 61)

This prejudice seems to be personally more than racially motivated. It could not have passed unnoticed that Seacole's warm, dry British Hotel, a 'recovery station' on the front, afforded soldiers many more comforts than Nightingale's Scutari hospital (Schama 2000: 221). Also, the rol-licking good times to be had at Seacole's hotel would have undermined the strict code of training and professionalism that Nightingale was attempting to associate with nursing.

Those who had no personal quibble with Mary Seacole, however, were universally complimentary. Far from exhibiting a racial preju-dice born of bitterness and fear, the men she had treated in Jamaica and the Crimea spread her reputation as an excellent nurse and a well-intentioned, kind woman. Their regard is demonstrated by the many excerpts from letters of praise that Seacole shamelessly includes in *Wonderful Adventures*. Significantly, those in a position of medical authority seem to have valued her mixed-race hardiness: as 'Late Medical Officer' A.G.M. attests in a letter reprinted by Seacole, 'Her peculiar fitness, in a constitutional point of view, for the duties of a medical attendant, needs no comment' (77). After her bankruptcy, Seacole's fans organised a lavish benefit in her honour at the Royal Surrey Gardens.[13] It spanned three days and was attended by several thousand people. *Wonderful Adventures* came out a month before the party, and was very well received. It 'sold out within eight months' and another issue was published in March of 1858 (Robinson 2005: 174).

The poem 'A Stir for Seacole', published in *Punch Magazine* on 6 December 1856, is a testament to her popularity and mainstream appeal. It portrays Seacole as a wartime heroine and encourages its readers to give her monetary support. Perhaps it does not present Seacole in entirely her preferred terms: she is repeatedly referred to as 'a kindly old soul' during a time of her life which she herself identifies as 'late summer' rather than old age; she is described as having a 'berry brown face', when she more often labels her colour throughout the *Wonderful Adventures* as 'yellow'; emphasis is placed on her role as hotelier and seller of goods before her nursing, when she identifies her true calling to be that of 'doctress', like her mother.[14] The piece is, however, unquestionably admiring in its treatment of Seacole. During a war when the British armed forces had been paralysed by decorum and red tape, *Punch* stresses that 'Dame Seacole's' service transcended prejudice:

> No store she set by the epaulette,
>   Be it worsted or gold-lace;
> For K.C.B or plain private SMITH
>   She still had one pleasant face. (Anonymous 1856: 221)[15]

A clue to the seeming contradiction between the potentially subversive content and form of her text and Seacole's reception may be found in the review of *Wonderful Adventures* published in the *Athenaeum Journal* on 25 July 1857. The author of this review lends his approbation to Seacole's book, calling it 'unpretending and affecting' (Anonymous 1857: 937). Like the *Punch* poem commending her ability to see beyond class and rank, the author of the *Athenaeum* review privileges Seacole's ability to avoid the niceties of decorous narration that might obscure the truth. During a war rife with spectacle and nationalistic rhetoric, Seacole may have used her otherness as permission to speak frankly and represent reality as she experienced it, a habit for which she found respect.[16]

Although full treatment of the Indian Mutiny is outside the scope of this study, it demands mention as a context relevant to the reception of Seacole's book, which was published the same year as hostilities broke out in India. Seacole's tone of national solidarity would not have gone amiss with an audience shocked by the political and social rifts within its most 'glorious' colonial holding. Further, many of the fatalities sustained by the Anglo-British army in India could be attributed to climatic factors such as forced marches in extreme heat, as well as diseases such as dysentery and cholera. Generals Anson and Barnard died of cholera, General Wilson replaced an ailing General Reed, and on 24 November Major General Havelock died of dysentery (Fremont-Barnes 2007: 11). Mary Seacole specialised in treating exactly these tropical diseases, which may have endeared her to a readership concerned with the viability of colonial expansion and maintenance in the face of hostile indigenous populations and endemic disease environments.

The nineteenth-century historian Alexander Kinglake suggested that 'it is with field-glasses, not prying microscopes, that people must watch a campaign' (1888: 334). During her first experiences in the Crimean War, Seacole's reports conform to this suggestion: 'It was very pretty to see [the troops] advance, and to watch how every now and then little clouds of white smoke puffed up from behind bushes and the crests of hills, and were answered by similar puffs.' However, she soon 'descends' and documents military skirmishes not from promontory outlooks above the field of battle but from amid the dying and fighting men (Seacole 1857: 148). When Seacole is not on the battlefield, she records the impermanence of life and the agonising pain suffered by those she tends at the British Hotel. There is no one better placed, she suggests, to witness the 'truths' of the Crimea.

By examining Mary Seacole's depiction of ailing white bodies, one discovers constitutionalism's potential to subvert, not merely reinforce, scientific colonial racism. Seacole deftly plays upon her readers' fears regarding their own physical superiority, positioning herself as indispensable to their ongoing survival. Seacole gains authority through depicting her first-hand experience of travel and medical practice. Both she and Africanus Horton, colonial subjects as well as practitioners of medicine, offer their expertise regarding local conditions and native remedies, ostensibly in order to improve the health of their white patients. Although they would seem thereby to facilitate colonial expansion, both Horton and Seacole imply that their medical knowledge can only prolong up to a point whites' habitation in the tropics. Seacole says that Britons 'struggle in vain' with the climate, and Horton asserts that Africa soon must be given back to the Africans because of the deadly climate (see Chapter 3). Even though Seacole arguably shares with Horton the subversive use of colonial medical narrative, she is the only subject under study in this book who posits mixed-race subjects as distinctively hardy. Seacole's self-valorisation through the manipulation of medical narrative, combined with her post-Crimean popularity, suggest that the status of Victorian mixed-race subjects was more multifaceted than has been previously thought.

Notes

1. Chadwick's 1843 *Report on the Sanitary Conditions of the Labouring Population of Great Britain* is the seminal text here. The *Report* goes to great pains to document, through census-taking and first-person observation, 'Proportions of Cases of Death from Epidemic Disease in the Provincial Towns and in the Metropolis', 'Instances of Disease aggravated by the retention of the Dead amidst the Living Rooms. . .' and many other pieces of data about death and dying. Chadwick then recommends that the queen lend her support to sanitary reform measures such as education, 'drainage, sewer construction, and building inspection' (Logan 1997: 152). The measures he suggests (some of which were adopted) involved developing a more sophisticated governmental infrastructure to monitor and legislate for public and individual health. Although the *Report* may have been well intentioned, unarguably performed the necessary function of bringing to wider attention the squalor and filth in which much of the labouring classes lived and was directly responsible for very practical, common-sense measures to 'clean up' select slums, still we can see in this and contemporaneous studies the roots of Foucault's 'biopower'.

2. Although acknowledged as an important figure during her time, Seacole was forgotten by historical accounts of the Crimea until the late twentieth century. 'The fact that her efforts were overlooked in later accounts of the war constitutes not only history's judgment of her role but, implicitly, a gloss on the position of its chosen heroine, Florence Nightingale' (Dereli 2003: 186). Seacole's popularity is currently in an upswing: a newly discovered portrait of her hangs in the British National Portrait Gallery, there is an exhibit dedicated to her in the Florence Nightingale Museum, and she is now presented as a historical figure of importance in the National Curriculum for British primary schools. She is also cited as an inspiration by contemporary nurses, who value her model of hands-on care, courage and initiative (see 'A role model for us all', 'Courageous and outrageous', Robinson 2005; Pearce 2004).

3. Unfortunately, contemporary readings of her work have tended to re-polarise her identity, labelling her as primarily a 'black woman writer', a proto-feminist or a colonial apologist. Race criticism continues to grapple

with how to theorise the rhetoric of hybridity – what one contemporary critic calls 'the problematic of multiracial pride' (Johnson 2005). Seacole's narrative, one of the first written by a free subject of mixed race, engages precisely this problematic by exploiting scientific discourse to prove her own unique abilities and strengths.

4. For a contrast, see Marlow's speech in *Heart of Darkness*: 'Now when I was a little chap I had a passion for maps. I would look for hours at South America, or Africa, or Australia and lose myself in all the glories of exploration. At that time there were many blank spaces on the earth and when I saw one that looked particularly inviting I would put my finger on it and say: When I grow up I will go there' (Conrad 1988: 11).

5. The theory that all races of humankind descend from a common ancestor; polygenists, conversely, believe that the races arose in different locations from difference species.

6. The tract eventually proved to be a hoax, written by theorists overstating their case in order to goad the opposite party into argument. Though an exaggeration, 'Miscegenation' expressed a serious perspective within scientific discourse of the time.

7. Review is of the pamphlet 'Miscegenation, or the Theory of the Blending of Races, Applied to the American White Man and Negro', published by Trubner and Co., 1864.

8. See Paul Broca, *On the Phenomenon of Hybridity in the Genus Homo* (1864) or Louis Agassiz, *An Essay on Classification* (1862). Foreshadowing of these theories can also be found in the earlier literature of 'natural history' and 'anthropology', such as Nott's *Types of Mankind* (1855) and Prichard's *Natural History of Man* (1843).

9. I use the term 'evolved' knowingly before its time as the best way to indicate long-term development of a race.

10. See Chapters 2, 3 and 4 for further discussion of the politics of acclimatisation.

11. See Chapters 4 and 5 for further discussion of the somatisation of disease.

12. Mary Kingsley navigates this issue by asserting that blacks are a permanently inferior species. Their constitutional strength is no threat, because they have no wish to 'climb the civilization ladder' (see Chapter 4).

13. As it turned out, the Royal Surrey Gardens Company could ill afford the luxury, as it was deeply in debt to begin with: after having paid its creditors at the rate of five shillings in the pound, the company was able to only give Mrs Seacole 57 pounds (Robinson 2005: 177).

14. I see an ironic parallel between how Victorian discourse simplified and re-labelled Seacole and how our contemporary treatment of her has accomplished much the same effect (continuing to call her the 'black Nightingale', for example, a nickname first given her by the soldiers she served in the Crimea).

15. This acceptance continued late into Seacole's life: Prince Viktor, Queen Victoria's nephew, sculpted a bust of Mrs Seacole as thanks for her care. Princess Alexandra of Wales, the queen's niece, seems to have been friendly with Seacole – there is some evidence Seacole served as her masseuse (Robinson 2005: 193).

16. See art historian Ulrich Keller's *The Ultimate Spectacle: A Visual History of the Crimean War* (2001). He argues that the Crimean War was the first 'media war' in history: battles were 'staged' choreographically, recorded through various media, and then re-staged in the realm of public discourse in order to enhance nationalist ideals of heroism.

Chapter 2

Mapping Miasma, Containing Fear: Richard Burton in West Africa

On 17 June 1864 Vice Admiral Sir John Hay addressed the House of Commons, severely criticising Lord Palmerston's government and proposing that a motion of censure be passed on the Cabinet. Emotionally overwrought by his brother's recent death on the Gold Coast, Hay asserted, 'The same men who ten years ago sent a British army to perish of cold, of hunger, of want of shelter in a Crimean winter . . . have now sent British troops to perish of fever, of thirst, and of want of shelter on the burning plains and fetid swamps of West Africa' (McIntyre 1967: 80). These two engagements – the war with Russia and the colonisation of Africa – are quite different in terms of geographical locale, date and national significance. However, Hay's speech suggests they were perceived as part of a similar trajectory of Britain's involvement abroad, about which many subjects felt deep worry and ambivalence.

Historian David McIntyre argues that Hay's speech, spurred by the government's decision to allot more troops to the protection of its trading colonies, was 'the first spark' in 'what became a blaze of publicity in criticism for the British West African settlements' (1967: 81). The result of this debate was that Edward Cardwell, the Secretary of State for the Colonies and head of the Colonial Office, 'called a halt to expansion' (96). He used the 1865 report of the parliamentary Select Committee on Africa (Western Coast) to formulate his policy (now known as the 'Cardwell Policy'). While discouraging expansion, the new policy also dictated that Britain encourage Africans to develop 'those qualities which may render it possible for [Britain] more and more to transfer to them the administration of all the Governments with a view to [Britain's] ultimate withdrawal'. Instead of being under British control, the ideal was for 'self-governing African states' to serve as 'agents of British influence' (100). Enforcement of this policy was extremely uneven. By the mid-1870s there was a renewal of intervention in native disputes and more aggressive colonial expansion. However, Cardwell's early 1860s investigation and the subsequent reform of colonial policy indicate the strength and volubility of the public's doubts regarding West African exploration. As evidenced by Hay's commanding speech, certain individuals who criticised imperial expansion wielded significant clout. In order to give force to their arguments, protesters portrayed West Africa as a hopelessly fatal environment for European subjects. According to their chain of reasoning, further investment of money, resources or manpower in the development of Africa was not only wasteful, but antithetical to the good of the nation.

Images in Victorian discourse of lonely, dying soldiers and colonists, exposed to danger by the parent nation, highlight such threads of ambivalence. Although the hunger and 'want of shelter' that killed British troops in the Crimea were mainly the result of government mismanagement, the 'cold . . . [of the] Crimean winter' was an inherent climatic challenge for which many felt British troops were unsuited, both in training and constitution. Hay's statement that men were 'sent to perish' implies that death is inevitable when subjects of a temperate climate travel to more extreme environments. The medicine of climate dictates that external elements such as heat and cold create an internal imbalance in the body and that this imbalance leads to disease. In the tropics, disease was often given the nebulous label of 'fever'. Hay argues that the troops were sent to 'perish of fever': by substituting 'fever' for heat, which would form a neater syntactical parallel with the 'cold . . . of a Crimean winter', he makes 'fever' as much an inherent fact of the West African environment as temperature is of other places.[1] To those who doubt the potential for 'acclimatisation', the 'burning plains' of West Africa become at least as, if not more, dangerous a threat to the British constitution as the cold of the Crimea.

As has been previously established, many explorers, doctors and scientists in the 1850s and 1860s believed that tropical illnesses were caused by climatic influences such as miasma, rotting vegetation, dampness or merciless heat. We now know that encountering new 'disease environments' means encountering bacteria, viruses and protozoa against which our bodies have limited defences, but many mid-Victorians thought that new disease environments were just that – foreign environmental factors hostile to their physiological balance. Travel writers had an especially acute motivation for deciding upon and following a disease prevention rubric, given that many believed their health was under constant threat. Acclimatisation can be defined as successful, permanent adaptation to a new environment. Whether or not a certain traveller thought his or her body could adjust to the new climate strongly influenced whether he or she deemed colonial expansion to be practicable or foolhardy.

Extremely high mortality rates in West Africa, which was popularly termed the 'White Man's Grave', catalysed debates about the viability of colonial expansion. The invocation of West Africa as potentially fatal for whites was not simply a rhetorical move. While regular quinine prophylaxis began to lower the white mortality rate from the 1840s, its most dramatic effects were not felt until after 1875 in British West Africa (Curtin 1989: 107). Curtin estimates that British military mortality in West Africa between 1859 and 1875 averaged 151 per 1,000 (1998: 70). Disease prevention during the latter decades of the nineteenth century gradually improved, especially after Ronald Ross's discovery in 1898 that mosquitoes transmitted malaria. Even by the period 1909–13, however, the rate of '6 to 24 deaths per 1,000 per year' still left tropical Africa 'the most dangerous region in the world' (Curtin 1989: 69). While the improvement in medical treatment was impressive, death rates 'were not low for Europe at that time'. Curtin asserts that, even as late as the beginning of the twentieth century, 'to send officials to West Africa . . . exposed them to a risk of death five to seven times higher than the expected death rate at home' (1989: 85).

Ambivalence regarding the colonisation of West Africa is evident in the political speeches, tracts and exploration literature of the mid-Victorian era. West African settlements, colonies and protectorates were alternately characterised as deathtraps or sites of unlimited trade potential. The Anglo-British citizens who depended on the region for their livelihood and lifestyle were understandably conflicted. Naturally, they were loath to agree with those who thought the area to be inherently unsuitable for whites. In order to explain their repeated illness and justify their continued presence abroad, mid-nineteenth-century travel writers creatively and selectively combined different strains of medical, racial and political rhetoric in ways that enhanced their own narrative authority. Such figures include the 'great adventurers' such as Livingstone, Speke, Stanley and Richard Burton, but also less frequently cited writers such as Winwood Reade, James McWilliam and Thomas Hutchinson, whose works have similar, though sometimes more extreme, rhetorical and stylistic hallmarks to those of their more famous contemporaries.

Some Victorian opponents of African colonialism asserted that the climate was irredeemably fatal to whites; others, such as Cardwell and Christian missionaries, claimed that Africans should be nurtured into self-sufficiency. African explorers and traders were among the most voluble and extremist in their opinions regarding acclimatisation and its relationship to race; within this group, Sir Richard Francis Burton was one of the most famous and prolific. Burton's personal investment in African colonialism, his subscription to certain medical and racial doctrines, and his hostility towards African natives are all interwoven within his travel writing. This chapter traces the arc of Burton's engagement with the tropical climate and its effects on the white body, from *Goa and the Blue Mountains* (1851), to *The Lake Regions of Central Africa* (1860), to *Wanderings in West Africa* (1863). When Burton visits the 'ghost town' of Goa in India, he forms conclusions that later influence his perception of Africa: races must be kept separate in order to guarantee imperial success. In *The Lake Regions of Central Africa*, he uses vivid sensory details and detailed first-person descriptions of illness in order to bolster his own heroic persona and also to de-authorise his companion, John Speke. Finally, in *Wanderings in West Africa*, he zooms out to create hygienic maps, allowing space for ongoing white settlement at higher African elevations.

This chapter considers how Burton struggles to reconcile the vulnerable white body with the colonial impulse. Sustained engagement with Burton's medical narration is noticeably absent from previous discussions of his work. Mary Louise Pratt famously cites a passage from Burton's *Lake Regions of Central Africa* in order to illustrate 'the conventional means which create qualitative and quantitative value for the explorer's achievement': the narrator often aestheticises the landscape, then imbues it with 'density of meaning', and finally assumes a position of 'mastery', gazing out across the landscape with a stance that Pratt calls 'monarch of all I survey' (1992: 204–5). However, Pratt does not fully connect the passage from *Lake Regions* with its immediate context. While she mentions that Burton's 'discovery' of Lake Tanganyika is 'particularly problematic' because 'he had been so ill he had to be carried much of the way by African assistants', she presumably does so only in order to draw attention to the often false or constructed heroism inherent in moments of colonial 'arrival' (204).

The fact of Burton's severe illness is not merely an ironic footnote to this passage, however: it is inextricable from the 'qualitative and quantitative value' with which he imbues the landscape. He romanticises his promontory position and outlook partly due to its contrast with the unhealthful jungle, swamps and marshes through which he has just travelled; he assumes that his readers will read the productive potential of the 'headlands' and 'capes' in terms of their healthful positioning, ventilation and elevation. Many of the most vehemently imperialist texts such as Burton's were written to counteract what explorers felt was Britain's sluggish imperial impulse. By focusing on concepts of environmental pathology in mid-century travel writing to Africa, one may witness how writers such as Burton attempt to depict and then delimit dangers to the white body.

Believing that Britain had the right to colonise and the right to benefit from colonisation was not the same as believing that Britons could survive abroad. In Burton's case, he first documents disease and then maps the space for possible health in order to encourage further West African colonisation. The imperial 'gaze' has been the subject of rich critical discourse. David Spurr believes this commanding view is the 'originating gesture of colonization itself, making possible the exploration and mapping of territory which serves as the preliminary to a colonial order' (1993: 15–16). I suggest that the 'gaze' of pro-imperial explorers such as Burton functions to map the healthfulness of the land and thereby to contain worries regarding the ability of the white body to survive in the tropics. The colonising 'gaze' is often a medical gaze: its process of knowledge-formation is inextricable from the diagnostic gaze of a medical geographer.

In analysing Burton's heroic manipulation of his own illness and his authoritative 'mapping' of health and the environment in West Africa, I assume that he helps to consolidate colonial knowledge and to change the course of colonial politics. Such a reading is in line with Ben Grant's assertion that 'The appropriation of foreign territories and people in the service of British imperialism was written as an appropriation by certain individuals, with their own interests and obsessions' and that the 'aggrandizement of the nation, therefore, went hand-in-hand with the self-aggrandizement of its subjects' (Grant 2009: 5). This chapter illustrates how Burton aggrandises the 'white man's burden' of tropical disease through first-person narration of illness in the service of empire.

When approaching Burton's African writing from this perspective, I take quite seriously the fact that both *The Lake Regions of Central Africa* and *Wanderings in West Africa* are framed by explicit discussions of illness. In the preface to *Lake Regions*, Burton says,

> I had intended this record of personal adventure to appear immediately after my return to Europe, in May 1859. The impaired health, the depression of spirits, and worse still the annoyance of official correspondence, which to me have been the sole results of African Exploration, may be admitted as valid reasons for the delay. (1860: vii)

This claim gives insight into what Burton hoped would be the outcome of his African travels – legitimate discovery and resulting fame. These hopes contrast with the devastating reality of shattered health, controversy and public conflict with John Speke. With this framework in mind, Burton's heroic depictions of his own illness become significant, as do his ominous portrayals of the African tropics. Further, Burton's disparaging remarks in *Lake Regions* imply that Speke was responsible for his own illness, which addled his brain: these passages show that illness from miasma could be used as grounds for moral judgement in a similar way as illness from contagion.

Burton also makes understanding illness and how it impacts on colonialism the frame for his 1863 work *Wanderings in West Africa*. In the Preface, Burton explicitly addresses his readers' worries about the fatal West African climate, asserting that he has satisfied the underlying purpose of his journey – 'to investigate the subject of West African mortality' (1863: xiv). He assures his readers: 'My conviction now is that the land might be rendered not more unhealthy than the East or West Indies.'[2] Currently, West Africa's 'fearful mortality' is caused 'principally [by] the bad positions of the settlements' – an error he seeks to remedy by documenting the problems inherent in their current position and suggesting methods for amelioration (xiv).

Ben Grant outlines Burton's 'geographical morality', or his tendency to superimpose racial and moral hierarchies on geographical locations. Such an approach effectively links Burton's study of racial anthropology with geography, but does not include colonial medicine within the understanding of both systems of knowledge. This chapter explicitly connects Burton's ideas of medical topography and climate with his experiences of illness, arguing that his texts create a kind of colonial medical map meant to facilitate the expansion of imperial power. For example, in the two-volume *Wanderings in West Africa* (written in 1862 and published in 1863, during the period of the Colonial Office debate on West Africa), Burton uses a long-range gaze in order to diagnose environmental ills and prescribe the hygienic reforms that he believes will make West African colonial expansion more feasible. Burton implies that whites have the capacity to acclimatise but blacks do not, thereby portraying natives as static and incapable of improvement. As demonstrated in Chapter 1, individuals who move successfully between disease environments wield power over other races: Mrs Seacole accesses this power by valorising her own hybridity. In contrast, Burton chooses to write landscape in a way that inscribes Africans within geographical boundaries, effectively trapping natives in a delimited characterological and geophysical space wherein whites are the conquerors, and blacks the conquered.

Burton's focus on images of rot, putrefaction and filthy water becomes significant for understanding his description of unhealthy locales. When not on land, Burton's mode of transport, the steamboat, gives him a comforting sense of separation from Africa's environmental influences. In Burton's writing, he first establishes that low-lying, damp land is unhealthy, as are the settlements located there; he then suggests that natives are well suited to such places, and should be kept there to do the manual labour necessary for colonial excavation of natural resources. Whites, however, should be moved to higher, cleaner places:

> When Sanitaria shall be erected, and the white population settled at an altitude above sea level, where it can regain its energy and resolution, when greater facilities of locomotion and intercourse are afforded, and, lastly, when the Africans are compelled by circumstances to become a working people, the 'Black Coast' will become a valuable possession. (1863: 237)[3]

Burton's various ideological subscriptions, to hygienic science and its techniques of medical mapping, as well as to white supremacy (based in polygenism), are far from coherent: these knowledge systems overlap and sometimes contradict each other, creating tension within his writing. Alan Bewell states, 'All disease representations can be said ... to be autobiographical, as expressions of an individual sense of pathogenic threat, and culturally specific, as they reflect the characteristic ways larger social groups see themselves and others' (1999: 5). By closely examining his description of health and the environment, one may observe Burton's emphatic attempts to resist, or at least to delimit, an 'individual sense of pathogenic threat'. Seacole's work provides examples of how to inspire fear of biological weakness in an audience, but close examination of Burton's work shows us that trying to contain, subsume or avoid such fear can lead to over-compensatory, racist rhetorical backlash.

Richard Burton

Richard Burton was born on 19 March 1821 to parents Martha and Joseph. His father was a former lieutenant colonel in the British army who took his family abroad after he fell into disfavour with his superiors.[4] The Burtons led a 'peripatetic existence', living in Blois, Lyons, Pisa, Siena, Florence, Rome, Naples and Pau during the span of nine years, which may explain Richard Burton's eventual mastery of over a dozen languages. After being expelled from Oxford's Trinity College, Burton served in the East India Company's army from 1842 to 1849. His exceptional ability at language acquisition made him well suited for gathering information from local subjects and reporting back to his superiors. He shifted from interviewing in army uniform to native dress, supposedly so as to obtain more accurate data.[5] He recorded his experiences serving in India in *Goa and the Blue Mountains* (1851), *Scinde, or the Unhappy Valley* (1851) and *Sindh and the Races That Inhabit the Valley of the Indus* (1851). Burton's travel narratives combine his formidable skill of translation with the attention to detail he cultivated while serving in the army, embellished by a preference for the salacious and dramatic.

In 1853 Burton accepted a challenge from the Royal Geographical Society, which was offering two hundred pounds to 'anyone who would explore the interior of Arabia' (Kennedy 2005: 58). He decided to go one step further, executing a trek to Mecca in the guise of a Muslim pilgrim. His choice was strongly influenced by his desire for maximum theatricality, fame and effect. These he achieved: his journey and the resulting narrative, *A Pilgrimage to Al-Medinah and Mecca* (1855), 'brought him into the national spotlight' (Kennedy 2005: 58). However, the attention was not all laudatory. Burton gained a certain notoriety by shocking his readers with details about infanticide, abortion and homosexual brothels in the lands he visited. Although some readers no doubt found these details titillating, many thought Burton went too far. His public persona took on a degree of the taboo associated with the practices and customs he delighted in describing.

Before graduating into a true man of the world, Burton still needed to assume the increasingly glamorous mantle of Victorian African explorer. Those elements of Africa that made it most intimidating – enormous uncharted territory, aggressive native tribes and hostile disease environments – also made it the ultimate challenge against which a traveller could test himself, afterwards laying claim 'to the status of national hero, an avatar of progress, reason, empire and civilization' (Kennedy 2005: 93). Burton's physical strength, willpower, linguistic and mapping skills and 'ethnographic curiosity' made him ideally suited to the role of African voyager (93).

First, Burton was engaged by the Royal Geographical Society to explore the Lake Regions of Africa; with Speke, he discovered Lake Tanganyika. Burton suffered greatly from his exposure to unfamiliar African disease environments: upon his homecoming, his fiancée Isabel described him as resembling 'a mere skeleton . . . his yellow-brown skin hanging in bags, his eyes protruding, and his lips drawn away from his teeth' (qtd in Lovell 1998: 305). During his travels, he told her, he had suffered from twenty-one attacks of fever, 'in addition to being partly paralyzed for some months and partly blind for others' (Lovell 1998: 305). After two years at home, Burton accepted the position of British Consul to Fernando Po. His voyage down the west coast of Africa to assume his post yielded a two-volume text, *Wanderings in West Africa*. In this book, Burton sought to explain why whites continually became ill in Africa. He chose to meet this challenge by focusing on images of miasma, rot and putrefaction, portraying portions of Africa's low-lying landscape as disease-ridden but higher elevations as healthy.

Acclimatisation was a fraught topic during the mid-Victorian era. Many anthropologists and scientific theorists held that groups of people became constitutionally accustomed to the climate in which they lived. Potentially, such groups adapted to local conditions more and more as generations passed, though such adaptation was not always articulated in evolutionary terms. However, certain individuals' constitutions were thought not to be suited for the location in which they resided, leading them to seek out the curative effect of locations with healthier atmospheres. As previously noted, terms such as 'race', 'species' and 'type' were in flux and under constant debate: theorists discussed whether groups of people adapted on the scale of country, continent or race. Of further concern was whether one group could change location and re-adapt, or whether each group was meant to range only within a given geographical area. Monogenists, those individuals who assumed one common human ancestor, were predisposed to believe in acclimatisation and evolution, since change over time was the obvious way to account for differences between races. Polygenists, imagining multiple centres of origin for the different races, often counted among their numbers the diehard anti-acclimatists, who believed that a given race's land of origin was its only natural habitat. Polygenism lent itself easily to racism through the oppressive gesture of labelling another race as an entirely discrete species, inevitably lower than one's own.

The colonial project short-circuited this rhetorical loop: it demanded that its proponents – often deeply racist, polygenist men – justify the appropriateness of travelling and settling in foreign, climatologically hostile lands. Burton's service in the name of Empire leads him to have an investment in the potential for acclimatisation: to live in Fernando Po for several years without such a possibility would seem to him tantamount to suicide. However, he emphatically rejects monogenism and resists sharing with blacks a common human ancestor. Perhaps, then, Burton's infamous bravado and authoritarian tone work to mask the contradictions and fissures within his scientific racism.

As a subscriber to humorally based hygienic science, Richard Burton believed that disease comes from noxious vapours and damp, low-lying air, not human contact. Hygienic science gained in popularity from the 1830s, and was at its peak when Burton travelled to West Africa. It slowly lost prestige as new discoveries bolstered the tenets of germ theory, but persisted as a major influence well into the dawning of the new century. Authors continued to use humorally inflected imagery to heighten the threatening quality of disease environments, as it allowed them a rhetorical flexibility that later contagionist imagery did not suit.[6]

Humanist reformers often embraced hygienic science and thereby did much good for the poor and downtrodden of English society. By trying to eliminate filth and its resultant 'poisonous vapours', such reformers often unwittingly removed pockets of cholera-contaminated water, flea-breeding rat nests and mosquito larvae-filled cesspools. But these reformers mainly focused on the dwelling places of the lower classes and refused to acknowledge that disease could be spread by the upper classes: thus began a policy of state-regulated health that selectively targeted specific sectors of society (see Foucault 2004; Gilbert 2004: xiv). Similarly, Burton exploits the elitist potential of hygienic practices by portraying the places where blacks reside as dirty and squalid. As some sanitary reformers in London assumed that the filth amid which the poor lived mirrored their inner debasement, so too Burton presents 'uncivilised' blacks as suited to their low-lying, dank settlements because they cannot know otherwise.[7]

In his African travel writing, Burton expresses the hope that white colonists can acclimatise to select 'healthful' regions of Africa; however, he holds that it is pointless for them to attempt to live in existing coastal settlements as the placement of most is 'execrable' (1863: 146). These should be left to the blacks, whose colonial masters govern from on high.[8] Richard Burton is the only one of the five authors under study in this book who both uses fear-inspiring images of climate and also encourages West African settlement. The foreboding elements he invokes are limited to specific locations, and he believes that he can offer practicable measures to counteract the poor climate. In case these 'scientific' and 'rational' suggestions are not enough to inspire enthusiasm for West African colonialism, Burton also shames, bullies and flatters his readers. He mocks measures inspired by contagionism, which he views as outdated and inhibiting free trade; he implies that France is better at taking advantage of the possibilities of West African colonisation than England; and he paints the native blacks as childish and lowly, far inferior to European subjects.[9]

Containing Illness: Environment and the Body

The sanitary reformers' tool for reform was the medical map. Upon this document they outlined low-lying areas of filth or decay and then sought to superimpose hygienic renovations. As Pamela K. Gilbert explains in *Mapping the Victorian Social Body*, 'Sanitary and medical mapping enabled mappers to both represent what they perceived before them and . . . an ideal to which the territory could hopefully be made to conform' (2004: xv). While Burton left the actual cartography to Speke, he uses his travel writing both to outline the unhealthy elements of the African landscape and then to prescribe measures for their possible improvement.

Burton uses concepts of 'environmental pathology' to justify the separation of races: a rhetorical move that is in line with the classic functions of colonial geography. In *Orientalism* (1978) and *Culture and Imperialism* (1993), Edward Said stresses that the practice of cartography helps colonisers to create geopolitical divides in new territories that benefit their national interests. Gilbert concurs: 'All maps are rhetorical. That is, all maps organize information according to systems of priority and thus, in effect, operate as arguments, presenting only partial views, which construct rather than simply describe an object of knowledge' (2004: 16). In his writings about Africa, Burton's gaze unites the functions of the sanitary medical map, meant to facilitate 'cleaning up' the landscape, with the colonial map, meant to facilitate the extraction of resources.

Burton uses visuality – what he sees and knows – to identify healthy and unhealthy climates: a seasoned hunter and adventurer, he casts his eye over a placid landscape. Scholars such as Dane Kennedy (1996), Judith T. Kenny (1997) and Mark Harrison (1999) have shown that the spatialising colonial gaze often read elevation as healthful in India. Indian hill stations provided racial separatism along with cooler climates for their residents and 'symbolized superiority and difference' (Kenny 1996: 656). In fact, Kenny claims, 'Europeans' oldest method of protection in the tropics was altitude' (656). Burton was influenced by this model of 'imperial geography' in India, 'with the natives in the plains and their British rulers in the hills', which informed how he engaged with other landscapes such as Africa (Grant 2009: 27). However, not all sources of tropical disease from climate can be seen – if one assumes that Burton's writing maps the effects of climate on the body and on the landscape, it becomes relevant to analyse his other sensory perceptions as well. Sensations of cold, clamminess, feverishness and exhaustion are all relevant, as are Burton's descriptions of taste and smell. This chapter traces an arc of Burton's sensory 'mapping' from his dire warnings in *Goa and the Blue Mountains*, through his heroic manipulations in *Lake Regions of Central Africa* to his large-scale analysis of land and environment in *Wanderings in West Africa*.

Burton wrote *Goa and the Blue Mountains* about his travels to the Indian hill station of Ootacamund, or Ooty, while on medical leave from army service in Sind. A significant portion of the book describes his journey through Goa, 'a Portuguese colony languishing in the ruins of past imperial glory' (Kennedy 1991: v). Goa had become a 'virtual ghost town' during the late seventeenth and early eighteenth centuries as a result of a succession of terrible cholera and malaria epidemics, which killed many and inspired many more to flee into the countryside (Kennedy 1991: ix). Burton draws lessons from Goa's fate regarding the 'danger of imperial decline' (xi), calling it a 'A city of the dead' (Burton 1991: 58). Although economic and disease factors played a part in Goa's downfall, these were merely the manifestations of the weak Portuguese constitution, undermined by over-indulgence and miscegenation. Burton intones,

> Pestilence, and wars with European and native powers, disturbances arising from unsettled home government, and, above all things, the slow but sure workings of the short-sighted policy of the Portuguese in intermarrying and identifying themselves with Hindoos of the lowest castes, made her fall as rapid as her rise was sudden and prodigious. (45)

Burton's book thereby enters into circulating debates regarding whether whites could survive over the long term in India: in the 1850s a parliamentary select committee concluded that Europeans should hold supervisory roles rather than widely settling in India (Kennedy 1991: xii). While in *Goa*, Burton seems to agree that whites risk degeneration from long-term colonial settlement, in his later African travel narratives he tries to carve out a space for British health. The dramatic contrast Burton creates in *Goa* between 'the moonlit scenery of the distant bay, and the dull grey piles of ruined or desolate habitations, the short-lived labours of man!' (61) establishes a pattern he will follow in *Lake Regions of Central Africa* and *Wanderings in West Africa*. These later texts are also haunted by spectres of imperial failure in the form of abandoned homesteads and mouldering colonial outposts, which are linked to the inescapable degenerative effects of climate.

Goa demonstrates how closely Burton feels climate is connected to disease: during his travels to Goa by ship, Burton complains that 'the wind that pours down the creek feels damp and chilly, teeming with unpleasant reminiscences of fever and ague' (20). His own sensory perception is the best tool of measurement here, as the 'damp and chilly wind' cues his body's memory, perhaps of an earlier exposure to similar conditions, which was then followed by malarial illness. Due to the nebulous sources of tropical disease, it is Burton's own sensitivity and his ability to connect present with past circumstances that proves his medical authority. No other 'test' is needed than his observation and experience.

Burton bolsters the lived experience of unhealthy climates with more general observations of India's medical geography. For example, he believes he knows better than those who attest to the healthiness of the hill station at Coonoor. He says,

> The situation is not considered a good one: its proximity to the edge of the hills, renders it liable to mists, fogs, and . . . the malaria which haunts the jungly forests belting the foot of the hills. Those who have suffered from the obstinate fevers of the plains do well to avoid Coonoor. (265)

The source of his superior knowledge becomes evident when he condemns the famous health resort of Ooty in similar terms: Burton believes himself to be more qualified to assess the Indian environment than governmental health authorities as a result of his status as a 'demi-Oriental': 'we demi-Orientals, who know by experience the dangers of mountain air in India, only wonder at the man who first planted a roof-tree upon the Neilgherries' (270).

One observes in his writings on India that, although Burton uses the example of Goa to justify the separation of Europeans from Indians, he does not support consistently the method of sending all Europeans to higher elevations as he does later in his writings on Africa. Burton prided himself on having passed as Arab during his journey to Mecca, and had a life-long fascination with Oriental culture: he styled his moustache in what he thought an exotic manner, sought out and translated cultural texts such as the Kama Sutra and collected Oriental erotic art. That he labels himself 'demi-Oriental' in the above passage, differentiating himself from the 'purely European reader', demonstrates how actively Burton sought to ally himself with certain marginal or other identities, cultivating an image of himself as 'outside the boundaries of class and custom' (Kennedy 2005: 57). If Ooty's mountain air is not healthful, then he may descend into the valleys of India, where he can spend enjoyable time with the natives.

Burton is much less predisposed to generosity of spirit with Africans than he is with 'orientals', and therefore much more absolute in his recommendations for the geophysical as well as cultural separation of whites from blacks. Dane Kennedy and Ben Grant have both observed that this may partly stem from Burton's inability to pass as an African native, which made him feel an outsider. When describing the African landscape, Burton falls back on traditional schematics: high altitudes are healthy and natives belong below. Burton applies his skill of colonial medical mapping to underscore the difference between Africans and Europeans. His literary methods work to keep blacks in their place – not just in terms of racial gradation, but in terms of geographical locale.

Any other kind of treatment could encourage the Africans to rise up: 'A ruling race cannot be too particular about these small matters. The white man's position is rendered much more precarious on the coast than it might be, if the black man were always kept in his proper place' (1863: 211).

The Royal Geographical Society funded Burton's 1856 expedition through central Africa, which was meant to help identify sources of viable trade. He was accompanied by John Hanning Speke, with whom he later had a very public feud over Speke's professed discovery of the source of the Nile. Burton's *Lake Regions of Central Africa* uses vivid sensory description, enhancing Burton's heroic persona through detailed first-person narrations of illness. Burton also depicts his knowledge of tropical 'fever' as more advanced than Speke's. Although both men become seriously ill, Burton implies that he uses better reasoning and intuition in order avoid or minimise illness, which demonstrates his superior knowledge of the African environment.

Overcoming tropical illness is a sign of heroism and a necessary step in colonial exploration. Burton says that the expedition guides, 'the Hindus', showed 'extreme unwillingness to open up the rich regions of copal and ivory to European eyes' (1860: 67). A brief 'coast-fever at Zanzibar' 'deceived' them that Burton's 'ardour for further adventure' had 'cooled', and 'their surprise at finding the contrary to be the case was not of a pleasant nature' (67). Burton both invests the African interior with the potential for untold riches and also implies that whites should not be discouraged by a 'seasoning' illness but rather continue on their course. He whets his readers' appetites for more adventure by casting his guides as the recalcitrant racial others who guard local treasures.

In his lecture 'To the Heart of Africa', presented in the 1860s and anthologised in the posthumous *Wanderings in Three Continents* (1901), Burton's travels through Central Africa are presented in a condensed manner. He uses sensory description in order to create for the listener a visceral experience of travelling from higher to lower tropical elevations. The following excerpt follows his trek from Rufutah to the Inenge basin. The beauty of higher elevations is linked in Burton's mind to their healthfulness, so that the gaze of the coloniser is also the gaze of the medical geographer. Like a pall cast over a fairytale landscape, the 'malarial' air of the lower jungle chases away health and good spirits:

> The dove, the peewit, and the guinea fowl fluttered about. The most grace-ful of animals, the zebra and the antelope, browsed in the distance. Then suddenly the fair scene would vanish as if by enchantment. We suddenly turned into a tangled mass of tall, fetid reeds, rank jungle, and forest. After the fiery sun and dry atmosphere of the plains, the sudden effect of the damp

and clammy chill was overpowering. In such places one feels poisoned by miasma; a shudder runs through the frame, and cold perspiration breaks over the brow. (1901: 113)

By invoking familiar, placid game animals at the beginning of the passage, Burton creates the sense of a non-threatening, bucolic landscape. The land's natural healthfulness is signified by the fact that the dove, harbinger of peace, and the zebra and antelope, identified as the 'most graceful of animals', favour these high plains. However, as he descends, Burton feels the unhealthy circumstances through his senses of touch, smell and his body's 'gut' responses. In the jungle, the reeds are 'rank', his skin 'clammy' and 'cold'. Miasma is mysterious and uncontrollable, mainly perceptible through its effects on the body.

In *Lake Regions*, Burton does not hesitate to write off entire districts through which he passes as unfit for colonisation by emphasising the inherent climatic factors that make settlement impossible, including polluted water, rotting tropical vegetation and 'sickly' sunlight. For example, he says that the water sources in the district of Muhonyera acquire 'from decomposed vegetation' an 'unnaturally sweet and slimy taste' (1860: 63). Although decomposing vegetation is nothing if not 'natural', the fact that it makes water unpalatable and perhaps unsafe for British consumption makes the entire area 'unnatural' for white habitation. He says that 'this part of the country' is 'little inhabited by reason of its malarious climate' but 'abounds in wild animals' (63). Similarly, in the 'malarious river-plain of the Kingari River', 'the water was bad, and a mortal smell of decay was emitted by the dark dank ground' (69). Burton echoes the common Victorian association of the tropics with 'excess' – an overabundant growth of vegetation may support large numbers of wild animals, but it also leads to rot and decomposition and is therefore unhealthy for whites. As Nancy Leys Stepan attests, the mid-century explorer believed that 'the heat and humidity of tropical places stimulated growth that was luxurious but also rank and wanton; tropical plants were wonderfully novel but at times bizarre; the animals were unusual but often deadly' (2001: 48). In contrast to the low-lying and unhealthy Muhonyera, the distant 'mountain-crags of Duthumi' are depicted positively as a place where 'the eye, long weary of low levels . . . rest[s] with a sensation of satisfaction' (Burton 1860: 64–5). The 'eye' being able to 'rest' when viewing the mountain implies the health-giving qualities of higher elevations; further, as Burton is able to 'sense' unhealthy locations through feelings of discomfort, so too a visual 'sensation of satisfaction' indicates the potential for well-being.

Burton depicts malarial environments as causing illness. At Tunda, he says, 'after a night passed amidst the rank vegetation, and within the malarious influence of the river, I arose weak and depressed, with aching head, burning eyes, and throbbing extremities' (1860: 71). He believes his illness is due to 'the alternations of damp heat and wet cold', fatigue, 'the exposure to sun and dew' and 'last, but not least, the wear and tear of mind at the prospect of imminent failure'. It is both the inconstancy of the climate as well as the insecurity of his position that makes Burton susceptible to fever, but he says 'it was too dangerous a place to show fear' and believes that because he has fought off worry, he has fought off the worst of the illness (72). The contrast this passage sets up between the nearly impossible odds against success and the narrator's determination to make the attempt can be heard through successive later narratives of exploration, including memoirs by Stanley as well as imperial adventure fiction, such as *King Solomon's Mines* (1885) by H. Rider Haggard.

It becomes a test of the explorer's character to understand and attempt to counteract the negative forces of the African climate. In Kiruru, where 'the weather was a succession of raw mist, rain in torrents, and fiery sunbursts; the land appeared rotten, and the jungle smelt of death' (82), Burton takes shelter in a warm and dry cottage while Speke 'remained in the reeking, miry tent'. Burton claims that Speke's poor judgement 'laid the foundation of the fever which threatened his life in the mountains of Usagara' (82). What Ben Grant calls Burton's 'moral geography' is also here a medical moral geography – the man who stays in a 'reeking, miry tent' is both less civilised and also to blame for his own resulting illness. Burton will use similar language in *Wanderings in West Africa* when he associates blacks with lower elevations. In both instances, only an inferior person remains in a poor location, because he lacks the refinement and sensitivity needed to 'sense' an unhealthy area and also lacks the motivation to leave it.

If each individual is responsible for becoming ill, then Burton must use very delicate rhetorical manoeuvring in order to maintain his own superior character when both he and Speke suffer from acute disease. Although a 'fever-fit' 'thoroughly prostrated' him, Burton is quick to stress that his experience of 'marsh fever' lasted only twenty days of what he calls the usual three weeks' duration, and that his 'companion suffered even more severely' (1860: 84). Burton claims that Speke 'had a fainting fit which strongly resembled a sun-stroke, and which seemed permanently to affect his brain' (84). This jibe is no doubt meant to call Speke's competence and thereby his later claim to fame into question, in contrast with Burton's own expertise, medical authority and physical resilience.

Although Burton invests Africa with much potential for trade, he believes it is dangerous for white subjects to linger too long in one place. It is evident that he fears degeneration through prolonged contact with tropical climates when he says, 'A prolonged halt causes general sickness' (1860: 94). Africa's sickly atmosphere corrupts the material symbols of Britain's military power and national virility:

> The humidity of the atmosphere corrodes everything with which it comes in contact; the springs of powder-flasks exposed to the damp snap like toasted quills; clothes feel limp and damp; paper, becoming soft and soppy by the loss of glazing, acts like a blotter; boots, books and botanical collections are blackened; metals are ever rusty; the best percussion caps, though labeled waterproof, will not detonate unless carefully stowed away in waxed cloth and tin bins; gunpowder, if not kept from the air, refuses to ignite; and wood becomes covered with mildew. (94)

The moisture of the atmosphere undermines the dual functions of the colonial expedition – to explore and to record. Forward momentum is stalled through the corruption of metal, wood, gunpowder and powder-flasks. The expedition is unable to contribute to colonial knowledge by taking observations and collecting specimens, as the climate makes paper, books and botanical collections 'black' or 'soppy'.

Historians of empire and science as well as postcolonial critics have shown how explorers often conflated local peoples with their environment. Specifically, imperialists were anxious about the potential of the jungle, forests and fields to 'mask' native bodies. As Richard Drayton observes in *Nature's Government* (2000), colonial expansion was often justified by the 'improvement' of tropical landscapes. 'Cultivation' of the landscape also functioned as a tool of control and containment of indigenous subjects. The following chapter, examining the writing of Sierra Leonean doctor Africanus Horton, shows a very different model for engaging with tropical vegetation. However, here Burton demonstrates characteristic imperial hostility towards native plants, which he thinks shelter native bodies. He is able to 'read' the riverbeds and shores, but stops short when he reaches the encircling brush. The lines of pebbles and seashells provide visual clues regarding how tides interact with the landscape, out of which Burton creates a kind of verbal topography: 'Especially near the estuary, river-terraces, like road embankments, here converging, there diverging, indicate by lines and strews of water-worn pebbles and sea-shells the secular uprise of the country and the declension of the stream to its present level' (1860: 103).

This rhythmic language and the bucolic depiction of this environment shift when Burton's eye is blocked by impenetrable marsh grasses: 'Produced by the black soils in the swamps and marshes', the grass 'rises to the height of 12–13 feet, and serves to conceal runaway slaves and malefactors: the stalks vary in thickness from a goose-quill to a man's finger' (103). The grasses thrive in an unhealthy marshland environment, nurtured by 'black soils' and in turn hiding black bodies. Burton depicts the brush as impenetrable and strong, blocking the intruding colonist with metaphorical hands made from stalks as thick as a man's finger. He lumps together 'runaway slaves and malefactors' by portraying both as fugitives from justice – a linguistic link that says much regarding his underlying ambivalence about slavery. Burton would not be alone among mid-century imperialists in implicitly condoning slavery. Even if slave trading had been abolished, Burton's scientific beliefs as well as his imperial politics justified the exploitation for British profit of goods obtained through inter-tribal warfare and slavery. Historian Anne Phillips claims that through much of the nineteenth century, 'British government turned a blind eye to local slavery in order to reap the benefits of agricultural production' (1989: 29). Finally, the foregoing passage recalls M'Cosh's representation of 'savage inhabitants' who look on 'composedly from the skirts of the woods' as whites face extermination from disease. Although natives are not pinpointed in these instances as the source of contagion, they are seen as complicit with, and perhaps even the will behind, the impenetrable and often fatal African environment.

In *Lake Regions of Central Africa*, Burton draws upon the structures of medical guidebooks in describing the progression of tropical diseases and then follows the same structure in his own first-person narration of illness. This superimposing of official description on to lived experience serves to enhance both Burton's medical and colonial authority as well as to bolster his brave and heroic persona. He describes in great sensory detail how it feels to suffer from severe malaria. I suggest that such narratives contributed to Burton's growing image as a man with extensive knowledge regarding African 'conditions': that is to say, to be familiar with the 'conditions' of the environment and the disease 'conditions' they engendered were skills as crucial to an explorer's authoritative reputation as his understanding of the political and cultural conditions of the colony.

When describing the Mgeta valley, Burton claims that 'the principal diseases' are 'severe ulcerations and fevers, generally of the tertian type' (1860: 104). Tertian 'fever' was identified by the life cycle of the malarial parasite, which causes fever to peak at intervals of more than two days. One sees a pattern emerging whereby Burton delimits the types of African 'fever' through a succession of labels. His initial bout of malaria he calls 'coast-fever', the illness in Dunkuru he calls 'marsh fever' and the following description is of 'seasoning fever'. He delimits all by place and period, though of course he cannot know when or where he first contracted malarial parasites. The 'Mkunguru', or 'seasoning fever', as Burton describes it,

> begins with coldness in the toes and finger-tips; a frigid shiver seems to creep up the legs . . . nausea ushers in the hot stage: the head burns, the action of the heart becomes violent, thirst rages, and a painful weight presses upon the eyeballs: it is often accompanied by a violent cough and irritation. Strange visions, as in delirium, appear to the patient, and the excitement of the brain is proved by unusual loquacity. When the fit passes off with copious perspiration the head is often affected, the ears buzz, and the limbs are weak. (1860: 105)

This passage shares many markers with Ford's description of fever as cited in the Introduction, including a strict chronological progression; an interrelationship between physical and mental symptoms, so that the observer can 'read' the progression of the disease through visual as well as behavioural indications in the patient; and a menacing overtone from words such as 'severe', 'violent', 'rages' and 'painful'. There are direct overlaps with Ford's diction – while Ford says that perspiration 'ushers in' (1856: 10) the resolution of the fever, Burton says nausea 'ushers in' the 'hot stage'; Ford says the first hints of fever are 'mental excitement' while Burton identifies 'excitement of the brain' as part of the feverish stage. The similarities between the language of both texts demonstrate Burton's familiarity with medical description, which he adapts to suits his own observations.

Burton's most sustained first-person description of fever appears as he approaches the town of Kajjanjeri in *Lake Regions*. He defines his illness as 'a formidable obstacle to progress' (1860: 403), a challenge to the momentum of imperial exploration. He decouples this episode of malaria from previous ones, claiming 'the miasmatic air of Sorora had sown the seeds of fresh illness' (403). By identifying the first sign of impending fever as a state of emotional distress – an 'unusual sensation of nervous irritability' – Burton is able to claim greater insight than would be accorded an external observer. He can sense the preliminary stages of illness in himself, observing both the irritability and the following 'general shudder as in the cold paroxysm of fever' with more acuity because he is living them.

The following narrative makes marked use of sensory detail, as Burton says 'Presently the extremities began to weigh and to burn as if exposed to a glowing fire' (404). He continues

> The whole body was palsied, powerless, motionless, and the limbs appeared to wither and die; the feet had lost all sensation, except a throbbing and

tingling, as if pricked by a number of needle points; the arms refused to be directed by will, and to the hands the touch of cloth and stone was the same. Gradually the attack seemed to spread upwards until it compressed the ribs; there, however, it stopped short. (404)

Burton writes his loss of health as a loss of agency and will. The rhythm of 'palsied, powerless, motionless' communicates his total debilitation, while the use of the third person ('the whole body', 'the hands', 'the feet', 'the arms') captures the disassociation Burton feels from his body as well as mimicking the objective detachment of a doctor or an experimental scientist. He builds suspense by saying 'the attack seemed to spread upward until it compressed the ribs' so that the reader may feel relieved when 'it stopped short'.

When 'the attack' 'reache[s] its height', Burton quotes Tennyson's poem 'The Princess' to illustrate his brush with death: 'I saw yawning wide to receive me "those dark gates across the wild/ That no man knows"' (403). The quotation paints Burton as a heroic lover, wounded while fighting for a maiden's love, rather than an imperialist on a quest for the source of the Nile, which lends romantic rather than political overtones to his 'quest' and suggests that readers should sympathise with him as they would with a man seeking love rather than the more worldly goal of riches and fame. He portrays himself as selfless and noble when he says, 'If one of us [he or Speke] was lost, the other might survive to carry home the results of the exploration. I had undertaken the journey . . . with the resolve to either do or die. I had done my best' (404).

Although the local guides minister to him, Burton dismisses their knowledge by saying his illness is 'beyond' their skills. He stresses that he is 'at a distance of two months from medical aid', which implies that qualified medical aid could only be found in the form of a European-trained doctor. Instead, he treats himself – 'I tried the usual remedies without effect' – and diagnoses himself as well – 'the duration of the attack presently revealed what it was' (severe malaria with paralysis) (405). Burton's service to empire takes a toll that extends past the duration of his expedition: 'The contraction of the muscles, which were tightened like ligaments above and below the knees, prevented me from walking to any distance for nearly a year; the numbness of the hands and feet disappeared even more slowly' (404–5). As the foregoing examples illustrate, in his early African travel writing, Burton maps disease on to the landscape and on to his own body in order to enhance his narrative authority and craft the persona of explorer and expert. He builds on this authority in *Wanderings in West Africa*, but focuses on hygienic maps of hospitals and landscapes rather than first-person illness narrative. This shift arguably is caused by his growing commitment to encouraging the consolidation of British colonial power in West Africa. Detailing personal experiences of disease could potentially undermine this purpose.

As miasma has a corporeally degenerative effect, according to climatism, in *Wanderings in West Africa* it also has a degenerative effect on the landscape. The mist helps perpetuate decay. One may imagine the houses and structures Burton depicts as metaphorically linked to the white body: both are unable to ward off the unhealthy environment at low elevations. His chapter 'A Day at St. Mary's Bathurst' illustrates these strategies. With this entry, he begins to describe the African environment as more foreboding, no doubt because he feels he has left behind 'the parallels, north of which . . . health and comfort [make] their home' (1863: 128). As Burton's steamer approaches the coast, 'the sun burst[s] through the thick yellow swamp-reek and the dew-clouds with a sickly African heat' (143). Miasmatic imagery is densely packed into this sentence: the air's smell and colour, 'yellow swamp-reek', metonymically stand in for the air itself; the clouds are damp 'dew-clouds'; and the sun is personified as strong enough to 'burst' through even thick billows of moisture. Combined with the adjectives 'sickly' and 'yellow', these images indicate a potent, unhealthy atmosphere.

Burton writes a hygienic map of the settlement at St Mary's, focusing on the climatic factors he thinks most important. Upon arriving, he notes the town's layout and low elevation: 'everything is horizontal, straight-lined, and barely above sea-level' (144). He locates the dwelling places, identifying their proximity to dirty water: huts 'rise from swamp and sand, terminating abruptly up the river'. He then observes select habitations more closely. He finds that 'the house walls' are 'stained and gangrened with mildew; a fearful vegetation of . . . palms [and] plantains . . . occupies every inch of soil, and the inundations of the river sometimes find their way into the ground floor' (144). He focuses on miasma surrounding the town and emphasises the resulting decay inflicted upon structures by the damp atmosphere. The buildings are like bodies in that they have become 'gangrened' with mildew: the wetness of the air, combined with the pervasive water, is making them sick.[10]

Much as the sun, earlier personified as forceful, bursts through the clouds, here the water 'finds its way' into the habitations. Both are pervasive and cause disease. Finally, excess water causes a riotous growth of native plants, the excess of which is 'fearful' to Burton. Instead of being life-giving, Burton labels this water 'brackish and bad' (145). He makes his assessment explicit: 'the island and settlement of St. Mary (of old a cemetery) seem to be selected for unhealthiness, for proximity to mud, mangrove, miasma and malaria' (145). Alliteration cleverly relates all these factors: wetness and mud grows mangroves, and miasma causes malaria.

In a hospital it is crucial for the beds of sick men to be as elevated as possible. Burton maps the disease environment of the military hospital at St Mary's, enacting in miniature the process he will then apply to the wider African landscape. He describes the military hospital as 'murderous': 'There is a sick ward upon the ground floor! – one night on the ground floor is certain fever' (156). Having addressed the unhygienic circumstances caused by damp, Burton turns his attention to the unhealthy air: 'In the first story the beds are crowded together, each patient having 800, whereas 2000 feet of air should be minimum . . . in these regions, no first story is thoroughly wholesome, unless a free current of air flows beneath it' (156).[11]

In fact, Burton believes 'the chances are that all the [European] Bathurstians are dying of dysentery and yellow fever' (146). Chapter 1 highlighted Mary Seacole's assertion that the Jamaican climate attempts to 'exterminate' whites; Burton uses similar rhetoric to a different end when he says 'All throughout the coast there are periodical clearings off of the white population' (149). Whereas Seacole includes all of Jamaica in her statement, Burton limits the negative effects of the African environment to the coast; and whereas Seacole implies that the climate's attempts to 'exterminate' whites are ongoing, Burton says whites are 'cleared off' only 'periodically'. Even the phrase 'there are periodical clearings off' removes any sense of an agent: whites are not the victims of an omnipotent force, according to this schema, just of their own stupidity. Observing the high death rate, Burton exclaims 'after looking at the settlements – no wonder!' (149). In other words, the 'clearings off' are avoidable by relocation.

As hospital patients should be kept as high as possible off the ground, similarly Burton believes it is critical that whites reside at high altitudes in Africa, away from miasma, damp and rot. In contrast to the hospital, he uses the 'old convalescent-house at Cape St. Mary's' as an example of an ideal location. An eight-mile trip inland from Bathurst, Cape St Mary's is higher and drier than the coastal town. Burton narrates his journey there: 'The scene at once improved: it illustrated on a small scale how much better is the heart of Africa than its epidermis . . . the swamp disappeared, and as the ground rose, the *coup d'œil* assumed . . . a "park-like" appearance' (163).[12] Once arriving at the sanatorium, Burton declares, 'I was charmed with the site after the horrors of St. Mary's' (165). The 'Cape House' is 'built upon the top of the cliff, ready to catch all the breezes that blow across the broad Atlantic' (164). This breeze is the antithesis of low-lying miasma: it is even called 'The

Doctor'. Residents believe that because it sweeps in directly from the sea it is not 'laden with the miasmata of the swamps' between Cape House and Bathurst (169–70). Burton proclaims 'A wonderment seized me – how long will it be before the Europeans of the settlement remove [here] *en masse*?' (165).

Fissures

Richard Burton's suggestion that the Europeans of St Mary's 'remove ... *en masse*' to the hills, to govern black Africans from a distance, was in line with contemporary, scientifically justified racial separatism. Written by 1862 and published in 1863, *Wanderings* entered directly into circulating scientific, anthropological and cultural debates about the 'Negro's place'. Burton was the vice president of the Anthropological Society of London, and its president was the British anthropologist James Hunt. Hunt gave the Society's inaugural address in 1863. The resulting paper, entitled 'The Negro's Place in Nature' (1864), was instrumental in setting the foundations of scientific racism, and was dedicated to 'My Dear Burton'. Hunt quotes Burton's earlier writings on Africa in his speech, wherein Burton also limits blacks within both defined characterological and geophysical space. In his speech, Hunt argues that scientific data regarding black individuals' skull shape, brain size and height prove their inferior intelligence, morality and culture. The 'Negro's place' is therefore at the bottom of the racial hierarchy, and their destiny is to be ruled. He believes any deviation from this fate is unnatural. Hunt says, 'From the most remote antiquity the Negro race seems to have been what they now are' (1864: 14). Physically, he asserts that there has been 'little or no self-migration of the Negro races since the earliest historical records' (14). Hunt joined a burgeoning group of polygenist racial theorists who argued that blacks were at an earlier developmental moment and were stuck there permanently.[13]

In his marginal notes on James Prichard's *Natural History of Man* (1843), Burton seems to agree that man can change and adapt through successive generations when he asserts 'some improvable some not' (qtd in Grant 2009: 103). However, black Africans, especially those Burton terms the 'Negroid' type, are emphatically not improvable. In *Wanderings*, Burton implies that Africans will never become 'civilised' or rise to the level of whites: 'The aboriginal American has not been known to slave; the African, since he landed in Virginia, has chosen nothing else ... has never, until egged on, dreamed of being free' (1863: 175). This 'type' of African subject is affiliated in Burton's work with low-lying, unhealthy landscapes. Just as they do not 'dream' of attempting to elevate their own political status, so too, Burton argues, do these blacks fail to raise their physical circumstance above the swamps and marshes. By associating 'Negroid' Africans with an illness-producing environment, Burton implies that they are themselves pathological as well as working to justify sacrificing blacks to the most malaria-ridden districts while Europeans decamp to the hills. For example, when speaking of the fatal colony at St Mary's, which he spends so long critiquing, Burton says '[it was] designed for the use of . . . Africans' (1863: 146).

Burton attempts to gloss over the fissures in his pseudo-scientific arguments for racial separatism. If he were to conform to polygenism's strictest interpretation, Burton would have to concede that whites were unable to travel beyond their 'zone' of origin – the temperate, northern climates – and thus colonial settlement anywhere in the tropics would be a foolhardy prospect. Instead, he says that if whites are 'unfitted to contend' against the climate of the African coast, it is 'by reason of their habits', not their innate constitutions. He believes that even the most civilised black is 'inferior to the acclimatised European . . . in enduring the fatigues of actual warfare' (1863: 168). Burton thus implies that whites can acclimatise to new environments, but that they should not take the risk of attempting to settle in notoriously unhealthy locations.

Certain of Burton's contemporaries, just as convinced as he was of Africans' inferiority and animalism, allowed for no such possibility. These writers' rhetorical differences may have stemmed from self-interest: Winwood Reade, for example, though a friend of Burton's, did not similarly depend on ongoing imperial expansion for his livelihood. In examining the ideologies of racial medicine within mid-century West African travel narratives, one comes across many moments when authors' rhetoric is in danger of breaking 'a serious sweat', as Elaine Freedgood describes it (2000: 3). Theories such as Burton's and Reade's are often self-contradictory and reveal the authors' underlying anxieties regarding the relationships between races and their suppressed doubts regarding the inevitability of white domination.

Thomas J. Hutchinson and Winwood Reade shared with Burton some key beliefs: that elevation is crucial to whites' health in Africa and that Africans are innately 'lowly'. In *Narrative of the Niger, Tshadda, and Binuë Exploration; Including a Report on the Position and Prospects of Trade up those Rivers, with Remarks on the Malaria and Fevers of Western Africa* (1855), Hutchinson's style and organisation is quite similar to Burton's. Both men's official position as British Consuls to Fernando Po causes them to evaluate each location they visit in terms of its potential usefulness to the British Empire. They both attempt to be empirically accurate and are stylistically blunt. One quickly notices a similar hygienic mapping, or ordering of visual and factual information. Each settlement's history is briefly summarised, along with its appearance, orientation and resulting healthiness or unhealthiness. For example, each of Hutchinson's chapters contains a subheading that reads 'Appropriateness of location', 'Geographical position of the town' or 'Sanitary character'. Hutchinson, like Burton, was also a sanitarian who believed that elevation was the key to health in Africa: for instance, in *Impressions of Western Africa. With Remarks on the Diseases of the Climate and a Report on the Peculiarities of Trade up the Rivers in the Bight of Biafra* (1858) he says malaria has 'no influence 2000 feet above the surface of its germination' (1970: 222). They also both assert that blacks should be compelled to become a 'working people'. Hutchinson is less vituperative in his characterisations of African natives. Perhaps this discrepancy is motivated by their differing perceptions of disease. Hutchinson, a firm believer in prophylactic quinine use, feels that he has a systematic tool with which to avoid disease. To Burton, African disease is threatening, invisible and inherent to the low-lying landscape. His impulse for self-preservation might have augmented his vehement racism, making him much less likely to look with any sincere human interest at blacks.

The histrionics in Winwood Reade's *Savage Africa* (1863) demonstrate the sensationalised use of medical rhetoric and give us some idea of the emotional impact even Burton's somewhat more subtle rendering of the African environment might have had on his audience. Reade makes no attempt at either objectivity or professionalism, but embraces wholeheartedly his role as entertainer for 'armchair explorers'. *Savage Africa*'s subtitle: *with notes on the habit of the gorilla; on the existence of unicorns and tailed men; on the slave trade; on the origin, character and capability of the Negro, and on the future civilization of Western Africa* proclaims its function as sensationalist travel narrative. Reade's journey took place at the same time as Burton's, and his book was published the same year as Burton's *Wanderings in West Africa*; however, *Savage Africa* displays more extreme and transparent scientific illogic. As Robbie McClaughlan observes, 'Reade simply glosses over the gaps in empirical understanding with imagined projections and creative conjectures marked by a spurious scientific rigour' (2012: 2). Its excess highlights the same oppressive project that motivates other, somewhat more measured texts.

Through examining passages that touch upon Africa's mortality for whites, one finds a certain kind of medical mapping employed in *Savage Africa* to create a threatening atmosphere. As a more self-consciously embellished text, Reade's book opens with lush, romantic images of the 'rosy bosom' of Madeira's hills. Uninhibited by a need to remain scientifically accurate or to maintain professional distance, Reade executes juxtapositions similar to those found in Burton's passage of 'descent', but adds unabashed melodrama:

> It is but a lovely charnel-house, this island of Madeira. It is a boudoir and it is a hospital – a paradise and a tomb. Here comes Death, with mock laughter and in tinseled robes. A garland of roses hides the cypress on his brow. He leads his victim to the tomb to the music of the spheres, and then all changes suddenly, like a horrible dream, and some weeping family, whose dear one is gone from them, fly from the scene of a bitter woe. For them Madeira is no longer beautiful; for them the sun is darkness, the flowers are ashes, the warm soft air is heavy with disease. (1863: 17)

Although similar to Burton's *Wanderings in West Africa* in its juxtaposition of the familiar with a darker reality (dove and peewit in the former, boudoir and roses here), Reade's passage could arguably be set anywhere, in any sensation novel that uses standard symbolism and archetype for effect. It has not the understated power Burton summons when describing his own physical sensations ('clammy', 'cold perspiration'). Further, Reade's Death is generic: though presented as mysterious and devious, it is not characterised as uniquely miasmatic or 'tropical'.

Thus, one observes that popular interpretations of travel to Africa drew upon their readers' awareness of the area's heightened risk for whites, but were not as scientifically explicit about the source of risk. Authors such as Reade use more foreshadowing, more melodrama and more foreboding when speaking of Africa, as merited by the region's reputation as wild and unhealthy. Explorers such as Hutchinson and Burton, in contrast, feel a professional duty to maintain the illusion of scientific accuracy because their observations may be earmarked for use by their government employers in determining colonial policy. Though more subtly, the contradictions inherent in Burton's deployment of illness narrative are just as linked with theories of race.

Reade proposes a far-fetched explanation for racial skin-colour difference. Like Burton, Reade is inclined to believe that higher races are drawn to higher elevations, far away from disease. However, although Burton refuses to acknowledge the two races' common ancestry, Reade not only acknowledges it but suggests that blacks are not at fault for their skin colour – they may in fact be a fairer, civilised race that has degenerated into blackness from residing in Africa. He casually mentions that full-sized animals dwelling on plains become smaller over generations after relocating to lower elevations, in order to suggest a similar dynamic in humankind: 'Thus animals can palpably degenerate in the lowlands of Western Africa. It is an additional argument towards proving the degradation of the men' (1863: 407).

In a frightening move, Reade then metonymically links blackness to sickness: 'I am inclined to believe that the black hue of the negro answers to livid color among us; that it is the color of disease' (409). He believes the 'constant and intense heat' causes what was originally red skin to become black, and that the dampness and moisture causes hair to curl tightly (408, 409). Coded in Reade's description is the view that successful acclimatisation is impossible – each race is meant for a certain atmosphere, and is depleted by atmospheres to which it is not suited. Reade differs from the most extreme anti-acclimatisation theorists in that he does not equate migration between climatic environments with immediate death, but with weakening over generations. Regardless, such beliefs make successful, long-term colonisation of Western Africa by whites foolhardy and improbable. In his longer text *African Sketch Book* (1873), based on three years' residence and travel in Africa, Reade is even more vehement on the subject. He asserts that every white person in West Africa will become ill with fever. The West African climate is 'uniformly bad' and he recommends that no trader or officer go there of his own free will (1873: I, 13–16).

Reade was in strong company: medical experts of the mid-Victorian era such as Henry Ford and J. C. Nott, as well as famous racial theorists such as Louis Agassiz, to varying degrees portrayed tropical climates as debilitating to whites (see Ford 1856; Agassiz 1859). As demonstrated at this chapter's opening, popular pressure was building in the late 1850s and early 1860s for the British government to restrict West African colonisation. Anti-acclimatisation theorists' voices were loud and stringent, and lent power to popular protest. These theorists argued that the African climate's incapacitating effect on European soldiers and explorers did not decrease with time. Their message would seem to directly undermine the viability of colonial expansion and settlement.

J. C. Nott, in his book *Types of Mankind*, expresses the anti-acclimatisation view most succinctly: whites, he says, 'deteriorate physically when moved to hot climates' (1854: 63). In order also to stay true to his ideals of white supremacy, Nott stresses that it is the enormous intelligence of whites that makes them want to wander the earth, and their innate superiority that drives them to civilise foreign lands: 'Some are born to rule, and some to be ruled' (79). In this way, Nott continues in the spirit of his theoretical predecessors who asserted that whites' impulse to conquer was generated by their superior natures, while tempering those predecessors' colonial enthusiasm with what Nott believes is current scientific knowledge. 'There is a limit beyond which [whites] cannot go with impunity,' he argues. Instinct 'ties them to the soil that witnessed their birth' (66). The link between his theory and colonial expansion becomes evident when he asks, anticipating Hay's 1864 address, 'How many are sacrificed annually to climates foreign to their nature?' (67).

Richard Burton's polygenism and supremacism would seem to predispose him to agree with Nott. After all, Nott's assertion that there are '[n]umerous centres of creation, wherein we find creatures fixed, with peculiar temperaments and organizations' is clearly polygenic in flavour (66). However, for Burton to agree with such an assertion would be to admit that his race makes him ill-suited to his job and to his lifestyle, and that he should curtail his travel. Instead, he allows for the possibility that whites can acclimatise to Africa's environment, especially at higher elevations. Further, though Burton might have been attracted by Reade's blatant conflation of blackness with a state of degeneration and disease, to acknowledge that both blacks and whites acclimatise represents a slippery slope down which he refuses to slide. After all, if blacks were once 'red' in skin, before they inhabited diseased lowlands, who can be sure they were not even lighter? Who is to say the races are really separate?

Burton's basic belief in blacks' inferiority predisposes him to mistrust the argument that posits their superior disease resistance. Instead, in *Wanderings in West Africa*, he propounds black subjects' increased weakness, as evident through the following passage's convoluted mixture of anecdote, stereotype and bluster:

> It has been a favourite theory that the Jamaican negro and others withstand the heat and miasmata of Africa better than the white man; the contrary is probably the case. The semi-civilized African dies of phthisis[14] much more readily than the Englishman; and if exposed to hardship, he becomes . . . rotten after the first year . . . Although negroes have a singular immunity from yellow fever the small pox is a scourge to them, and they die like sheep of dysentery and bilious remittent . . . They are very far from being brave. (158–9)

To predict that a black person will become rotten after a year is, of course, patently unspecific and unscientific. Burton also uses the language of religious superstition rather than fact when he says that 'small pox is a scourge to them', in order to indicate that he believes blacks to be doubly cursed. Smallpox damages the skin permanently, marking its victims as cursed with ill health just as blacks' skin colour marks them as racially inferior; further, that blacks are singled out by a 'scourge' implies that they have incurred God's wrath. Burton believes that trying to civilise an African native will do more damage than good, as the native is restricted by his own inferior intelligence.[15] Finally, he makes a misguided conceptual leap from blacks' susceptibility to certain diseases to cowardice when he says 'they are very far from being brave', thereby conflating their emotional and physical constitutions. 'Negroes' easily become ill from smallpox: they have not enough grit in their character to withstand disease. Such a scientific muddle shows the inherent contradictions and obfuscations at the heart of much colonial discourse.

There are very few instances in which Burton expresses doubt and despair; however, these instances give a clue as to the inner struggle necessary to maintain such relentless confidence in the colonial project. Passing from the West African settlement of Frederiksborg to James Town, Burton sees the ruins of two old stone houses where former colonists resided. Such moments may bring to his mind those earlier days, when he visited the 'ghost town' of Goa and blithely laid the fault for its downfall at the feet of its European subjects. As Burton's colonial medical map of St Mary's seems to equate the state of the 'gangrened' houses with colonists' illness, so here he equates the empty houses with their death. He says,

> The beauty of the view, the contrast of ruin and perennial growth, the terrible sereneness of Nature, unchanged, inexorable . . . filled my mind with a sudden and profound sadness. Like the builders of these deserted homesteads, I have sought this coast, determined to show what can be effected by energy not undirected by intellect. And now, under that glowing sun, and with that ever-smiling prospect before me, a voice seems to say that all my efforts shall be in vain, perhaps even vainer than theirs. (1863: 161–2)

Burton's goal in *Wanderings* was to prove that the potential existed for whites to seek their fortune in Africa. They had the power to explore foreign territories and also to apply hygienic remedies to the landscape in order to make it habitable. When Burton focuses on the low-lying vapours and dampness of the west coast, he is able to perform imperial optimism. However, when he is faced with deserted homesteads whose inhabitants had probably died under the 'glowing [African] sun', he feels a 'sudden and profound sadness' for which he can offer no remedy.

Notes

1. For a more detailed discussion of West African fever see Chapter 4 on Mary Kingsley's *Travels in West Africa* (1897).
2. Notice that Burton is not saying that the West African environment can be made salubrious, just that it can be made tolerable: the 'West Indies' was a region also known for high white mortality rates.

3. By saying that whites can regain their 'energy and resolution' at higher altitudes, Burton is drawing upon the idea that 'malaria', or 'bad air', depletes and corrupts Europeans' natural vigour.

4. Burton's father refused to testify in the divorce proceedings of King George IV and Queen Caroline.

5. The information-gathering and reporting skills he developed during this time set the stage for the structure of his works. In his Burton biography entitled *The Highly Civilized Man* (2005), Dane Kennedy describes these early texts as 'encyclopedic' in their in-depth treatment of native 'terrain, crops, land holdings, taxes, languages, literatures, education, medicine, intoxicants, religions, customs and ceremonies' (42).

6. There is a certain amount of slippage between the two theories, because 'attention readily shifts between agency and process in disease' (Pelling 1978: 21). Sometimes a difficulty can arise in distinguishing 'concepts of contagion, infection and miasm[a]': 'Confusion arises from the failure to distinguish between the material or influence (living or non-living), which is transmitted between persons or environments, and the process of transmission or affection, direct or indirect' (21).

7. Kingsley makes a similar gesture, as discussed in Chapter 4. She refers to the African native's 'place' as 'his own . . . swampy valley' (1897a: Appendix I, 680).

8. Burton subscribes to the 'doctrine of ethnic centres': he believes the 'European to be the brains, the Asiatic the heart, and American and African the arms, and the Australian the feet, of the man figure' (1863: 175). Racial hierarchies manifest in his writing as hierarchies of geophysical elevation.

9. For example: '[France's] warlike imperial colonial policy contrasts strongly with our Quaker-like peacefulness; about Gambia the natives have sneeringly declared that they will submit to the French, who are men, but not to us' (1863: 137). He also makes multiple derogatory references to contagionist practices of quarantine and health inspections that have 'not been pulled down' since the cholera outbreak of 1856. He finds the regulations to which both travellers and residents are subjected 'arbitrary and exclusive'. He mocks extensively the 'old, toothless, nut-cracker-chinned health-officer . . . forbidding any more daring soul to near the gangway' until thorough inspections have been made (1863: 18).

10. Gangrene is 'A necrosis or mortification of part of the body, extending over some considerable area in a visible mass. Sometimes used to denote the first stage of mortification' (*OED* online).

11. Burton identifies the air itself as the disease-causing factor, not the bacteria or viruses carried by the air. However, when he says '[o]n the second floor are the quarters of the medical officers, within pleasant distance of an atmosphere fraught with small-pox and dysentery, typhus and yellow Jack', one observes how the measures proposed by hygienic reformers often incidentally did lessen disease (1863: 156). Of these four listed diseases, dysentery would be decreased by eliminating polluted water sources; yellow fever might decrease when standing water where mosquitoes breed was eliminated; and smallpox would decrease the further away a contagious individual was from others. These benefits would be accomplished even without the practitioner's full understanding of how diseases worked.

12. For further discussion of the imagery of membranes, skins and borders in *Wanderings*, see Jessica Howell 'Fatal Skins: Richard Burton's Colonial Lexicon', MA thesis, University of California, Davis, 2004.

13. The cross-pollination between Hunt's ideas and those of other theorists mentioned in his paper deserves brief explanation. While not emphatically polygenist, Hunt agrees with and quotes Josiah Nott's assertion that inter-breeding between blacks and whites may produce subjects with decreased fertility. According to this idea, mixed-race offspring would have further degraded 'natures' or characters. In her book *The Origins and Growth of the English Eugenics Movement* (1985), Lyndsay Farrall argues that eugenics, or the belief that social problems such as poverty and crime can be eliminated through selective breeding, also has its roots in Darwinian thought. The eugenicists' goal was to produce fitter subjects. When combined with racist bias that dictated that 'mixed breeds' were degenerate, the goal soon became to produce racially pure subjects, which would hopefully be more 'fit'. Many argue that such thinking fed directly into later Nazi propaganda.

14. 'A wasting disease, especially one involving the lungs; specifically, tuberculosis' (*OED* online).

15. See Chapter 4's discussion of Mary Kingsley's polygenism, which inspires her to similar rhetorical moves. She argues that teaching the native and 'giving him' white religion is in fact quite damaging.

Chapter 3

Africanus Horton and the Climate of African Nationalism

James Africanus Beale Horton described Richard Burton as '[t]he most determined African hater' of their time (qtd in Fyfe 1972: 60). Burton's work, Horton wrote, was '[p]ersonally abusive, turgidly illustrative, and illogically argumentative' towards Africans, Creoles in particular (61). Further, Horton felt that the tenets of racial anthropology, as explained in James Hunt's 1863 speech 'The Negro's Place in Nature', were fundamentally 'pro-slavery' (62). A writer, army officer and physician born in Sierra Leone and trained in Britain, Horton wanted economic independence for Sierra Leone and to exonerate his race from the accusations of backwardness and savagery levelled by Burton, Hunt and their colleagues.

Horton's life embodied several contradictions. Although he is now posited as one of the forefathers of African nationalism, Horton's education and his role within the British military was made possible by the same racial science that underlay Burton's tracts and many policies of the Victorian empire. Horton was trained as part of a movement by the British War Office to replace white doctors on the West Coast of Africa with black Africans, who, it was thought, would survive tropical health challenges better than their predecessors. The mid-nineteenth century, 'in spite of all the confident European belief in Progress', was still 'the period of "the white man's grave" in West Africa' (Shepperson 1969: ix). Although the rising prophylactic use of quinine from the 1840s had ameliorated the death rate somewhat, as Philip D. Curtin has documented in his book *Disease and Empire*, 'the change was more modest' for British land troops. The previously cited statistic of 151 deaths per 1,000 between 1859 and 1875 was gleaned from military mortality records of British non-commissioned officers in West Africa, specifically the West India regiments in which Horton served (Curtin 1998: 26).[1] It was thought that Horton and his fellow West African doctors could mitigate these risks through their supposedly superior disease resistance and knowledge regarding local conditions.

However, Horton became ill as often as his white compatriots, since they were all exposed to the same unhealthy garrison conditions, and his recommendations regarding improvements to sanitation and treatment were followed only haphazardly. Horton remarks, 'I urged the necessity of sanitary reform on the coast, and I was harshly remarked upon by many of those whose lives it was my chief object to spare' (1868b: x). The Deputy Secretary of the War Office, Benjamin Hawkes, had recommended in 1853 that selected Africans be trained to serve as medical officers for West African imperial garrisons. Horton learned the difficult lesson through the course of his career that this was not intended to set the stage for African independence, but merely to sacrifice black rather than white doctors through exposure to the most fatal locations. Richard Burton's assertion that unhealthy locales were 'designed for the use of . . . Africans' (1863: 146) did not mean that Africans were to be given power over their land, but that they were expected to help exploit those locations for imperial gain.

Despite these challenges, by the time of his death Horton had become a man of consequence, holding the position of Chief Commandant in Gambia and the Gold Coast and Justice of the Peace (Adeloye 1992: 3). He also laid the foundations for an African-owned bank. His publications included *Physical and Medical Climate, and Meteorology of the West Coast of Africa* (1867), *West African Countries and Peoples, British and Native, . . . and A Vindication of the African Race* (1868), *Guinea Worm: its Symptoms and Progress . . . and Radical Cure* (1868), *Letters on the Political Condition of the Gold Coast* (1870) and *The Diseases of Tropical Climates and their Treatment* (1874). Horton's position in the army allowed him to make close observations of major political conflicts on the Gold Coast during the 1860s and 1870s and to use these observations, along with his medical training and experience, to make recommendations regarding how health and disease would impact the political future of West Africa. Many perceived the inroads that Horton made towards African independence with distrust. Not coincidentally, he and his fellow students were the first and last West Africans to be trained in medicine and commissioned by the army (Adeloye 1992: 4).[2]

The 1865 motion in the House of Commons, mentioned in the previous chapter, stated that British 'policy should be to encourage in the natives the exercise of those qualities which may render it possible more and more to transfer to them the administration of all the Governments, with a view to our ultimate withdrawal' (qtd in Nicol 1969: ix). The 'intelligentsia of West Africa' took this recommendation quite seriously (Nicol 1969: ix). Horton's work traces an arc of hopefulness for West

African self-governance, which peaks with *West African Countries and Peoples* and *Letters on the Political Conditions of the Gold Coast* and subsides in his later works. In fact, Horton addresses *Letters* to 'To the Right Hon. E. Cardwell, Secretary of State for War', author of the Cardwell policy. In *Letters* Horton lends his support to the 'Fantee' appeal, which claims that 'our wisest and safest policy lies in our adopting, without delay, some measures for our self-government, and our self-defense' (against the Ashanti) (1870: 31). Horton's expectations that Britain would grant West Africa political freedom were disappointed. After the mid-1870s, he focused his energy instead on creating a financial and educational infrastructure to inspire African development for the future. While his more overtly political works have been studied within the context of African nationalism, this chapter takes up the 'guides' as well in order to demonstrate that even within these supposedly more neutral texts, Horton marshals the rhetoric of environmental medicine in order to promote change.

Although Horton was well known during his own lifetime as a scholar and intellectual, his work has been largely forgotten until recently. His name was rarely mentioned during the colonial era, and only with David Kimble's *A Political History of Ghana* (1963) and the subsequent reprinting of Horton's works did he begin to receive sustained scholarly attention (Fyfe 1972: 157–8). As Charles Ambler wonders in his article 'African Studies: Engagement and Interdisciplinarity', 'How [is] it that this body of work did not form the basis of the intellectual foundation of our discipline – African studies?' Ambler regrets that Horton and his contemporary Edward Blyden have 'somehow found themselves . . . marginalized as Westernized elites' (2011: 3). Rather than characterising both men as equally Westernised, Ngũgĩ wa Thiong'o has placed Blyden and Horton into opposing 'camps' of early African nationalism. Horton proposed the first West African medical school in 1861; after his proposal was denied, in 1871 he advocated the formation of a West African university run by African subjects. Wa Thiong'o takes issue with Horton's university model, based as it was on European-style education and English-language instruction. He regrets that because eventually 'it was the Horton vision that triumphed', English became 'the foundation of excellence' for an early generation of black British writers, including Chinua Achebe (wa Thiong'o 2000: 2).

While Horton, along with many of his fellow Victorian African intellectuals, did express respect for certain Western values, one must keep two caveats in mind. First, historical definitions of racial and cultural purity may continue to influence our contemporary readings of colonial discourse. When one dismisses a writer who 'professed admiration for elements of white culture' as 'inauthentic' or practising 'mimicry', one must take care not to perpetuate nineteenth-century 'denunciations' of Westernised Africans, such as Burton's own mockery of Sierra Leone Creoles (Bickford-Smith 2011: 76). Instead, when evaluating Horton's contribution to African letters, it pays to remember the set of historical exigencies within which he worked: as Abiola Irele observes, to cite Western values served not only to 'appeal to the moral conscience of Europe' but also 'to refute the European thesis of [Africans'] non-participation in a human essence' (1991: 79). Further, Edward Blyden's cultural 'purism', which wa Thiong'o now idealises, rested on a concept of the African 'nature' as static, while Horton believed that cultures change over time and civilisations are cyclical.

This chapter is interested in the spaces for subversion within Horton's role as doctor, scientist and social theorist. His superiors moved Horton relentlessly from one garrison to another, ostensibly based on staffing needs but also probably as a result of race-based hostility. Rather than demonstrating the constitutional fortitude often ascribed to Africans, Horton grew ill from the repeated relocations and the new disease environments he encountered. He suffered repeatedly from malaria and dysentery, and died a premature death from an inflammatory skin condition, erysipelas. In contrast to Mary Seacole, whose writing stresses her constitutional hardiness, Horton's writing offers the opportunity to observe how an African nationalist represented his own illness as a source of first-hand knowledge and authority.

Horton claims intimate knowledge of the West African environment by citing his own extensive observations of climatological measurements and his knowledge of the endemic diseases that he believes arise from exposure to climate. While most criticism has focused only on Horton's later, explicitly political work, one may find the development towards African nationalism nascent in Horton's earlier writing on medical climatology. In his medical 'guides', such as *Physical and Medical Climate, and Meteorology of the West Coast of Africa* (1867) and *Diseases of Tropical Climates and their Treatment* (1874), Horton depicts West Africa as potentially fatal for both black and white subjects, but implies that local populations have a unique and irreplaceable familiarity with their own environment. Critics such as Richard Drayton (2000), Nancy Leys Stepan (2001) and Beth Fowkes Tobin (2005) have illustrated that the natural sciences, especially botany, were used as a tool for imperial exploitation. However, I posit that Horton's work stands as a counterforce to the imperial 'evaporation of history and culture' from depictions of the natural environment, especially through his 'discussion of plant life' (Tobin 2005: 24).

Sources and Limits of Authority

James Beale Horton was born on 1 June 1835 in Gloucester, a hillside settlement four miles from Freetown, to parents of Ibo descent. His father, James Horton Senior, was a recaptive slave who converted to Christianity, educated himself, and worked as a carpenter and gardener.[3] His parents probably took the name Horton in honour of the first Christian missionary to visit Sierra Leone in 1816, John Horton (Adeloye 1992: 1). James Horton Junior was educated first at the village school in Gloucester under the careful tutelage of the Revd James Beale, who recognised the boy's intelligence and recommended in 1845 that Horton be transferred to the Church Missionary Society (CMS) grammar school in Freetown. Horton later adopted the name 'Beale' as a demonstration of his gratitude for this early mentorship.

The Revd (later Sir) Henry Venn, the CMS Secretary, selected Horton as one of three West Africans to be trained at King's College London in the study of medicine. The CMS had chosen King's College in particular because of its 'Christian atmosphere' (Adeloye 1992: 2). Horton achieved a Certificate of Honour in Comparative Anatomy while in London. The subject was of especial interest to him as he sought evidence to contest 'allegations of Negro inferiority' (Nicol 1969: 24). His goal was to prove that Negro 'backwardness' was based on adversity and exploitation rather than biology (24).

Horton continued his studies at the University of Edinburgh, where he completed an MD. In Edinburgh, Horton specialised in medical geography: his thesis (1859) was on 'The Medical Topography of the West Coast of Africa including Sketches of its Botany', and was split into two sections, 'Topographical and Botanical Records' and 'The Seasons and Meteorology of West Africa' (Fyfe 1972: 34–5). The thesis draws heavily on the published work of previous medical authors, but more than half of the evidence is drawn from Horton's own first-hand observations (35). It also demonstrates Horton's strong interest in botany. As proof of his close attention to this subject, Horton names a species in his thesis that he 'claimed to have identified, Clerodendrum Hortonium' (35). He and his fellow West African medical student, William Davies, were elected 'foreign members' of the Botanical Society of Edinburgh. Although there is no evidence that Horton participated in political activism while studying in Edinburgh, it was on the cover page of his thesis that he first adopted the name 'Africanus'. Biographers believe that Horton adopted this name both to indicate pride in his origins and accomplishments as well as perhaps to confer on himself a sense of traditional grandeur derived from a Latinate forename (Adeloye 1974: 280).

Horton's health while in England and Scotland appears to have been good (Fyfe 1972: 32), in contrast to the third African medical student, Samuel Campbell, who developed bronchitis upon arriving in London, and was never able to complete his studies but returned to Sierra Leone and an early death. It was not until Horton's military service commenced that his health began to suffer. On 5 September 1859 the British army commissioned Horton and Davies as staff assistant surgeons in West Africa (Fyfe 1972: 36). Arriving in Sierra Leone, they found a city suffering from epidemics of yellow fever, measles and smallpox which had killed '500 in Freetown alone in a few months', including 'forty-two Europeans, half the European population' (39). Horton and Davies wanted to stay in Sierra Leone, as the resident doctors were also ill and the region was seriously understaffed; however, they were sent on to Ghana, to serve in the Gold Coast garrisons (39).

Horton faced both direct personal as well as systemic discrimination during his career in the army. The Director General of the Army Medical Services, Thomas Alexander, asked Horton for a report on the conditions at his first station. Within the first three weeks in post, Horton sent a complete account of the 'town and geology of Anomabu' and its fort. He included measurements of 'all the rooms' and 'four drawings of the fort courtyard', also listing 'broken windows, roofs, and doors which let in the rain and made the place damp and unhealthy' (Fyfe 1972: 41). Although these circumstances were not greatly remedied, the exercise seems to have stimulated Horton to further observations, which laid the groundwork for his future publications.[4] While Horton received modest promotions throughout his career, when he applied for leadership positions his requests were declined primarily due to his race.

Horton was sent to a succession of unhealthy stations in West Africa. As Christopher Fyfe states, 'the continual movement' between 'one after another of the damp, tumbledown old forts where the garrisons were quartered' told on Horton's health, to the extent that the author of his obituary in the *Lagos Observer* of 8 November 1883 suggested that he had been 'deliberately moved about' from 'prejudice and malice' (Fyfe 1972: 40). Letters written by members of the colonial administration document the challenges Horton faced: for example, in 1861 Governor Richard Pine admitted to the War Office that there was 'prejudice and objection on the part of the European medical officers to the introduction of men of colour who may become their seniors on the Coast'.[5]

Horton also encountered day-to-day prejudice from his superiors. The commanding officer of the fort at Anomabu, Captain de Ruvignes, took an especial dislike to Horton and 'persecuted and humiliated' him from the first (Fyfe 1972: 41). After he had been transferred from his first station, in a letter dated 3 February 1860 Horton recounts the troubles he had encountered there to his mentor, Sir Henry Venn. His letter suggests that both Horton and Venn had anticipated that Horton would be poorly received by the whites with whom he was to work; however, Horton may not have been prepared for the frequency or severity of the attacks. He says, 'Little did I think that I will be compelled at such an early period of my entrance into the Army to represent to you the unbearable treatment I have received from one of Her Majesty's officers' (de Ruvignes). Venn initially must have counselled his protégé to 'turn the other cheek', as Horton assures him 'I have born in mind + thank God (been) able to carry out your last admirable advice to "never stand out too much for your rights – be patient + time will bring it to you".'[6]

This model of Christian behaviour led Horton to endure 'brutal treatment' at the hands of his superior, whereby he was 'tormented, annoyed, disturbed and vexed'; however, Horton's passivity only seemed to 'encourage' his tormenter. Silence in this case was not a tactical response but the only one Horton felt was available to him, given the important precedent set by his education:

> It is a matter of paramount necessity that as I am amongst the first of the native Africans who have been educated by H.M. Government in the medical profession and sent out as Staff Asst Surgeon to practice that noble art amongst my countrymen + those of the Europeans who may require our attendance ... [I] must not to give in to the dictates of passion, or to take rash measures ... [or] thousands of those here who are hostile to the plan will have grounds to complain, [and] they will use every means to dissuade the Government from going on in that noble Cause which is fraught with blessings for Africa.[7]

Unfortunately, it was not his mentor Venn but Major Hector Smith, another leader of the Missionary Society, who replied to this letter. Rather than lending a sympathetic ear, Smith answers in a threatening and didactic tone:

> we hope that instead of tracing your uncomfortable and unhappy position to those whose authority you must obey – and to whose defects you attribute your uneasiness; you will now look within and compare your proud spirit with that of Him who washed the feet of his disciples. (qtd in Fyfe 1972: 43)

Smith adopts a superior stance by exhorting Horton to 'look within and compare your proud spirit' to that of Jesus. The injustice of the reply was exacerbated by the fact that Horton had already refused to bring charges against his superior de Ruvignes, and had waited until after transfer to write the foregoing letter. Most important for the purpose of this analysis is Smith's overt scepticism regarding the veracity of

Horton's remarks, which he makes evident by suggesting that Horton is uncomfortable, unhappy and uneasy as a result of his own pride rather than the actions of his superiors. The inverted structure of the phrase 'to whose defects you attribute' deflects those defects from the superiors to the more proximate 'you'. By referring to Horton's superiors as 'those whose authority you must obey', Smith elevates them to the status of an untouchable power that needs only be invoked rather than named.

Throughout his career, objections to Horton's promotion or advancement were often couched in similar language, calling his authority into question. In 1861, when Horton proposed the establishment of a West African medical school with himself as its head, the Director General of the Army Medical Department asked Dr Charles O'Callaghan, Principal Medical Officer on the Gold Coast, for his opinion as to Horton's medical authority. O'Callaghan replied that neither William Davies nor Horton possessed 'the confidence of the European community nor even the confidence of the native community in the Territory in the same degree as the European Medical Officers' (qtd in Fyfe 1972: 48). As Christopher Fyfe observes, this excerpt demonstrates a common tactic of colonial rhetoric, whereby the white speaker uses African subjects to ventriloquise his own 'antagonism' towards educated Africans (1972: 48). In 1872 Horton applied to be administrator of the Gold Coast, but his application was rejected by the Colonial Office. A Mr Meade concluded 'Dr. Africanus Horton (a pure black) and a native born African, is a good medical officer but I don't think it would do to make an Administrator of him' (qtd in Adeloye 1992: 6).

Horton attempted to appeal against the dismissal of his university proposal by sending back two letters of recommendation. The first was from S. C. Brew, a Fanti trader. Brew responded to O'Callaghan's denigration of Horton's authority thus: 'I can only say that the person who advanced such a statement must know next to nothing of the Coast as such is diametrically opposed to the truth' (qtd in Fyfe 1972: 48). Governor Richard Pine, whom Horton had treated during the abortive conflict with the Ashanti (1863–64), wrote the second recommendation. Pine had initiated a standoff with the Ashanti over two captives in his possession and then refused to back down in order to avoid humiliation. The confrontation lasted into the rainy season, and illness began to wreak havoc within the West India Regiment. Pine left Horton in charge of the medical services when he himself was forced to withdraw due to illness, and after all the other medical officers had either died or withdrawn. When the British finally retreated, the Ashanti king claimed 'The white man bring many cannon into the bush, but the bush is stronger than the cannon' (qtd in Fyfe 1972: 55).

Horton's liminal and ambivalent role in the Ashanti conflicts characterises much of his army career: he was on both the side of the cannon and the bush. He understood the reasons why the Ashanti defended both their territories and their traditions, but was ordered to support the health of the troops fighting against them. His political tendency was towards pan-African nationalism, as he believed that all African tribes deserved the benefits of education and the opportunities it allowed, but he was encouraged to take the side of tribes such as the Fanti in their conflict with the Ashanti as a result of underlying colonialist policies of 'divide and conquer'. Although according to our current scientific knowledge Horton's explanations for the sources of disease were fundamentally flawed, nevertheless he understood the health risks posed by fighting during the wrong season and in the wrong locations. However, his superiors did not heed his advice, and he was left to minister to the dying. When such conflicts did not result in success, as with Pine's Ashanti debacle, Horton's reputation arguably was damaged by association; when they did result in success, as with the Ashanti War of 1874, he was passed over for commendation in favour of white colleagues (Fyfe 1972: 118).

These biographical details set the stage for the following discussion of Horton's published work, which includes regular and repeated references to his own personal and medical observations as a source of authority. Such a technique places him squarely in a tradition of travel writers who cite first-hand knowledge to bolster their assertions and impressions (Thompson 2011: 98). Were all things equal, Horton's extensive experience might have cemented his position as an expert in West African medicine and politics. Many white writers traded on much sparser knowledge to much greater effect. For example, Richard Burton's assertions regarding West African peoples were 'concocted out of trivial gossip and prejudiced, superficial observation, by a stranger to the country' but were nonetheless 'extremely influential' (Fyfe 1972: 61).

Although Horton drew upon more formal training and cultural awareness of West Africa than Burton, there was a great disparity between these two figures' popularity. This was a result not only of their different races, but arguably also because Burton's often shocking subject matter and imperialist bluster drew a large audience for his opinions. Also, the goals of their texts were different – Burton aimed to entertain as well as influence his readers, and his risqué reputation enhanced the mystique of his writing, while Horton's texts read as assiduous and conscientious studies. It is nonetheless incongruous that Burton was identified as 'the most qualified Englishman or indeed European living . . . to give an opinion on a question of African character and conduct', when men such as Horton and Edward Blyden were so much better placed to make such judgements (Elliot qtd in Fyfe 1972: 61).

African nationalists of the Victorian period were aware of this incongruity, and celebrated Horton's contribution to West African letters. The African Aid Society was founded in 1860 to further business and philanthropic interest in West Africa, and its journal *The African Times* (1862–1902) became an important forum for educated Africans to voice their opinions. The journal was edited by self-professed 'friend of Africa' Ferdinand Fitzgerald and produced in London; Edward Blyden was a frequent contributor (Shepperson 1969: xiv). The *Times* printed a publication notice for Horton's *West African Country and Peoples* in July 1868 and a full-length review in September, both of which demonstrate the significance of Horton's writing to his contemporaries. The 'Literary Notice' of 23 July announces,

> We hail this work with pleasure. We have long wanted books on Africa written by Africans, and it is a most evident sign of progress that there should now be at least one educated West African entering the literary lists for his country, his race, and those honours which attend successful authorship. (Anonymous 1868a: 9)

Horton's book is seen as a nationalist enterprise because its arrival represents progress for Africa – progress as judged within the construct of metropolitan publishing.

The 23 September review commends Horton's subject matter more explicitly as 'calculated to remove many misconceptions as regards the peoples and countries of which it treats' (Anonymous 1868b: 38). It depicts Horton as a more legitimate authority on West Africa than white explorers, with a well-placed barb clearly aimed at Burton:

> The author is not a man who has taken a run down the West Coast and back again in a mail steamer, and then written a book chiefly valuable as an evidence of the extent to which the boasted European intellect, when it has a wrong bias, can be gulled as to facts, and be made worthless as regards conclusions. (38)

These white explorers undermine their own criteria for exactitude and completeness in observation, which seems to make their intellectual contribution 'worthless'. However, by taking at face value some of the stated goals of colonial exploration literature (discovery, reportage, understanding), the reviewer wrongly assumes that a counter-text written with exactitude and completeness will be more believable to these same false authorities. Therefore the review stresses Horton's training and his 'eight years at the different British settlements on the

West Coast' as the sources of his authority: 'he ought to know what he is writing about' and 'does know' (38).

This reviewer believes that Horton's 'facts' will trump those invoked by racist science, 'clearing away the thick haze of prejudice in which the West Coast countries have been shrouded'. 'Vulgar falsehoods and aberrations of intellect' can now be 'demolished by real scientific facts' and 'a clear and lucid reasoning'. These facts will 'establish the truth': that 'the mental superiority of the civilised European over the uncivilized African is . . . the result of circumstances, and not of natural diversity' (38). The difficulty with pinning the book's authority on 'fact' and 'clear reasoning' is twofold. First, the facts of racial science were in flux and subject to manipulation and interpretation, as demonstrated throughout this book; therefore, either as a result of new discoveries or someone else claiming more scientific exactitude, biased readers are likely to discount Horton's assertions. Secondly, the reviewer simply reverses prejudicial colonial rhetoric by attaching to racist writers labels such as 'vulgar' and aberrant, labels which these writers had previously associated with educated Africans.

The *Times* reviewer hopes that *West African Countries and Peoples* will have 'a large circulation in England' and 'arouse sympathies for Africa where they have never yet been felt'. It is ironic that the literary notice commends Horton's 'successful authorship', since Horton financed the publication of the book himself. Because his book was not written 'to attract the fancy or to excite wonder, by recording acts of heroic enterprise, like the gorilla hunting etc.', Horton felt it was unlikely to be profitable (qtd in Fyfe 1972: 68). However, he may have hoped that the book would be taken seriously by policy makers, or be passed around circles of influence. The reviewer in the *Anti-Slavery Reporter* (a vehicle for the British and Foreign Anti-Slavery Society) is perhaps more realistic:

> We fear that the spirit of indifference to the interests and welfare of the natives which has so long disfigured the policy of Great Britain in this quarter of the world will still operate to retard, for many years, the introduction of any comprehensive plan for the government of her West-African settlements and dependencies, such as is submitted by Dr. Horton. (Anonymous 1869: 187)

The reviewer's fears proved well justified. All the 'influential political and literary journals – *The Edinburgh Review*, the *Quarterly Review*, the *Fortnightly Review* and *Blackwoods Magazine* – ignored' *West African Countries and Peoples*, whereas the British medical press had 'welcomed *Physical and Medical Climate* as an original and useful contribution to medical knowledge' (Fyfe 1972: 89–90).

It is not the purpose of this chapter to contend that Horton broke down the walls of Victorian prejudice, but rather to suggest that his writing yields fruitful examples of a subject of colour intervening in the linked discourses of racialised medicine and African national identity. Further, by analysing Horton's self-positioning, one may observe room for subversion and protest within the genres of the medical guide and geographical survey. In Horton's seemingly documentary texts one may trace the rhetorical uses of illness narrative by a subject of colour, who invokes first-hand knowledge of tropical illness in order to advise his readers as to the viability of colonialism. Horton also makes a case for himself in both his scientific and political writing as an expert on West Africa, based on his intimate understanding of the West African environment, especially tropical plants and foliage.

Environmental Medicine, Authority and the First Person

In 'Physician Autobiography: Narrative and the Social History of Medicine', Donald Pollack observes, 'the life stories of physicians' do not only 'describe medicine', they are also 'forms of the constitution and reproduction of medical domains' and 'highly sensitive to historical changes in the social system' (2000: 109). For doctors to tell their own experience 'is a powerful form of referential practice' and 'conveys a profound sense of experientially based truth that can be exploited politically' (109). Although Pollock's study is concerned with contemporary physician autobiographies, his assertion can be applied productively to earlier texts as well. However, one must keep in mind that the social prestige and power affiliated with medicine as a profession has varied over time, and so therefore has the credence given to doctors' 'experientially based truth'.

Africanus Horton does not identify his work as physician autobiography – his stated purpose is to document his environment rather than his life. However, he draws upon first-hand experience as the basis for his authority and includes condensed narratives of illness within the longer texts to illustrate his assertions. Further, his work is driven by the desire to reconstitute the 'domain' of tropical medicine in a way that will reflect the experiences of African subjects rather than the imposed systems of racial anthropology and other biased Victorian 'sciences'. Therefore, when Horton writes about his life as a doctor and a scientific observer, he creates a form of autobiographical writing that serves to demonstrate his masterful knowledge of his surroundings and their effects on racialised bodies. I trace the development in Horton's invocation of climate and disease alongside the political engagement of his work.

In *Physical and Medical Climate*, Horton reframes his frequent relocation as providing him breadth of observation:

> My opportunities of observation have been such as to enable me, from personal experience, to make accurate statements with regard to the climate from Bight of Benin to Senegal . . . I served from time to time, during several years, at all the military posts on the Gold Coast. I am a native of Sierra Leone, where, fifteen years ago, I made thermometrical and pluviametrical observations . . . (1867: x)

This self-commendation includes a laundry list of place names and locations as well as a sprinkling of technical terms such as 'thermometrical' and 'pluviametrical', which lend Horton the air of a seasoned expert on West African climate.

In the Preface to *Physical and Medical Climate*, Horton highlights the ominous reputation of West Africa. Although he claims that the book's goal is to propose 'sanitary reforms' and 'prophylactic measures' to decrease both 'native' and white mortality (1867: v), it is the current cost to European lives that he stresses the most. No doubt this is because the majority of his readers, and those who would authorise and effect change, were Europeans, and so the urgency of the situation had to be impressed upon them. However, a secondary purpose might well have been to raise questions in his readers' minds regarding whether the extent of the proposed improvements was worth the cost and effort, and the ongoing loss of life. Horton says that, heretofore, the 'European on leaving home' has had 'a melancholy foreboding of a speedy termination of his existence'; further, 'his relatives and friends reckon him, from the day of his embarkation, as amongst the dead' (v). This dramatic statement depicts death as so unavoidable that it can be pinpointed from the moment of departure from England – although it is this situation that Horton purportedly wishes to change, nonetheless in the foregoing passage he rhetorically kills off all Europeans who leave their homeland. He drives home his point by saying 'to what extent these forebodings have been realised, I leave the death-rate of the few Europeans who visit the coast to tell' (v).

Less narrative passages can also have strong rhetorical effect. As evident in Mary Seacole's work, writers of colour could subtly condemn their readers as unsuitable for tropical climates by blaming the white 'constitution' for its susceptibility to disease. Similarly, Horton includes a list of 'constitutional diseases' that he observed in Anamaboe station on the Gold Coast in 1861, along with the number of sufferers. These include 'Debility (38)' and 'Anaemia (10)' (1867: 211). More surprisingly, he includes diseases he terms 'zymotic', such as dysentery, and 'local diseases', such as influenza and gastritis, as affected by the constitution. The incidence of these can be decreased through sanitary measures, but they cannot be avoided completely if one is of the wrong constitution.

Horton dedicates the fifteenth chapter of *Physical and Medical Climate* to 'Hints for the preservation of health by Europeans in tropical climates'. He begins by depicting European subjects as naive and foolhardy and posits himself as a local authority whose advice must be heeded by those who care to survive. The newcomer 'must conform to certain rules and regimens', Horton says, 'regulating his habits to that of the climate he intends to reside in, and if he expects to keep his health, must endeavor to profit by the experience of those who have resided some time in it'. He shows open scepticism regarding his readers' ability to manage their own health:

> Europeans fresh from Europe are very generally found to praise the climate in the tropics as the best in the world; especially if they have been in the south of Europe ... and they will unnecessarily expose themselves to a great many injurious climatic influences, and pooh-pooh any advice to the contrary offered them by persons whose long residence and experience in such matters should carry with it great weight. Such individuals have generally within a few weeks or months to pay most dearly for their folly, and should they be lucky enough to outlive their opinions, soon tell a different tale. (269–70)

In this passage, it is the European traveller's privilege that is his undoing – he wrongly believes the African climate is similar to temperate climes with which he is familiar, and so does not perceive it as a threat. He is reckless, 'unnecessarily' exposing himself to 'injurious climatic influences', and arrogant, 'pooh-poohing any advice to the contrary'.

The passage is metonymic for Horton's larger political project, to be recognised as an authority on the West African environment and to implement measures of benefit to his country's people. He suggests that his own opinions be heeded when he advocates for 'persons whose long residence and experience in such matters should carry with it great weight'. Horton continues threateningly, claiming that those who do not heed his advice 'pay most dearly for their folly' and, if they survive, have no choice but to believe in his greater wisdom. As with Seacole's 'boys', who swore by her teas and remedies, so Governor Pine and others whom Horton has cared for show him admiration and attest to his skill; hence, his warning is not without basis. However, by using the plural, Horton also sanctions the opinion of other 'persons' who have 'experience in such matters', thus creating the space for a pocket of educated West African authorities.

Horton underscores the foregoing warning by following it with a specific case that he observed. The subject, 'an eminent judge who had resided for some time in the south of Spain', should epitomise Western rationality but instead he acts impulsively upon arrival in Africa:

> Finding that the south-west sea breeze was very bracing, and the air tolerable, he walked about from one part of town to the other under the noon-day sun. He could not endure the slow pace of a carriage, which in that part of Africa is drawn by men; and on one occasion he jumped out and raced with the native drivers. What was the result? He soon took fever, congestion of the brain followed, and he became a victim of the climate,– or rather of his infatuation, within six weeks after his arrival. (269–70)

One of the judge's crucial mistakes is to test his physical prowess against 'native drivers', who demonstrate superior endurance. Further, Horton not only denounces the judge's impulsive behaviour but his underlying 'infatuation' with the Gold Coast. The judge acts like a cocksure colonialist, who believes he can dominate the tropical environment. The passage echoes common warnings against excess in travel literature about the tropics. These warnings are so common that Mary Kingsley is later able to mock the truism of colonial travel literature that one must 'avoid chill, excessive mental and bodily exertion' (1897a: 684). Unlike these typical Anglo-British narratives, Horton does not displace blame from the colonists themselves on to the heady climate that 'corrupted' them. In fact, he shows that it was not the climate but the judge's response to it that proved his undoing.

Horton's description of the disease progression – excess leading to fever, fever causing 'brain congestion' and then death – is vivid. In Joseph Conrad's African fiction, fever and 'feverish' behaviour in white colonists often foretell their death from tropical disease. In this case, it is as if the judge's excess is made physically manifest through an inflamed brain. Later in the same chapter, Horton describes in more detail the sensations that one must be on watch for in cases of this kind:

> When there is a feeling of tension, heat, headache, throbbing, and other unpleasant sensations in the head, we should lie down quietly, and endeavor to get a sleep, for it is certain that something wrong is going on in the brain, and rest and quietude are most likely to relieve it. (281)

There is a disquieting mixture of certainty and uncertainty in this excerpt: it is 'certain' that there is 'something wrong', but unclear what is 'going on in the brain'; further, to 'lie down quietly and endeavor to get a sleep' is far from a comforting suggestion, or one that inspires much confidence in a cure. Horton seems to sympathise with the patient's predicament by saying that 'we' should lie down quietly, but this may be as much a patronising 'we' ('do we feel like having some broth today?') as an affinitive 'we'.

Horton follows the foregoing case with a strict set of measures that whites must take in order to avoid illness, from wearing a white turban and cotton waistband in order 'to keep the bowels from sudden impression of cold', to having food plain with no condiments or spices in order to avoid overstimulation (276). He also advises against exercise for newcomers to the tropics, 'as it will soon prove injurious to the constitution' (280), especially 'in the damp and rainy season'.[8] The implicit critique within these excerpts was skimmed over by Horton's Anglo-British readers, who welcomed his book as a legitimate attempt to facilitate white health in the tropics. In the *Athenæum* of 2 November 1867, the reviewer cites Horton's extensive rules as evidence that 'the loss of life to which Europeans are exposed in tropical climates is not so much a want of adaptability of constitution as ignorance and defiance of the common laws of life'.

Only one year later, Horton made it more evident that his advice was meant to warn, not encourage. For one of his two more sustained interventions into colonial politics, *West African Countries and Peoples, British and Native: and a Vindication of the African Race*, he entered into debate with men such as Richard Burton and James Hunt regarding race and the environment. A monogenist Christian who believed that races improve over time through civilisation and opportunity, in his book Horton asserts that 'civilised' races can degenerate or collapse after reaching their zenith. He plays upon British fears of degeneration by asserting that European children cannot thrive in the tropics.[9] 'When delicately and carefully brought up', he says, these children can 'possess a great delicacy of colour and complexion; but when thrown into the world at a very early age, and subject to the climate and other demoralizing influences' they 'become exceedingly dark, and show a marked difference in their form, proportion and features'. Both the sun and the challenges of colonial life 'negrify' young Europeans. This depiction turns the language of racial anthropology on to the progeny of its inventors, by stressing the change in children's 'form, proportion and features' (1868b: 69–70).

Horton then likens the long-term effects of the tropics on white children to black Africans' appearance and behaviour: 'If this is true among European children born in the tropics, how much more true is it with those who have been subjugated for numberless centuries to the baneful influence of demoralization?' Although a sympathetic inversion of racist thought, this excerpt nevertheless recalls Winwood Reade's shrill worries about the 'negrification' of whites in *Savage Africa*. However, Horton attempts to mould the rhetoric to support his conclusion that 'it is only when the negroes are in possession of privileges and advantages equivalent to the rest of mankind, that a fair comparison can be drawn between the one and the other' (69–70).

As the foregoing excerpts demonstrate, even when adopted in the service of African nationalism, the language of environmental degeneration can both damage the author's logic and undermine his assertions. However, the true thrust of Horton's argument appears in his notes: 'The yearly death-rate is so great, that the [House of Commons Committee] could not contemplate the continuance of such slaughter; in fact, tropical Africa must be left eventually for the Africans' (68). Horton's rhetoric is pointed, as he highlights the threat to children and calls the results of continued colonisation 'slaughter'. In comparison, he claims that 'wherever the African race has been carried to, except, perhaps, the East Indies, they increase, no matter under what depressing and burdensome yoke they suffer' (68–9). Although Horton mentions his own illness in later texts, and stresses that individual Africans can acquire fever and other tropical diseases when forced to travel through different disease environments, here he clearly wishes to depict the African race as hardy and built for survival. He continues, 'the African people is a permanent and enduring people; and the fancies of those who have determined their destruction will go in the same limbo as the now almost defunct American slavery' (69).

Horton writes European extinction in explicitly environmental terms. He says:

> A European race may exist for a short time in any part of Africa, but, ultimately, in tropical Africa, the reverse of what we find in Australia and New Zealand happens to them, and in the course of a very short space of time they die out . . . their offspring suffer seriously from birth to manhood from internal diseases, the result of miasmatic and climatic influences. (68)

Here he draws upon the colonial truism that weaker indigenous races are decimated by disease, using the same example of Australia and New Zealand as in Darwin's *Descent of Man*. However, Horton makes Africans the exception to this rule, as they survive and thrive in spite of oppression and abuse. In fact, 'In the tropical countries of Western Africa, the idea of a permanent occupation by European settlers, if ever entertained, is impossible of realization; it is a mistake and a delusion' (68).

Unlike Mary Seacole, Horton does not deflect attention away from his own instances of poor health. Indeed, it would be difficult to do so, as he was unwell for so much of his military career. However, he takes rhetorical control of his own illness in a few key ways: he chooses when to mention it and in what context; he uses it to shore up his own reputation as an experimental scientist; and by addressing it explicitly, he also tries to save future generations of educated Africans from being used as fodder for the unhealthiest colonial outposts. Christopher Fyfe observes that Horton 'brought overwhelming evidence, from his own experience with the West India Regiments and in treating Africans, against the theory . . . that the people of African descent were immune to malaria. His own case history would have been equally conclusive' (1972: 121). Although this assertion holds to a certain extent, one could probe further by asking when he introduced this evidence of his own 'case history' into his work, and what form it took.

There is a detailed description of Horton's health struggles in his army medical records, held at the University of Birmingham. Entitled 'Abstract of case of Staff Asst Surgeon Horton', the document begins 'This officer arrived on the Gold Coast on the 18th October 1859.' A pattern of illness emerges, which it pays to quote in full:

> during the time that he was stationed at Quittah, he suffered from several relapses of fever . . . [Subsequently] he was located at Accra and Anarwabae, [where he] had attacks of Remittent Fever, lasting from 1st December 1860 to the 13th January 1861. Early in June 1861 he was again attacked by fever and remained on the sick list during that month – being brought up to Head Quarters at Cape Coast Castle for treatment – when his health had been re-established he was ordered to Dixcove – During the tedious journey he had another relapse of fever, and was reduced to a state of excessive weakness. On the 11th November 1861 – Diarrhea supervened after obstinate constipation, and on the second day assumed a dysenteric character. The local pain of the bowels and febrile action increased for some days – and as no abatement of symptoms became apparent, Dr Horton left Dixcove for Cape Coast Castle on the 22nd November 1861 – [At] Cape Coast Castle, Mercurial preparations with opium were given internally, and counterirritation set up on the abdomen to relieve the local distress and pain – the disease was subdued, but as Dr Horton is reduced to a state of great prostration, and has suffered from so many relapses of Remittent Fever, the Board have arrived at the opinion that this officer should have leave of absence for three months to visit Sierra Leone, his native place, for the purpose of recovering his health.[10]

From this description, Horton appears to have had recurring attacks of malaria as well as a bout of dysentery, no doubt compounded by exhaustion. There is of course great pathos in this case. It emerges from this report that Horton suffered debilitating illness on and off throughout the first two years of his career, was moved five times during the same period, and was treated with mercury, opium and 'counterirritation' (probably cupping) before being sent home to 'his native place' to try to recover. From this it would not be difficult to write an account, barely embellishing upon the facts, that would touch many readers' emotions and inspire sympathy.

However, the first sustained mention of Horton's own illness appears in his *Diseases of Tropical Climates*. After there was 'no further prospect of immediate self-government for British West Africa', Horton 'returned to medicine and geology' (Fyfe 1972: 119). The Fanti Confederation had failed, and the last vestiges of Cardwell's policies were being abandoned in favour of more active British sovereignty, which was to lead in the next decade to the 'Scramble for Africa'. In *Diseases of Tropical Climates*, Horton puts aside the vehement political argumentation that characterised his earlier work, and instead invokes his own illness as dispassionate scientific observer. He claims,

> The lagoons of India, China, Japan, Africa, and other tropical countries, may be safely regarded as the source of the most deadly malarious emanations. I experimented on myself, when stationed in the unhealthy region of Quittah, on the bank of the extensive lagoon on the Guinea Coast of Western Africa; and the result was that, at a certain period, the lagoon is not only a generator of malaria, but that it exists in a very concentrated form. (1874: 20)

Rather than a moving first-person narration of illness, this appears to be a detached and passing reference to his own illness, mainly in order to substantiate the dangerousness of a particular locality. Yes, this area is dangerous, and yes, one may become very ill with malaria there at certain times of the year.

By saying 'I experimented on myself', Horton enters into a rich legacy of nineteenth-century scientists famous for self-experimentation, who were often known for their selflessness and successful discoveries. Historical surveys of such experiments have suggested that over 89 per cent proved their hypotheses (Weisse 2012: 51; Altman 1987). Self-experimentation can also be a cause for concern, however: if the experiment goes wrong, the only scientist qualified to set it right may be too compromised to do so. *The Strange Case of Dr Jekyll and Mr Hyde* (1886) is one fictionalised imagining of the possible horrors that can result from this scenario. Horton next marshals data in order to prove that black Africans are also susceptible to malaria, 'especially when brought into contact with it in a strange country' (1874: 22). This statement adds more layers to his preceding claim.

Horton himself was an African 'brought into contact' with malaria 'in a strange country' through the exigencies of his post. Perhaps he began to see patterns in his own illness and hoped that the displacement and suffering could serve a purpose. He offered observations of the unhealthy conditions in each successive post in order to form the foundation for sanitary improvements and win greater respect for local Africans. Although his reports did effect small and gradual changes, and started the ripples in motion that would lead eventually to the founding of a West African university and bank, during his lifetime his success was not as conclusive as he must have wished. By saying 'I experimented on myself', then, Horton claims agency – he is no longer part of the larger colonial experiment, placing Africans rather than whites in harm's way, but a scientist proving a theory of his own.

Tropical Vegetation

While much of the extant scholarship on Africanus Horton focuses on his role as a forefather of African nationalism, his contributions to medical science also inform Adelola Adeloye's biography *Doctor James Africanus Beale Horton: West African Medical Scientist of the Nineteenth Century*. Adeloye claims that '[t]he most important contribution' of Horton's MD thesis from the University of Edinburgh was 'its reference to many examples of West African plants with medicinal properties' (1992: 11). Horton was 'one of the first doctors' to make 'respectable reference to West African traditional and herbal medicines', and he encouraged their use by modern doctors (14). Plants that Horton recommends as therapeutic include the bark of the mangrove tree (febrifuge), castor oil plant (purgative), *bofaruna* extraction (galactagogue) and *ochro* fruit (respiratory aid) (qtd Adeloye 1974: 14).

Adeloye claims that Horton's early writings 'kindled the aspirations and expectations of medical science when he affirmed that there were numerous examples of such medicinal herbs in Sierra Leone "which for want of able investigators are still unknown"' (1974: 11). As has been well documented by colonial historians and postcolonial ecocritics, the widespread exploitation of indigenous botanical resources was a main driver in colonial expansion. For example, in *Nature's Government*, Richard Drayton calls the mapping of these resources 'phytogeography', a practice based on the belief that 'European power, joined to the scientific mastery of nature, would necessarily confer the greatest good on the greatest number' (2000: xv). Drayton demonstrates that 'waves of botanists' travelled to West and East Africa after slavery was outlawed, each expedition carrying a 'chief botanist' whose job it was to catalogue the area's natural resources and 'potential for agriculture'. The goal was to find a 'legitimate commodity to replace slaves' (Drayton 2000:

203). In fact, the Colonial Floras scheme (1863), which was intended to build 'systematic knowledge of plant distribution', produced a full 'seven tomes' just on 'the *Flora of Tropical Africa*' by the end of the nineteenth century, 'as the formalization of Britain's *imperium* swept new territory into the reach of its collectors' (206). The expansion ironically was facilitated by the agricultural exploitation of other colonies, as Lucile Brockway observes in her book *Science and Colonial Expansion*. In the final decades of the nineteenth century, for example, cinchona bark from Indian and Ceylonese plantations was 'processed in England, and shipped to West Africa as quinine powder', in order to support the health of whites as they grew Britain's colonial territories (Brockway 1979: 131).

By shining a spotlight on West Africa's medicinal herbs, Horton may have participated in this process. He highlighted a resource that that he thought, through development, would enhance the life quality of both black and white residents of the Coast. By contrast, throughout his life Horton discouraged the colonial exploitation of mineral resources in favour of West African financial independence (Fyfe 1972: 128). However, Horton's discussion of native plants complicates the binary division that critics often associate with eco-colonialism, whereby indigenous peoples are 'naturalised' and 'at one with nature' and colonists are outsiders who tame the tropical environment. His work stresses the therapeutic and aesthetic qualities of local plants but also pinpoints 'malaria' as emanating from decomposing vegetable matter. He claims that African subjects possess extensive knowledge regarding their environment, but associates this knowledge with their untapped intellectual capacity rather than with their emotionalism and intuition. This nuanced representation of tropical nature serves to underscore Africans' authority over their own environment.

In *Physical and Medical Climate*, Horton encourages more colonial engagement with the African environment than in his later texts. He advocates 'a more general planting of umbrageous trees in the highways of the towns', due to the 'delightful properties of trees': they 'exhale a certain quantity of aqueous vapour' and thereby 'cool the atmosphere'. While 'an effort in this direction has been made by the planting of a large number of trees in the front street at Bathurst' and other places, there should be 'a more general' planting, and under 'a well-directed plan' (1867: 72–3). Horton here advocates the planting of trees on a practical as well as an aesthetic basis.

Postcolonial eco-critics are right to consider the historical as well as ideological significance of writers' engagement with specific parts of the natural environment, but one must be wary of recreating the wild/savage versus cultivated/civilised binary of nineteenth-century perceptions of nature. In the volume *Postcolonial Ecologies*, Lizabeth Paravisini Gebert analyses forests in a postcolonial Caribbean context, where she says they can symbolise 'notions of indigeneity': 'immersion in forests', she claims, can be 'the means of recovering a cultural authenticity that was lost on contact with the plantation' and can stand for 'the idealization of the plot system of agriculture as an alternative to the plantation system' (2011: 100). As demonstrated in Chapter 2, colonists were often anxious about the ability of local peoples to navigate forests, hide in them and use them as a means of escape or as a base for counter-attack. In response, many Europeans sought to remove the forest and reshape the environment into a more normalised and non-threatening space, reminiscent of their homeland. Sir Walter Raleigh, the sixteenth-century explorer and writer, is an example of someone whose life and work embodied the 'impulse to reform the landscape by turning it into a space of agricultural production that recreated the known British model' (Paravisini Gebert 2011: 101).

However, these is still more room to understand colonial subjects' own complex engagement with and depiction of their natural environment. For example, when Horton advocates the 'well-directed' and systematic planting of trees along highways and central streets, he neither seeks to recreate an untamed space for indigeneity nor to replicate an English park. Instead, he advocates a beneficial measure that would both increase the comfort of all inhabitants and, at the same time, probably undo some of the deforestation perpetrated by colonial settlement. Most importantly, he believes that trees cool the air, which decreases sun exposure and resultant illnesses.

Africanus Horton arguably takes a similar stance in his work as Mary Seacole when she asserts 'so true is it that beside the nettle ever grows the cure for its sting' (1857: 60). These writers locate both the irritant and the cure within their local environment, and by displaying familiarity with the interrelationship between the two, claim for themselves a privileged status as the most qualified 'doctor' of tropical ills. In *West African Countries and Peoples*, Horton implies that these abilities are nascent within many of his country's people. Falling after his first appeal in 1861 to the War Office for a West African medical school, but before his final proposal in 1871 for a West African university, *West African Countries and Peoples* combines idyllic imagery with details regarding Africans' capacity for observation and calculation in order to advocate their further education.

Horton begins an extended passage on Africans and their relationship with nature by disqualifying 'the anthropologists of these days' (1868b:

21), who he says are blind to how well local subjects can interpret 'the book of nature'. Africans possess 'wonderful powers of observation', Horton claims, that only need enhancement with 'necessary information respecting natural objects' and the cultivation of 'patient attention' in order to 'rivet' the observations 'in their memory'. He continues by depicting the richness of the tropical environment as only discernible by Africans:

> the majestic trees of the forest, covered with their evergreen foliage of a thousand variegated colours; the numerous gay tropical birds with beautiful plumage; the solitary and melancholy grandeur of many of the scenes with which they are surrounded; the magnificent rivers which run through their country; the ocean, in all its forms of sublimity and terror; the tremendous rocks which resound with the ceaseless roar of the billows, and the numerous shells which stud the shores of their country, form in a scientific point of view but a small portion of their consideration, from their seeming insignificance, and from a want of scientific knowledge in the beholders; yet still, the brilliant stars, the splendid midday sun, the resplendent full moon, and the terrific tornado, with its thunder and lightning, all call into exercise the peculiar disposition and talents of their mind. (21)

Although Horton invokes Africa's great aesthetic beauty – 'evergreen foliage of a thousand variegated colours', 'gay tropical birds', 'brilliant stars' and 'resplendent full moon' – he also repeats 'scientific' twice in quick succession at the end of the passage. His use of the word shifts, however: first, the Africans' brain capacity is the subject of scientific quantification, as Horton explains that they currently only use a 'small portion of their consideration'; secondly, Africans become the potential consumers of 'scientific knowledge', which would allow them to make the most of the innate 'dispositions and talents of their mind'.

Crucially, Horton does not make Africans' 'talents' dependent on education. Their ability is innate, and is already triggered by 'the brilliant stars, the splendid midday sun, the resplendent full moon, and the terrific tornado'. Rather than characterising their talents as depending on intuition, Horton uses the word 'observation' and thereby associates the process with intellect and rationality. Horton also repeats 'their country' in order to illustrate that this is a personal relationship between African subjects and their native land. He invokes the scope and grandeur of this land by describing 'the magnificent rivers which run through their country . . . and the numerous shells which stud the shores of their country'. Sweeping arcs of land and water indicate that all within their bounds belong to the African.

By the time *Diseases of Tropical Climates* was published in 1874, Horton's proposal for a West African university had been declined and his hopes for West African independence dashed. His guide to tropical medicine seems the most neutral of his texts, but significantly his representation of tropical nature has become more foreboding. He defines malaria as the 'exhalation of a certain invisible effluvium from decayed vegetable as well as animal matter' (1874: 18). He cites a series of names for this 'effluvium', three of which contain references within them to the tropical environment: '*phyto-septic matter, vegeto-putrescent matter, miasma, marsh-miasmata*'. He claims darkly that malaria's presence can be 'detected solely by its action on the constitution' (18).

Trees have shifted from a beautifying and comforting presence to a threatening one. Horton states, 'Marsh poison has been observed to be attracted by, and to adhere to, the foliage of many umbrageous trees, which makes it dangerous to sleep under them' (25). It is unlikely that his readers would find themselves making camp under the trees in Africa. Instead, this passage brings to mind dark and mysterious forests, impenetrable to colonial forces, which critics such as Paravisini Gebert have located primarily in postcolonial literary works. By using the language of climatic illness, Horton is able to create these associations under the guise of an informational text.

Emile Pasteur hypothesised in 1874 that microbes cause putrefaction. Evidence in favour of germ theory was building. The 1869 Annual Report for the Medical Department commended the work of B. Sanderson, who had found evidence that contagion was spread through 'living, self-multiplying organic forms' (Worboys 2000: 128). Although Horton was intrigued by Sanderson's idea of 'zymotes' – the 'spherical particles' that cause disease – in *Diseases of Tropical Climates*, he associates these 'zymotes' with putrefaction. This allows him to continue blaming 'remittent fever' on 'vegetable sporules' or 'cryptogamic vegetation' (1874: 78). The very undergrowth of Africa can poison you, Horton seems to warn his readers. Based on his previous recommendations, the sewers and drainage of colonial outposts such as Sierra Leone had been improved; however, it was unlikely that the colonial administration would be able to eliminate all vegetable matter.[11]

British exploration discourse often stereotypes tropical climates as abundant, and local peoples as reaping the benefits of their surroundings without expending any effort (Tobin 2005: 4). In the tradition of Linnean botany, the bounty of tropical nature was catalogued not only through botanical surveys but also through arts and letters. Beth Fowkes Tobin demonstrates how these catalogues 'decontextualize tropical nature' (2005: 12). Through this process, she argues, 'the knowledge and skill of the local producer are lost in the catalog's celebration of nature's bounty and the elevation of the [white] writer as expert about agriculture, botany, geology, and the natural world' (12). The work of Africanus Horton redresses this imbalance by claiming for a black African subject expertise regarding his own environment. Horton undoubtedly draws upon some traditional European depictions of the tropics. However, he mixes these strains of rhetoric so that West Africa emerges as beautiful but forebidding, fecund but also fatal, and fundamentally comprehensible only to the African eye.

Notes

1. At the beginning of the nineteenth century, both France and Britain 'tried to increase the proportion of Africans' in their armies, and so formed the West India regiments. Many of the soldiers were slaves 'recruited by purchase, often bought directly from slave ships' in the Caribbean, though the officers 'and many non-commissioned officers' were European. The West India regiments were 'organized from the beginning as a regular part of the British army' (Curtin 1998: 17). After the 'legal slave trade' was abolished in 1809, many slave recaptives were 'landed in Sierra Leone', where 'with a degree of coercion, they could be persuaded to enlist in the West India regiments' (17). In the mid-1840s local 'corps of African troops' were merged with the West India regiments and served in West Africa 'in rotation of four to five years at a time' (17). The history of the West India regiments highlights the patterns of migration between West Africa and the Caribbean that caused both their political and disease environments to be interrelated.
2. His example did, however, usher in a new cohort of West African men who sought medical training in the United Kingdom, including Nathanial King (qualified in 1874), Obadiah Johnson (1884), John Randle (1888), Orisadipe Obasa (1891), Sodeinde Akinsiku Leigh-Sodipe (1892), Oguntola Sapara (1895), Akinwande Savage (1900) and W. A. Cole and Curtis Crispin Adeniyi-Jones (1901) (Adeloye 1992: 21).
3. For more information on recaptives, see Spitzer (1975).
4. His text *Physical and Medical Climate* (1867), based on these observations, did effect change by inspiring the foundation of a Board of Health for Sierra Leone.
5. Pine to the Colonial Office, 7 December 1863, CMA papers C.A. 1/0/117–20, National Archives. Letters of J. A. B. Horton.
6. University of Birmingham Church Missionary Society Archives, CMS/B/OMS/C A1 O117 1–4.
7. Ibid.
8. Although this advice might prove helpful through preventing contact with mosquitoes, Horton believes it important to avoid exercises especially in the morning because 'Due time should be allowed to the sun to disperse the malaria which accumulates on the surface of the earth' (1867: 281). Horton's conceptualisation of malaria and its relationship to plant matter will be discussed further in the final section of this chapter.

9. However, he walks a fine line when he seeks to discourage racial inter-marriage. Although he staunchly defended mulatto women from Burton's condemnation, Horton also hurriedly says that the progeny of intermarriage do not thrive. While he may be seeking to defend West African racial and cultural purity, Horton also haphazardly, perhaps accidentally, invokes polygenism and its belief in the fertility test for species distinction.
10. University of Birmingham Church Missionary Society Archives, CMS/B/OMS/C A1 O117 6–21.
11. Once Ronald Ross had linked malaria to mosquitoes, he organised 'mosquito brigades' in Sierra Leone to empty pools of standing water, but also to eliminate disease hosts and rotting vegetation. His discovery gave scientific justification to the clearing and reconfiguration of local landscapes, which Horton might have hoped would be impossible (see Ross 1902).

Chapter 4

'Climate proof':
Mary Kingsley and the Health of
Women Travellers

Ten years after the death of Africanus Horton, a white woman who was eventually to be called 'the Prophet of Africa to her own people' landed in Sierra Leone. This illustrious label was given to Mary Kingsley by Horton's fellow African nationalist, Edward Blyden (Blyden 1901: 15). The mutual respect between Kingsley and Blyden grew out of their shared belief that white British culture should not be imposed on Africans. Although Kingsley was idealised by Blyden and many of her contemporaries in African affairs for this seemingly progressive cultural relativism, her recommendations were undergirded by some troubling and complex theories of racial science. Kingsley was quite happy to study African practices such as fetish and polygamy without an eye to reforming them, because she felt that the less African social structures were changed by whites, the more economically productive would be Britain's colonialism. She accorded black Africans greater disease resistance and thought they should be used accordingly for labour in the service of empire. Most fundamentally, she asserted that the Christian mission to improve African culture and religion was deluded because of her polygenist conviction that the races were irrevocably separate.

Kingsley's travels to Africa occurred during a key historical period when much had been discovered about the transmission of disease, but a few key links were still missing. As the 1893 guide *Hygiene & Diseases in Warm Climates* demonstrates, 'It is only within recent years that the *rôle* of parasitic diseases in tropical pathology has been fully understood' (Davidson 1893: v). Andrew Davidson describes Laveran's 1880 discovery of the malarial parasite, and even cites the parasite's life cycle in the blood, but still believes that this parasite is 'generated only in connection with the soil' (1893: 130). Until and even after Ronald Ross documented the transmission of malaria through mosquito bites in 1897, writers drew freely upon a mixture of infectious and environmental metaphors, and many continued to invoke the fatal tropical climate as the source of disease. In order to block widespread European settlement of Africa, which she believed would be both inimical to the welfare of African subjects and counterproductive to England's economic interests, Kingsley depicted the West African climate as irredeemably fatal for most whites.

Both Blyden and Kingsley were aware of the 'fatal climate's' rhetorical potential. Blyden cites a personal letter that Kingsley sent him in his lecture *Miss Kingsley and the African Society* (1901). He claims that, though Kingsley was thankful for scientists' 'efforts to study and deal with tropical diseases', still she 'believed that there are physical or material disabilities or obstructions which are amenable to moral influences' (1901: 22). It is worth citing both Kingsley's original 'unpublished letter' to Blyden and his own interpretation of that letter. Kingsley writes, 'human nature ... will act upon its physical environments in [*sic*] your behalf; the air and all nature will fight for you, as Wordsworth said about Toussaint' (22). Blyden chooses to emphasise the possibility inherent in the foregoing passage that moral, non-intrusive engagement with Africa could 'go a great way towards curing Climates' – that choosing the right course of action, rather than acting upon 'coarser passions and brutal instincts' of colonial domination, could save whites from death. He underscores this point by saying 'Miss Kingsley's moral force and moral intentions made her climate proof in the most malarious regions in West Africa' (22).

While Blyden hopes that his readers will be swayed by the possibility that a change in perspective might save them from malaria, there is another possible reading of Kingsley's letter. Not able to trust that 'moral force' alone would rein in Joseph Chamberlain's plans to expand England's West African colonies, Kingsley may be hinting to Blyden that the very real obstruction of the tropical climate could work as the best deterrent. Although the line in Wordsworth's 1802 sonnet 'To Toussaint L'Ouverture', 'the air and all nature will fight for you', is often cited as an example of the romantic sublime (Persyn 2002), as invoked by Kingsley it takes on more threatening overtones. Wordsworth wrote the poem for L'Ouverture, a West Indian revolutionary jailed for his role in supporting slave rebellions. The original line naturalises a native subject by implying that his home environment sympathises with his plight. However, within the context of Blyden's discussion of African malaria, Kingsley seems to be using Wordsworth's poem to suggest that 'the air and all nature' will fight for the cause of non-intervention by causing the illness of interloping colonisers.

This chapter takes up Blyden's assertion that Kingsley was 'climate proof'. Specifically, I argue that Kingsley was aware that her unusually strong health during her African travels could be a source of authority and narrative power when writing her book *Travels in West Africa* (1897). Therefore, she contrasts her own disease resistance with the vulnerability of the other white subjects she encounters. Blyden celebrates what he calls Kingsley's 'abundance of heart', which in combination with her 'affluence of experience' allowed her to say 'with unfaltering accents' what was 'just and right' (1901: 23). As opposed to the representation cultivated by Blyden that Kingsley's writing was unaffected, I am interested in the ways she crafts her work with an acute awareness of its intended audience.

Mary Kingsley's conscious reframing of the discourses of gender and health are evident when her private and public personae are contrasted. In a March 1899 letter to Sir Matthew Nathan, Kingsley claims that with the death of her parents she lost what was her main life purpose: homemaking and domestic duties. She says that in travelling to West Africa she embraced her own probable death: 'I went down to West Africa to die. West Africa amused me . . . and did not want to kill me just then. I am in no hurry. I don't care one way or the other, for a year or so' (qtd in Lane 2003: 96). When considering this seemingly off-hand remark, one must take biographical context into consideration. Intended for Nathan, the object of Kingsley's unrequited love, this comment was made more than four years after Kingsley's safe return from Africa (Lane 2003: 96). Kingsley draws upon a well-established discourse of 'suicide by Africa' in her letter: in his *Guide to Health in Africa*, Thomas Parke says it was commonly thought to be a 'slower form of suicide to take up residence' in Africa (1893: 2). However, it seems more likely that a drive for adventure, novelty and usefulness motivated Kingsley's travels rather than any suicidal impulse. This letter serves as an example of Kingsley both performing culturally accepted modes of feminine self-sacrifice (I had no domestic role as sister and daughter, which took away my will to live; I still have no domestic role, which leaves me similarly dejected) and enhancing her own stature by demonstrating bravery in the face of certain death. As this chapter demonstrates, Kingsley's apparent lack of concern for her own well-being could be a benefit rather than a liability to her health. She implies that only a person with nothing to lose may successfully travel through the land known as the 'White Man's Grave'. Her life circumstance, humour and light-hearted constitution all work together to make Kingsley at home in the climate of Africa.

Kingsley's ability to draw upon different identities has been well documented. She relished being called 'Sir' while travelling in Africa and referred to herself as an 'Englishman', but she remained a vehement anti-suffragist who slogged through marshes in full skirts; she was an avowed polygenist and believer in white supremacy, but demonstrated more cultural relativism and respect for African traditions than many of her contemporaries. Many critics have linked her multivalent rhetoric to tropes of travel and liminality – as Kingsley crossed geographical borders and boundaries, so too are readers interested in the ways in which her writing crosses and revises identities and roles.[1] Further studies have explored Kingsley's non-linearity in terms of both geographical travel and scientific methodology (see Blunt 1994; Early 1997). Perhaps it is logical, then, that Kingsley's own body has often been read as intangible, fragmented or diffuse. In order to prove that Kingsley's writing erases her individual body, privileging instead 'nothingness and the sublime', Christopher Lane cites Kingsley's own self-depiction as 'part of the atmosphere' and 'like a gale of wind' (2003: 96–8). Laura Ciolkowski argues that Kingsley mobilises discourses of white female sexual vulnerability, portraying herself as a British woman 'violently threatened by foreign cultures' through repeated invocations of 'cannibalism, bodily dismemberment and physical fragmentation' (1998: 339, 46).

Indeed, Kingsley carefully crafts a narrative persona that revises notions of linearity and melds characteristics of different gender identities. However, one should not take her practice of self-renunciation at face value. This chapter suggests an alternative reading of Kingsley to that of physical vulnerability or diffuseness. Rather, Kingsley depicts herself as at one with the African atmosphere while representing other white subjects' disease and death, thereby suggesting that she is singularly impervious to climatic illness. In contrast, she manipulates ominous images of climate in order to inspire fear of West African fever in her readers, portraying Africa as a potentially rich source of raw materials but also as inherently dangerous to most whites. 'Miasma' and the fevers it causes are nebulous enough deterrents for this purpose. According to the constitutional profile Kingsley creates, the only whites eligible for travel to West Africa may be Kingsley herself and certain traders, the 'old Coasters'.

Richard Burton sought to rehabilitate the reputation of West Africa by recommending that whites relocate to higher elevations, in order to contain the risk of disease within topographical 'zones'. In contrast, Mary Kingsley mocks the belief that living on a mountain will save you. In *Victorian Writing about Risk*, Elaine Freedgood argues that domestic texts attempt to 'locate risk according to the consoling geographical scheme of a safe England in a dangerous world' (2000: 171). In contrast, the literature of empire may 'suggest that safety and danger traverse borders and boundaries with the same peripatetic flair exhibited by so many of [its] authors' (171). As they move through changing landscapes, authors such as Mary Kingsley draw and redraw 'borders' around 'geography' that are 'always being breached or failing' in an 'endless attempt to create cultural artifacts capable of containing risk and anxiety' (Freedgood 2000: 171). In fact, I would suggest that Kingsley highlights the very permeability and insecurity of these borders by focusing on the insidious and pervasive effects of the tropical climate, specifically miasma, tropical currents and tides. Kingsley's goal is therefore not to 'manage' and 'contain' risk in order to create a 'fantasy of security' for her readers (Freedgood 2000: 169), but to prove that she is unique in her ability to travel through these porous boundaries of safety and danger. While certain 'ephemeral texts', as Freedgood terms them, may 'provide their readers with immediate and portable ideas of security' (171), they often do so by first articulating risk; and some, such as Kingsley's *Travels in West Africa*, never convincingly contain that risk at all.

This chapter begins by tracing how Victorians perceived the risk of 'fever', especially in the context of West Africa, in order to establish how Kingsley uses this malleable group of illnesses to stimulate readers' worries. The section 'Trading on Health' outlines those subjects whom Kingsley exempts from tropical illness, including the 'old Coasters', black Africans and herself, and how this grouping works to her benefit. Her own resistance to the effects of 'miasma' allows her greater freedom and mobility than her readers. However, Kingsley does not ascribe physical strength to black Africans in order to liberate them from the yoke of colonialism, but to justify their ongoing use as beasts of burden.

The chapter then considers more closely Kingsley's own relationship to the African environment. How and why does she depict herself 'at home' in the tropics? Although Kingsley was an avowed polygenist, by examining her references to disease and diseasedness one may read much ambivalence regarding the relationship between whites and blacks in her texts. For example, when she says that 'the fascination of the African point of view is sure to linger in your mind as the malaria in your body' (1897a: 441), she both pathologises the African 'point of view' and also implies that both her mind and body have been 'colonised' by the African environment. The final section of this chapter considers how Kingsley creates a vision of a healthy, white female body in the tropics, impervious to the negative influences of climate because it is already 'in sympathy' with them.

Fear Digs the 'White Man's Grave': West African Fever

Kingsley reminds her readers of West Africa's high rates of white mortality through her repeated descriptions of fever, thereby entering into a longstanding rhetorical tradition reaching back to the earliest exploration of the African continent.[2] During the sixteenth, seventeenth and eighteenth centuries, the west coast of Africa primarily functioned as an exchange point for human cargo: black slaves were captured in Africa and sold for slave labour in other countries. With the abolition of slave trading throughout the British Empire in 1807, and of slavery itself in 1833, Britain decided to explore further the natural resources of West Africa in an attempt to make its coastal colonies pay as points of trade. It also hoped to encourage other colonial powers, such as France and Portugal, to abolish slave trading in favour of trading ivory, gold, copper, indigo and spices (Carlson 1984: 2). Britain therefore greatly increased the number of its representatives on the coast of West Africa during the first three decades of the nineteenth century; however, it met with little success in counteracting the slave traffic or in encouraging legitimate trade. It was during the 1820s that the British popular press named Africa the 'White Man's Grave', as more and more reports of exploratory missions wiped out by disease began to filter back (Carlson 1984: 10).

Throughout the 1830s, independent merchants and businessmen tried to make inroads in West Africa to find valuable natural resources. Their missions suffered high mortality rates. The members of the government-sponsored 1841 expedition to explore the interior of West Africa via the Niger River included 'geologists, mineralogists, chemists, botanists, church representatives and staff to run a model farm', who were no more immune to disease than the commercial representatives. The scientists analysed samples of river water in an attempt to identify the 'disease-producing effect in the "miasms"', but by the time two months had elapsed, 130 of the 145 whites on the expedition had been ill with fever, and 40 had died. No indigenous Africans on board had been ill (Carlson 1984: 10).

Of some help was the widespread use of quinine from the mid-nineteenth century. However, quinine dosage and use patterns were inconsistent and far from universally successful. West Africa was still a very dangerous place to be. As Philip D. Curtin asserts in *Disease and Empire*, it is a 'historical problem' to 'discover why people were willing to go to a place where the probability of death was about fifty per cent in the first year and twenty-five per cent a year thereafter' (1998: 1). Curtin attributes the early nineteenth-century British migration to West Africa to ignorance, coercion and unhappy conditions of life at home. Although Britain's enthusiasm for African exploration was checked somewhat after death rate statistics began to be made available in the mid-century, in the popular imagination Africa still represented an infinitely fecund source of raw materials needed to feed the growing demands of Britain's industrial-capitalist economy.[3]

However, a cluster of diseases labelled 'fever' stood between Britain and this seemingly inexhaustible source of materials. Currently, we know that fever is a symptom, not a disease in itself: the body raises its temperature as a response to infection. During the Victorian age, however, fever was considered a disease in its own right. Although theorists attempted to classify different types of fever by their geographical location ('Bulam' fever, or 'African' fever) or by their cycles ('remittent, intermittent', 'Tertiana', 'Quartana', 'Quotidiana'), many still felt that all fevers were linked. While the distinctions between fevers became more refined during the latter half of the nineteenth century with the advent of greater scientific knowledge, the hygienic theories of Southwood Smith and Edwin Chadwick remained influential in the conceptualisaton of tropical disease. It is understandable that ideas of environmental pathology had such staying power: the diagnostic waters were muddied, considering that it is often difficult by observation alone to distinguish yellow fever from other forms of jaundice, malaria or influenza. All of these disease groups produce fever as a symptom, whereas the dominant feature of malaria and yellow fever is fever. According to statistical reports from the 1830s, 94 per cent of all European deaths in West Africa resulted from malaria, yellow fever and gastrointestinal infection, with at least 85 per cent from 'fevers' ('combining malaria and yellow fevers, among others'). These remained 'the dominant cause of death throughout the nineteenth century' (Curtin 1998: 5).

Most native Africans achieve acquired immunity to malaria by contracting the disease early in life. While infection as an infant or young child can be fatal, those who survive have greater disease resistance.[4] White Victorians, however, had no childhood acquired immunity to those diseases found in Africa, and were therefore physiologically vulnerable to the new disease environment. Upon arriving in West Africa, many of them quickly became ill and died; others were worn down by cyclical malarial attacks. Most British white Victorians interpreted the contrast between their own disease rates and those of natives to mean that West Africans had an 'innate, racial immunity' (Curtin 1998: 11).

There was still some uncertainty in the 1890s regarding the origins and modes of fever transmission. Heretofore many people had believed that noxious gases, exhalations from decomposing organic matter or damp night air, often labelled 'miasma', could bring on fever. Over-exertion and exposure were also thought to leave the subject vulnerable. These symptom-exciting factors were thought all the more potent if the subject's underlying temperament was nervous, extremely sensitive or anxious. Even by the late Victorian period, many scientific discoveries were not translated into common health practices during tropical expeditions. Some travellers might filter their drinking water; a very few might boil it. Many would use quinine, albeit inconsistently. However, these measures were usually added to other longstanding techniques, such as wearing cotton flannel and avoiding night air. Victorians travelling to West Africa knew that they had a significant chance of contracting an often-fatal disease of nebulous origins and ambiguous symptomology. Native Africans appeared much more resilient, and in some cases impervious to such illnesses. When white travellers tried to arm themselves with knowledge as to how disease could be prevented, they heard conflicting theories propounded by various medical authorities and received staggeringly long lists of preventative measures that included rules for dress, behaviour, food and drink.

Victorian writers made equally good use of fever's uncertain aetiology in order to maximise suspense. This suspense had an edge – not only did fever make readers nervous, but they also thought nervousness laid them open to disease. Athena Vrettos in *Somatic Fictions* (1995) and Jane Wood in *Passion and Pathology in Victorian Fiction* (2001) have analysed Victorian fictional narratives of nursing, hysteria and delirium in order to demonstrate how authors write the somaticisation of disease. Wood outlines the nineteenth century's dominant concern with hyper-sensibility and hypochondria (2001: 3). She asserts that Victorian writers of fiction 'exploited the contested aetiologies of disease in order to incorporate uncertainty into their narratives of physiological collapse' (115). Authors of nonfiction use the rhetoric of medical uncertainty in a similar manner: while narrating their adventures in foreign lands, writers can make those lands seem sinister or accessible to their readers by pinning down fever's causes or emphasising its mystery and omnipresence.

I return to Ford's *Observations on the Fevers of the Western Coast of Africa* (1856), because it provides a clear model of how Victorian travel narratives and advice texts characterised fever. Ford's book, quoted extensively by Burton and other Victorian explorers, outlines the types of fever, their progression in the body and their treatment. Ford further provides suggestions for those newly arrived in Africa regarding the bathing, eating and exercise habits they might employ to avoid becoming ill. Tellingly, Ford calls coming down with fever the 'invasion' stage. The patient's early, instinctive desire to shield himself from wind, cold and exposure to draughts is useless, according to Ford, as he has already been invaded by fever, which is working its way through the body. The patient is described as having a pale face, shrivelled skin, contracted nose, blue lips and dull and heavy eyes during the first, chilled stage of the disease, which quickly passes into the second, feverish stage. Then the patient 'begins to complain of heat. He throws off the bedclothes and asks for air; the skin becomes red and hot; the face loses its shrunken appearance, becoming turgid; the eyes appear bright and watery; thirst becom[es] urgent' and nausea 'comes on'. Urine becomes red or black, and delirium or paroxysms are common, before the fever resolves in healing or death (Ford 1856: 9–10).

This is merely the progression of one attack of 'uncomplicated' fever: 'complicated' fevers, according to Ford, involve damage to the spleen, liver or brain. Ford uses ominous language to explain the sad results of ignoring or misinterpreting one's own symptoms of African fever: 'new residents with first fevers', he says, often suppose they have a '"cold," or are weary, and do not admit that they are sick, until the fully developed hot stage forces them to apply for aid, though . . . the delay until the use of remedies becomes vain, and death follows as the penalty'. To avoid such fatal error, Ford impresses upon his readers 'the necessity of a careful observation of one's own feelings' (1856: 8).[5]

The characterisations of fever found in medical advice texts such as Ford's *Observations* and James Martin's *The Influence of Tropical Climates on the European Constitution* (1861), combined with their laundry list of avoidance measures and disease causing factors, no doubt inspired fear and uncertainty in their readers. Simultaneously, these experts told their readers that fear of acquiring disease often brings it on. Medical authorities warned travellers to be on constant watch for symptoms of fever in themselves, while the circulating rhetoric of masculine hardiness in the service of nation dictated that the admirable adventurer should not become obsessed with his body's state.[6] This contradictory rhetoric surrounding African fever reflects Victorian ambivalence about the biological viability of the imperial project. Further, when their narratives are made public, the extent to which explorers have let their actions be determined by fear of fever begins to have broader ramifications. As explorers selectively interpret Victorian medical advice texts and explanatory systems in ways that reflect their own personal opinions about colonialism, they thereby suggest how much England should let fear of fever dictate its colonial settlement of Africa.

Trading on Health

Mary Kingsley's readership was made up of both legislators and the general public who influenced them: her books had both 'popular and specialist' appeal (Birkett 1992: 82). *Travels in West Africa* went into five editions, financing her next journey to West Africa; *West African Studies* 'sold 1,200 copies in the first week' (Birkett 1992: 82; Thiesmeyer 1994: 157). Kingsley's manipulations of the medical rhetoric of climate thus had a wide audience and political impact. She expresses strong opinions about which individuals should be encouraged to pursue the development of West African trade. She feels nostalgic for an earlier time of African exploration with less governmental interference. Although she admits that she had initially been predisposed against the West African traders, during her travels she comes to respect them and, in fact, to make their political causes her own.[7] Her books advocate what she feels to be the best interests of the 'old Coasters', and her writing also draws upon a precise vocabulary taught her by the traders relating to African cultural traditions, boating, navigation and geography.[8]

The traders held a specific set of economic and racial ideologies to which Kingsley also subscribed, and which give insight into her deployment of medical rhetoric. Her biographer Dea Birkett has aptly called the philosophy that Kingsley and the traders shared 'Free trade economic Imperialism' (1992: 4). One could term Kingsley anti-colonial but pro-Imperial, as she neither believed in strict government management and control of trade, nor the process of attempting to reproduce British culture in foreign lands; however, she did believe in whites' innate superiority and their right to use those lands for economic gain.

Two of the traders most influential on Kingsley's thinking were Sir George Goldie, of the Royal Niger Company, and John Holt, of the Liverpool traders. Britain had given Goldie a Royal Charter to develop trade in Nigeria in 1886, but took it away again in 1895. When Joseph Chamberlain entered the Colonial Office, he began a movement to reinstate government-controlled trade in West Africa. Supporters often justified government control by claiming that Africans could be raised to a higher level of civilisation, and that contact with a European country was therefore beneficial. The trade bosses such as Goldie and Holt had no such motivation. According to them, Africans could, and perhaps should, stay as they were; after all, these men had become rich with the system as it stood. Although she disagreed with some of the details of Goldie's philosophy (for example, he was against the liquor trade and she was for it), both men's economically motivated race theories greatly informed Kingsley's own. They valued black Africans in so far as the Africans made trade possible by providing manual labour and workmanship. Allowing natives a certain amount of cultural and religious autonomy seemed to men such as Holt and Goldie the way to maximise productivity. Further, to exploit or abuse natives too blatantly was bad business: as the Company officials say of Kurtz's methods in *Heart of Darkness*, such techniques 'ruin the district' (Conrad 1988: 57).

Holt's biography attests that '[t]here was nothing in the least sentimental about John Holt's attitude towards the natives of West Africa'; this fact 'commended him to Mary Kingsley' (John Holt & Co. 1962: 40). His attitude 'was compounded of the most practical elements'. Of the native Africans, Holt said 'They made me what I am. Their labour, their muscles, their enterprise, have given me everything I possess. I am bound to try and protect them against outrage and injustice' (40). Goldie, in turn, stressed the 'fecundity and vitality of the negro races', and showed a similar gratitude for the trade goods made possible by their 'docility, intelligence, and capacity for work' (qtd in Wellington 1977: 168). Goldie recommended 'ruling on African principles through native rulers' (qtd in Wellington 1977: 176). These men's 'compassion' and 'sympathy' for African natives depended on their function as workhorses. Such words as 'docility' and 'capacity for work' are most commonly used to describe beasts of burden. To treat the blacks any other way might be 'sentimental', in contrast to the ideal attitude of practicality. In a telling reversal of slavery language, the white trader is here 'bound to try and protect' blacks from the encroachment of white society: in this case, if the black man earns the white man money, the white man is bound to him in gratitude. This interpretation of the 'White Man's Burden' simply works to justify whites' ongoing domination as a kind of protection by conflating the traders' best interests with those of their workers.[9]

Similarly, the trader in Kingsley is motivated to perceive native subjects as hardy and disease resistant, no doubt in part because their 'fecundity and vitality' are key characteristics that make ongoing trade possible. She says, 'for one thing I am glad to say the African does not die off as do those weaker races under white control, but increases' (1897a: 677). Rather than celebrating native Africans on their own merits, Kingsley is glad that they are hardy because the natives represent Britain's best chance of having access to Africa's natural resources, which 'lie protected against the miner by African fever in its deadliest form' (631). Africans should be encouraged to extract their own land's resources in exchange for traded goods, including liquor.[10] The primary racist impulse of imbuing blacks with the brute strength of beasts is reminiscent of slavery discourse.

Kingsley uses polygenism, which dictates that the races are discrete species with different points of origin, to support her political goals. She clearly articulates her race ideology in opposition to that of Christian missionaries, many of whom are monogenist. Both missionaries and the Colonial Office held as a tenet the idea that blacks could be 'lifted' towards white civilisation. In contrast, Kingsley claims that blacks are 'inferior in kind, not degree' (1897a: 659). If Kingsley could convince her readership that the ideas of these two factions were incorrect, they would have less of a foothold in Africa's development. Hence, she argues that whites should leave native culture alone. Her attacks on missionaries and the Colonial Office are 'built from anthropological foundations'. To inculcate the African with Christian doctrine, Kingsley believes, is to ruin him by giving him a 'second-hand rubbishy white culture' (17). In order to make this claim, she seeks to prove that African tribal societies have their own internal organisation and religious beliefs, which have developed in response to the demands of their environment. Polygamy functions to create an even distribution of labour, she argues, and as for that other practice – cannibalism – most cited as sinful by the Western world, Kingsley argues it to be vastly over-reported and exaggerated. Kingsley believes that the practice of 'fetish' or taboo provides a 'wholesome restraint' on the African. In other words, blacks are not a blank slate, or 'so many jugs only requiring to be emptied of the stuff which is in them and refilled with [a] particular form of dogma' (659). While Kingsley's respect for certain African traditions may appear refreshing in the face of the vindictive racism of Richard Burton and others, it pays to remember that though Kingsley allows Africans a certain amount of respect, she believes the races to be firmly divided. This division paints indigenous peoples as irrevocably inferior, not simply 'savage' as a result of circumstance. She says, 'I feel certain that a black man is no more an undeveloped white man than a rabbit is an undeveloped hare' (659).

Kingsley grew up reading about and being inspired by Burton's travels in West Africa. One may see echoes of Burton's thought in Kingsley's spatialised racial ideology, Kingsley opines,

> the African is not keen on mountaineering in the civilization range. He prefers remaining down below and being comfortable . . . And if he is dragged up into the higher regions . . . he falls back damaged, a morally maimed man, into his own swampy country fashion valley. (1897a: 680)

Of note in this passage is the conflation of the African subject with 'his own . . . swampy valley': the places of miasma and disease are where he is most comfortable. Unlike Burton, however, Kingsley does not conflate the two in order to then disapprove of or verbally abuse the black African.[11] In contrast to Burton, Kingsley underscores the unremitting fatality of Africa's climate for most white subjects by ruling out acclimatisation (690). Also, though Kingsley does associate African subjects with lower elevations, she does not subscribe to Burton's belief that health is possible for whites on Africa's higher elevations.

Kingsley cites the example of the current governor of Fernando Po, whom she meets and finds charming but mocks for his withdrawal to the hills. Upon becoming ill, she says, the man 'withdrew from the Port of Clarence and went up the mountain to Basile, which is in the neighbourhood of the highest native village, where he built himself a house'. He 'profoundly believed in' the 'advantages of the superior elevation' she says, and encouraged all other whites in the region to join him. While Kingsley acknowledges that 'undoubtedly the fever is not so severe at Basile as in the lowlands', she says there are instead 'the usual drawbacks to West African high land': an 'over supply of rain', 'saturating mists' and 'sudden and extreme alternations of temperature'. The colonists who have retreated to the hills still 'fall off', and their children 'die continuously from the various entozoa which abound upon the island' (44–5). In one fell swoop, Kingsley eliminates the comforting possibility of healthy mountain outposts as well as stimulating readers' instinctive fear and protective instincts towards 'continuously' dying European children.

As previously demonstrated, Edward Blyden and his contemporaries made much of Kingsley's sympathy with Africans. However, both Blyden and Kingsley argued for British non-intervention by portraying blacks as static – Kingsley by stating that they are a different species and Blyden by claiming there is a reducible African 'character' that is distinct from the European character. Although he has since been idealised by postcolonial Africanists, Blyden's schema is potentially troubling because he builds it around a set of stereotypes such as blacks are emotional and intuitive (for example; Blyden 1903). Kingsley's schema is troubling because, by affiliating blacks with their own 'swampy valley', she associates their mentality as well as their bodies with disease.

One observes a certain ambivalence in this portrayal, however, when she says that 'the fascination of the African point of view is sure to linger in your mind as the malaria in your body' (1897a: 441). Kingsley herself was not immune to disease: in letters she writes about having a 'touch of the West Coast fever' long after she has left West Africa (qtd in Frank 1986: 320). However, she depicts her illness as non-debilitating rather than acute: it has become a part of her body and her life. Further, when she conflates the African 'point of view' with disease, she also cannot help but write herself as colonised by 'malaria' through her sympathy with blacks, naturalised within the environment she inhabits. However, she also seems to anticipate criticism from her readers that she over-identifies with black subjects by implying that this sympathy is not her fault. Like a patient who does not know conclusively from whence malaria comes and therefore cannot protect against it, Kingsley is powerless to fight the 'fascination' Africa exerts on her.

'My people are mangrove swamps': Female Health and the Tropical Environment

Critical discourse does not seem to have a well-developed language with which to describe the healthy Victorian female body, perhaps because much of Victorian scientific discourse pathologised women. From figuring a woman's physical health in terms of her childbearing abilities to idealising the feminine subject as 'weak, pale and not hungry', Victorian medicine seemed calculated to reinforce female subservience and passivity (Horne 2004: 264). Literature often reflected and perpetuated these values, using the 'injury and eventual inspirational death' of female characters as 'a characteristic means of spiritual education' for female readers (Nelson qtd in Horne 2004: 260). Readers of Victorian literature are accustomed to encountering domestic martyrs and angels in the house, or subversive female characters who are punished with illness or death. Small wonder, then, that scholarship about nineteenth-century women and health is commonly concerned with the female anorexic, hysteric, sentimental, invalid, madwoman or criminal. This chapter suggests that here is a different model of nineteenth-century female health to be found in Mary Kingsley's work, which depends on the woman's climatic invulnerability. This vision of health transcends childbearing and domesticity, and also refuses to adopt wholesale either contemporary ideas of masculine vigour or feminist visions of the 'New Woman'.

It is useful to outline the discourses of female tropical illness before examining how Kingsley writes female tropical health. Medical guidebooks outlined the myriad ways in which women were vulnerable to disease abroad. As with many models of colonial health, the observations and hints given in *Tropical Trials: A Handbook for Women in the Tropics* (1883) were based on English subjects' experiences in India, but generalised to all tropical environments. Written by Major S. Leigh Hunt, Madras Army, and Alexander S. Kenny, 'demonstrator of anatomy at King's College London', this book claims that 'the physical resources of women in withstanding the hardships and discomforts imposed upon them by the exigencies of tropical life' are 'limited, as compared with the greater strength of constitution possessed by the other sex' (6). Although the authors are sympathetic to the distress women must feel at the lack of 'home comforts' and 'nameless social fascinations' provided them in the colonies, Hunt and Kenny suggest that they should determine to 'maintain body and mind in a healthy state by anticipating the difficulties' of their new lives (1, 6).

The ominous warnings offered by Ford's guidebook are augmented by Hunt and Kenny with patronising sexism. The authors feel the need to repeat and italicise phrases as if speaking to an audience in 'a state of mental chaos' (1). Hunt and Kenny also are adamant that women should submit to the superior medical authority of men. They admonish, 'You must not imagine because the atmosphere around you may happen to be cool and refreshing, that you can dispense with your ordinary pith topee during the day-time – *you have still to guard against the rays of a tropical sun*' (114). If a woman were to find herself in the 'exceptional circumstances' of being 'beyond the reach of medical aid', she should refrain from depending on the 'resources of the family medicine-chest', through which she may cause 'much harm', creating or augmenting 'symptoms . . . which too often end fatally' (177). The authors reiterate 'the imperative duty' of seeking 'the skill and experience of medical men', who are 'acquainted with the special local peculiarities of the climate', and therefore 'better able to appreciate the severity, and understand the symptoms of each particular case'. Those whose health has 'completely broken down from the effects of climate' often have 'themselves alone to blame for the pitiable state to which they are reduced', because they have not sought reputable medical advice. Familiarity with 'local peculiarities of climate' grants one superior status – Burton exerted this superiority over Speke, and in the foregoing example men exert their superior medical authority over women. Kingsley co-opts this authority for herself, not through dominating her environment but by showing her own comfort and pleasure in her surroundings.

Accordingly to colonial medical authorities, taking pleasure in Africa is the last thing Kingsley should do. The most culpable women, according to Hunt and Kenny, are those who 'foolishly persist in *enjoying*, as they say, the "cool night air"'. The authors' disdain is related to such women's sensual pleasure in their environment, which they punish most swiftly and severely: 'every breath' the women take 'is laden with the malarial poison'. Hunt and Kenny tellingly label women's self-exposure to the tropical environment as an 'indiscretion', a word layered with associations of sexual wantonness, which they stress will cost the victims 'hours and days of suffering for the rest of their lives'. These women are forever marked: once 'the malarial influence has got a "hold" upon her constitution, she will never entirely shake it off – *once malarial, always malarial*' (267–8).

Although she conforms to certain stereotypes of the female colonial traveller – depicting herself as 'distracted' and scatter-brained in her packing, for example (1897a: 4) – Kingsley directly contradicts and subverts many of the other warnings offered by these medical 'authorities'. She is physically active during all parts of the day, matter-of-fact rather than sentimental, disdains social frippery and travels in pursuit of scientific knowledge. Most importantly, however, Kingsley displays sensory enjoyment of the African environment and claims rather than disavows its 'hold' on her. For example, in the previously cited letter to Matthew Nathan of 1899, Kingsley claims 'It is the non-human world I belong to myself. My people are mangrove swamps, rivers, and the sea and so on. We understand each other' (qtd in Frank 1986: 293–4). As outlined at this chapter's outset, previous critics have argued from this passage that Kingsley's body is fragmented or diffuse. However, through close consideration of the passages from *Travels in West Africa* that are especially rich with imagery of climate, one observes that her 'sympathy' with local environments gives Kingsley an emotional and physical resilience that allows her to survive in the 'White Man's Grave'.

However, Kingsley does deftly apply discourses of female vulnerability in the tropics to the other white women she meets on her travels. Kingsley knew and respected Mary Slessor, a Scottish missionary in Calabar during the late nineteenth century. In discussing Slessor and other white women she encounters in Africa, Kingsley echoes common tropes of female martyrdom. In his biography of Slessor, W. P. Livingstone briefly introduces her difficult childhood and upbringing. He then highlights Slessor's heroism by emphasising the fatality of West Africa: 'conditions [were] formidable. Calabar exhibited the worst side of nature and of man . . . it was one of the most unhealthy spots in the world – sickness, disease, and swift death attacking the Europeans who ventured there' (1923: 31). He states grimly, 'For Europeans it was a foodless country, in which they had to face hunger, fever, and death' (31). Slessor is depicted as a martyr to the African climate:

> She was frequently attacked by fever, and laid aside, and on one occasion was at the point of death. But she never lost her confidence in God. So many attacks weakened her constitution . . . [that] she began to have a longing to look again upon loved faces, to have grey skies overhead, and to feel the tang of the clean cool air on her cheek. 'I want my home and my mother,' she confessed. (54)

Of note in this description are both the romanticisation of the cooler British climate – the 'tang of the clean cool air on her cheek' – and the characterisation of the African climate as malignant through the repeated word 'attack'. Summing up Slessor's life, Livingstone names his subject 'A sufferer from chronic malarial affection, and a martyr to pains [whose] days were filled with unremitting toil' (8).

In *Travels in West Africa*, Kingsley reinforces stereotypes of feminine physical delicacy with regard to other women, but not herself. She portrays the African environment as potentially fatal for other white women, including missionaries and functionaries' wives. She also depicts the majority of white men, especially those constitutionally predisposed to upset and fear, as susceptible to tropical illness. A vision of Africa emerges as rich with material resources and a worthy venue for trading, but also as dangerous and unwelcoming for missionaries, colonial officials and most laymen. Kingsley uses contrasting registers to paint herself and other 'old Coasters' as accessible yet heroic. These are the only subjects fit for travel in Africa because they do not fear death.

Under the rubric Kingsley establishes, with herself as the model, only those who have no other reason to live should come to West Africa. Most of her readers are thereby disqualified. In her article 'West Africa, from an Ethnologist's Point of View' (1897) she argues that only those 'who have not got a wife and family, and whose friends feel prepared to bear their loss with resignation' should venture to the Coast (1897b: 68). Without being so explicit, she communicates the same sentiment through her portrayal in *Travels in West Africa* of two women more delicate than she. Kingsley asserts that Lady MacDonald, a wife and mother, possesses 'courage in going to the Coast . . . far greater than my own, for she had more to lose had fever claimed her' (1897a: 12). Mme Forget is portrayed as similarly unsuited for life in the tropics: '[she] is a perfectly lovely French girl, with a pale transparent skin and the most perfect great dark eyes . . . It grieves me to think of her, wasted on this savage wilderness surrounded by its deadly fever air' (152).

It is certainly no accident that these two women, for whom Kingsley feels such acute concern, are the wives of a government representative and a French missionary, respectively.[12] As demonstrated in Chapter 1, Seacole performs a similar concern for her white 'sons', compassionately observing that they do not belong in foreign climates; here Kingsley expresses similar concern for the wives of colonial officers and missionaries. This rhetoric has a double effect: it paints the speaker as on the side of her readers and patients, while deftly calling into question their fitness for travel. A colonial officer or a missionary reading Kingsley's book might well be inspired to seriously question the wisdom of taking his wife to West Africa. Indeed, he might well wonder whether he should go himself.

Mary Kingsley is exceptional – at least, in her self-representation – in that she is not afraid of fever because she is not afraid of death. She is able to manipulate this to her advantage, in much the same way as Mary Seacole does: both are unafraid of fever on their own behalf, but wish to inspire fear of fever in their readers. Seacole portrays herself as unafraid as a result of her hybrid disease resistance and Kingsley portrays herself as unafraid because she does not care if she dies, and it suits both for the British public to remain where they are, as armchair readers, continuing to allow these two extraordinary women the freedom they have come to prize. One can imagine Kingsley's horror if Sierra Leone were to be sanitised and touted as a vacation destination like the Mediterranean, complete with Christianised Africans dressed in trousers and cummerbunds.[13] Outposts of civilisation would hem her in. Neither would it suit her to witness the wholesale destruction of native environments and cultures in the name of progress. Although 'Kingsley's visual-spatial methods coincide with a bourgeois interest in furthering economic imperialism in West Africa', Deborah Shapple Spillman believes that Kingsley is unaware of the unavoidable links between 'economic' and 'cultural imperialism' (2012: 92, 94).

Kingsley portrays in her books other whites' constitutional vulnerability to the African climate, but she herself remains psychologically and therefore physically immune, as she does not have a fearful nature. While Kingsley's unique perspective may exempt her personally from the hypochondriac thought patterns inspired by Ford and other medical advice authors, she still chooses to demonstrate to her readers how the disease environment of West Africa may inspire hypochondria. She sets the stage by directing readers, 'before you elect to cast your lot in with the West Coasters', to 'remember that 85 per cent of them die of fever or return home with their health permanently wrecked' (1897a: 690). Truly thorough fever 'hygiene', according to Kingsley, is hopeless: 'you must avoid chill, drinking polluted water, excessive mental and bodily exertion . . . never get anxious, or excited, or lose your temper. Now there is only one – the drinking water – of this list that you can avoid' (684). Instead, she suggests, one should think positively:

> Let the new-comer who goes to the Coast take the most cheerful view . . . and let him regard himself as preordained to [survive]. Let him take every care short of getting frightened, which is as deadly as taking no care at all, and he may – I sincerely hope he will – survive. (690–1)

Far from being confidence-inspiring or providing comfort to her readers, Kingsley's rhetoric actually seems calculated to inspire anxiety. She treats the list of 'do-not's' with humour, emphasising how impossible it is to follow such a regimen, but does not invalidate its usefulness. Further, Kingsley mirrors Ford and other medical advice authors when she underscores how crucial it is not to be frightened. The West African traveller cannot win for losing, according to Kingsley's schema, as any worry or fear negates his most conscientious preventative measures. It is difficult not to be afraid of something that is indeed fearsome.

Kingsley recommends that the traveller avoid fear by employing a relentlessly positive outlook 'and let him regard himself as preordained to [survive]' – though she has avoided fear by doing quite the opposite, representing herself as ostensibly reconciled to death. In *Illness as Metaphor*, Susan Sontag demonstrates that nineteenth-century doctors advised their patients to 'avoid over-taxing their strength, and to bear the ills of life with equanimity' (1979: 52). During the 1970s, when Sontag wrote, doctors were prescribing 'self-expression', assuring patients that cancer stemmed from repressed emotions (53); more recently, patients are again commonly advised to employ a relentlessly positive outlook in order to counteract their illness – what cancer doctor Jimmie Holland has called the 'tyranny of positivity'.[14] Regardless, one observes that the tendency to apply moral judgement to illness, and to hold the patient responsible for his or her own survival, transcends historical explanatory systems of disease.

It would suit Kingsley if most of her readers felt they could not survive African fever due to their race and susceptibility to fear. She paints a vivid picture of a man – a 'new Coaster', not an 'old Coaster' – who came to West Africa to be a bookkeeper and was nearly killed by 'shock'. His emotionalism and apprehensive nature predisposed him to illness. When sent to an 'isolated out-of-the-way' factory, he expected to meet the 'Agent he had come to serve under'. Encountering no one upon arrival, the young man 'made a tour . . . round the verandah' of the agent's house and 'noticed a most peculiar noise in one of the rooms and an infinity of flies going into the Venetian shuttered window'. 'Plucking up courage' to enter the house, he found 'What was left of the white Agent, a considerable quantity of rats, and most of the flies in West Africa.' Kingsley states he 'then presumably had fever' and was 'taken off'. Kingsley portrays the bookkeeper's response as normal. In fact, she pronounces portentously, 'some men would have died right out from a shock like this' (1897a: 85–6).

This passage both represents the deleterious effects of extreme fear on white subjects' health and is calculated to inspire fear in the reader. The author uses darkly humorous hyperbole – 'an infinity of flies', 'most of the flies in West Africa' – to represent the horror of finding a decomposing body. The bookkeeper can function as a symbol for those of Kingsley's white 'unseasoned' readers considering a trip to Africa. According to this passage, even when white Europeans pluck up the courage to visit West Africa, they cannot imagine the revolting circumstances that await them upon arrival.

Kingsley portrays the established traders, the 'old Coasters' as she calls them, as immune to this horror and therefore protected against somatic illness:

> On your first voyage out you can hardly believe the stories of fever told by the old Coasters. But a short experience of your own . . . soon demonstrates that the underlying horror of the thing is there, a rotting corpse which the old Coaster has dusted over with jokes . . . but which, when you come yourself to live alongside, you soon become cognisant of. (85)

Kingsley portrays the old Coasters as infinitely brave: far from being horrified themselves, they collect incidents of death and make stories out of them. Kingsley admires and mirrors both the traders' no-nonsense, humorous tone and their bravery in the face of death. Kingsley is quite aware of inspiring fear in her readers: early in *Travels in West Africa*, she gloats that she, like the traders, has a stockpile of stories that could 'damage the nerves of the cultured of temperate climes' (41). No doubt the tale of the bookkeeper is one such.

Certainly, images of corpses, flies and rats can make readers want to avoid the place described. However, Kingsley also portrays the African environment as mysterious and dangerous through her invocations of miasma. In describing African fever, Kingsley draws upon miasmatic theory. Kingsley wrote after the heyday of Koch's and Pasteur's microbial discoveries, and published *Travels in West Africa* mere months before Ross identified the malarial parasite in mosquitoes.[15] She even acknowledges these recent discoveries of the malarial microbe's life cycle but believes that 'malarial microbes' can be acquired through polluted drinking water (1897a: 686). Kingsley was interested in medical science – '[she] had thought of taking up medicine' (Gwynn 1932: 48) – and took a 'brief' nursing course at Kaiserworth Medical Institute in Germany before going to West Africa, to 'enable' her 'to care for herself and others' (Frank 1986: 76). She acknowledges the recent advances in tropical medicine in an appendix to *Travels in West Africa* when she says 'the peculiar microbes of everything from measles to miracles [have recently been] "isolated"' (681). However, her scepticism regarding some of these discoveries is made explicit in the pairing of measles – a real disease – with miracles, which are inexplicable.

Generally anxious as she is to be accurate and up-to-date and reasonably attuned to medicine, it is notable when Kingsley uses images of miasma rather than contagion to describe the ominous, fever-ridden landscape of West Africa. This is not to say that Kingsley is wilfully anachronistic. However, until something more effective than quinine is discovered, she asserts that explorers are still at the mercy of the African climate (1897a: 682). Also, miasma's qualities – its omnipresence and mystery – suit her rhetorical goals. If there were rhyme and reason to African fever – if one could identify its precise causes and control them – then the land that she so values for its openness and freedom would be destined for widespread settlement. As reducing miracles to science denigrates the miracles, so too does piercing the mystery of West Africa cheapen Africa itself. If African fever continues to remain mysterious and fearsome, however, then Kingsley can continue to mediate between her readers and the Coast. In trying to maintain her own free space, Kingsley places Africa outside the purview of colonial rule both in terms of scientific knowledge and trade.

Kingsley's role collecting African species of fish, first informally and then for the British Museum, is reflected through a marked attention in her book to the patterns of tides and currents, which she connects to the healthfulness of the land. While authors such as Burton and Horton advocate hygiene, drainage and sanitary reforms to clean up the African environment, by focusing on the influence of warm currents on the African climate Kingsley implies that substantial improvement is impossible. When describing the islands of Principe, Anno Bom and San Thomé, she states that Principe is 'the most unhealthy' as a result of its position 'on the Guinea Current – a hot current', whereas Anno Bom is healthier because it is 'on the Equatorial, which averages 10° cooler than its neighbour'. San Thomé and Fernando Po are under the influence of more than one current, and so 'in a mixed and uncertain state'. She says the effect of currents on the climate 'is very marked'. Her wish that 'we could arrange for some terrific affair to take place in the bed of the Atlantic, that would send that precious Guinea current to the place it evidently came from, and get the cool Equatorial alongside the mainland shore' is obviously tongue in cheek. However, it does imply that the 'cooling off' of Africa would have to happen on a macrocosmic level – which is impossible to effect – in order for West Africa to be made 'quite another place' with a climate amenable to whites.

Kingsley links the fearfulness of West African fever to miasma. When describing her progress up the Bonny river, she focuses on 'the breath of the malarial mud, laden with fever' and assures her readers that if they see it, 'chances are you will be down to-morrow'. She paints an eerie scene of witnessing the miasma

> become incarnate, creeping and crawling and gliding out from the side creeks and between the mangrove-roots, laying itself upon the river, stretching and

rolling in a kind of grim play, and finally crawling up the side of the ship to come on board and leave its cloak of moisture that grows green mildew in a few hours over all. (1897a: 97)

This mist is personified as a kind of deadly beast, 'creeping', 'crawling' and 'gliding', 'stretching' and 'rolling'. Its sinuousness is both beautiful and frightening, as it 'plays' with its victims. The toxic effects of the malarial 'breath' are visible in its effect on the boat, which it coats with rot.

Kingsley reinforces miasma's fatality in an 1893 letter to her friend Mrs Skeat. The lush beauty of the jungle during the day contrasts with the 'miasmatic' evening time:

it is getting dangerously near 6 o'clock . . . and you are cramped from sitting for hours and none too well fed, and the person steering begins to express a doubt about which creek is which, and the thick, white, wooly miasma-laden mist comes stealing out from among the tree stems floating in ghostly trails along the surface of the River, winding itself round the tree stems like a soft material – and now and then wrapping up the boat in its fold so that you can hardly see the bow – . . . the crocodiles which swarm along the Rivers break the silence with a whining roar, or howl, you wish you had taken the advice of your friends and were well home at dinner in Cambridge, a place it is borne upon you that it is extremely unlikely you will ever be privileged to see again.[16]

The verbs 'steals', 'floats', 'winds' and 'wraps' make the mist seem insidious, ominous and wraithlike. That it is 'thick, white, wooly' and obscures the vision further adds to this impression of ghostliness. Finally, the mist is 'miasma-laden': the reader must assume that disease-causing foul air is inextricably a part of the West African environment. The vapour is a ghost and also creates ghosts. Rather than affiliating the danger with specific West African locations, instead Kingsley links it to the time of day itself. 'Dangerously near 6 o'clock' implies that the evening time is inherently hazardous to the health of white travellers. Ford, Kenny and Hunt order their readers to avoid being out during dusk and dawn, as the lingering 'night air' is thought to be particularly miasmatic. While Kingsley's characterisation of the mist creates an ominous vision of West Africa's climate, she must be out in the night air in order to describe it, 'wrapped up in its fold' within her boat. She is stimulating fear in her readers while simultaneously transgressing her own warnings.

Kingsley's healthfulness is defined by responsiveness to and oneness with the environment. Bruce Haley has outlined three characteristics of a healthy state. First, he says, 'health is a state of functional and structural wholeness' (1978: 20). Secondly, all physical and mental structures must not only work but also work usefully: this he terms telicity (purpose). Finally, and mostly importantly for our discussion, Haley outlines a third element necessary for health: vitality, or 'activity, growth and responsiveness' (20). He quotes 'widely published' Victorian 'doctor-philosopher James Hinton', who claims a man is healthy

> when his blood is in harmony with the ceaseless activity of nature; when his body is warm with the soft kiss of air . . . The living body should thrill with every thrill of the wide earth, as the aspen leaf trembles in the tremulous air. (qtd in Haley 1978: 20)

We are most accustomed to nineteenth-century literary models of female health that are based on masculinist models. As Jackie Horne notes, Victorian educational stories for girls, when they (infrequently) provide an active and physically healthy female character, often do so in masculinist terms. Eleanor, the healthy girl in Juliana Horatia Ewing's *Six to Sixteen*, copies the actions of boys 'particularly in regards to the body' (Horne 2004: 261). Eleanor demonstrates 'masculine' ideals of health such as direct, intentional action, determination and intellectual 'substance' – specifically, a desire to discuss issues that really matter. This type of girl is more likely to forego crinolines and other feminine attire that will restrict her activity. Kingsley, however, draws upon several different strands in crafting her own model of female health. As is well known, she maintained traditional dress while trekking through the African wilderness. Also, as has been previously noted by critics, she does not privilege either linear scientific knowledge production or linear progress through landscape: her main focus is not on directionality and final products.

Most notably, she does not portray her body as a fortress threatened by climatic attack. Rather, she is in sympathy with much of the African atmosphere. Even when she canoes in blazing heat or trudges through an icy downpour, Kingsley's reactions are matter-of-fact, normal and proportional, and she does not link her climatic exposure to any resultant illness (1897a: 277, 403). She is not a victim of a hostile, external environment, but rather in synch with the climatic forces around her. Kingsley does not use a gaze of mastery but of appreciation when she says that when looking at scenes of beauty she becomes 'part of the atmosphere' (qtd in Lane 2003: 97). Although Lane and others read these moments as Kingsley privileging emptiness and defamiliarisation, I want to suggest that she may instead be privileging her own ability to harmonise with rather than fight against climate. Perhaps this ability is a result of her hardy emotional and physical constitution, or perhaps it is due to her assumption that it is futile to fight for one's health when disease causation is still so nebulous. Regardless, she keeps with Hinton's definition of health as being 'in harmony with the ceaseless activity of nature' (qtd in Haley 1978: 20).

In the passage previously cited, the reader is named 'you' and encouraged to be afraid of the 'miasma-laden mist'. Critics such as Deborah Shapple Spillman have noted Kingsley's striking use of the second person. Although it can be used as a device to create immediacy in travel guides ('you will see', 'you should visit'), Spillman notes that 'Kingsley's approach seems less conventional given the expectations of [ethnography]'. She argues that 'Kingsley's adoption of the second-person pronoun, which, at times, enters in to an extended second-person narrative, disrupts the familiar perspective of nineteenth-century ethnographic narratives' (2012: 88). I would like to suggest that Kingsley employs the second person in order to immerse the reader in the experience of becoming ill in Africa. For example, in *Travels in West Africa*, Kingsley uses visceral description to portray nineteenth-century African fever. She warns anyone travelling to Africa to watch for tell-tale symptoms – an 'aching head and limbs and a sensation of a stream of cold water down your back and an awful temper'. When she senses she may be coming down with fever, the traveller should 'take a compound calomel and colocynth pill, fifteen grains of quinine and a grain of opium, and go to bed wrapped up in the best blanket available'. 'When safely [in bed],' she says, 'take lashings of hot tea or, what is better, a hot drink made from fresh lime-juice, strong and without sugar.' If the fever is not handled correctly, or if the patient receives a slight chill, she emphasises that the sufferer will most probably die (1897a: 689–90).[17]

Imagine the surreal and strange experience a fit of fever must have been if one followed Kingsley's regime. To be ill, uncomfortable, having ingested both a mercurial preparation and opium, wrapped like a mummy and drinking lime juice must have been quite enough to alienate the senses. Even with our knowledge of the merits and demerits of such measures, present-day readers, addressed in the second person, can picture as vividly as Kingsley's original audience just how lonely and desperate an episode of tropical fever must have felt. Her readers must have been none too eager to experience at first hand the feelings she describes, which may be exactly the effect she intends.

Unlike both the delicate women and the fearful men whom she describes succumbing to tropical illness, Kingsley cultivates for herself a narrative persona defined by modesty and ironic humour. Through her books, Kingsley (and the traders) are both made heroic by implication – they meet dramatic and unusual circumstances with practical and productive action, when most people would become overwhelmed or panicked, and thereby vulnerable to disease. Humour is widely acknowledged to be Kingsley's 'sharpest weapon, and one she handled with skill' (Birkett 1992: 82). In *Imperial Eyes*, Mary Louise Pratt asserts, 'Estheticization in Kingsley is replaced by a relentlessly comic irony applied to herself and those around her … Africa is a rousing jolly good time. Above all, Kingsley's book owes its enduring popularity to this masterful comic irreverence' (1992: 215). Kingsley describes a canoe trip up the rapids of Ogowe to collect fish as follows: 'I had to jump at a rock wall, and hang onto it in a manner more befitting an insect than an insect-hunter … [Afterwards] in we got again and paddled away until we met our next affliction' (1897a: 114). Far from seeming heroic in a conventional sense, Kingsley treats with off-handed humour what were doubtless precarious circumstances. Her statement 'in we got again and paddled away until we met our next affliction' assumes matter-of-factly that the next 'affliction' is right around the corner, and that she and her crew are dauntlessly paddling towards it. Any 'befitting' manners fall by the wayside in the urgency and immediacy of Kingsley's adventures.

Several contemporary reviewers took issue with Kingsley's comic irreverence. 'The offhand way in which some rather serious subjects are treated is hardly fair', wrote the reviewer for *Science* of 27 August 1897. The book 'is further marred by coarse flippancy and jocular smartness of a low masculine type' complained the reviewer for *Dial* (qtd in Birkett 1992: 82). Kingsley might have argued that this 'low masculine type' of humour was uniquely adapted to the formidable challenges presented by West Africa, which leave no room for rarefied manners. She certainly represents the 'palm oil ruffians' or 'old Coasters' as displaying this same kind of humour. They are both matter of fact about death – 'Did you know poor B–? Well! he's dead now' – and matter of fact about the physical realities of their chosen home (1897a: 30). Kingsley adapts such humour to her situation as a woman: for example, she jokes that her full petticoats protected her from being skewered when she fell into an animal trap, or that she felt ready for a new adventure after getting a full set of hairpins. However, by both reproducing the traders' 'low' humour and using her own brand of 'flippancy', Kingsley shows that, though she is not above the details of mundane, corporeal existence, she is above the fear of death.

West Africa is the only place that Mary Kingsley felt agreed with her: she believed that she thrived in Africa's physical environment. Kingsley herself suffered much less from fever than most. In a letter to her friend Violet Roy, written on 26 August 1893, she says,

They are having bad luck with fever this time. 5 of them have been down with it – I have not had the least touch so far, and am getting fat and young again so that if it keeps on you won't know me on my return.[18]

Whereas Africa destroyed most white constitutions, in some ways Kingsley felt it healed hers. Even when she does return to England, it is with acknowledged expertise and authority. In Mary Kingsley's African travel narratives, then, we witness a writer mobilising the multivalent disease rhetoric of climate and fever to protect and close off the setting that nurtured her independent identity: the African West Coast.

Notes

1. Recent treatments of Kingsley's work examine it as a potentially rich source of insight regarding the intersections of gender, genre and imperialism in late Victorian ethnographies by women. Critics such as Lynette Turner argue that Kingsley's work is defined by the slippage between masculine and feminine, public and private language (2000: 55). Jules Law, in 'Cultural Ecologies of the Coast' (2003), examines how coastal spaces represent the 'edge of cultural practice' in *Travels in West Africa*. He agrees with Mary Louise Pratt in *Imperial Eyes* (1992) that Kingsley does not privilege the classic 'bird's-eye' view so often employed by colonial travellers.
2. For discussion of fever in eighteenth-century literature, see Ward (2007).
3. This diminished enthusiasm was legislated through the Colonial Office's 1855 recommendation to cease aggressive expansion in West Africa and to pursue the goal of 'elevating' the native African sufficiently that he might eventually take over much control of his own country. Hays spoke in support of this change in policy. Burton and Kingsley react against it: specifically, Kingsley feels that Britain never did pull out of West Africa in any meaningful way, but instead twiddled its thumbs while other major European powers started making inroads into unexplored regions, laying the foundation for the 'grab for Africa' from which Britain did not emerge as the dominant colonial presence she would have wished it to be.
4. There also exist very real genetic adaptations to malaria, such as sickle cell haemoglobin, which are common among those from malaria-endemic areas and probably survived as genetic traits because of their protective effect against a greater original danger. The protective effect of variant blood does not rely on previous infections in the individual to 'protect' them, but is in fact 'built in' by 'racial' (really long-environmental) origin.
5. See Chapter 5 for further discussion of how travellers to Africa are encouraged to monitor their own mental equilibrium.
6. The character of Tom Thurnall from *Two Years Ago* is an extreme example of this ideal (see Chapter 1).
7. 'Divorced from the moral and social restrictions of middle-class British

society, [West African traders] were thought to lead drunken and debauched lives among people far removed from European civilization.' These 'palm oil ruffians' were 'single men', many of whom 'were the inheritors of those who had made their money by slave trading' (Birkett 1992: 24). They formed a dispersed community with a strict code of ethics that dictated that they help each other against any common enemies, whether violent natives or disease. Although the traders showed scepticism about Kingsley's scientific project in West Africa (collecting unknown species of tropical fish for the British Museum), they supported her endeavours as best they could, shuttling her to various places in their steamboats, offering her their well-meant tips and sharing their stories. The traders' brutal honesty, crass humour and unalloyed bravery in the face of danger appealed to Kingsley, who felt nonplussed amid the finery and delicate manners of English society.

8. Her anxious focus on accuracy perhaps stemmed from her humiliatingly spotty childhood education. She had admired her own father from afar, but believed he had never taken the time to educate and mentor her properly. Self-educated from his library, which included random travel narratives and outdated scientific tomes, Kingsley was deeply dissatisfied with the result: '[When a child] . . . I developed a passionate devotion for the science of chemistry, and I went in for it – experiments not being allowed – in the available books in the library. Most of them were books on alchemy, and the rest entirely obsolete. After most carefully getting up all the information these could give me, I happened on a gentleman who knew modern chemistry and tried my information on him. He said he had not heard anything so ridiculous for years, and recommended I should be placed in a museum as a compendium of exploded chemical theories, which hurt my feelings very much, and I cried bitterly at not being taught things' (qtd in Gwynn 1932: 16).

9. 'The White Man's Burden' is the title of a poem by Rudyard Kipling (1899).

10. Kingsley disapproved of the Hut Tax on liquor imports to Africa (1897a: 496–7).

11. For further discussion of Kingsley's spatial and geographical metaphors, see Blunt (1994).

12. Lady Ethel Macdonald was the wife of Kingsley's friend Sir Claude Macdonald, who governed the Niger Coast Protectorate. Kingsley accompanied Lady Macdonald on her first journey to West Africa to join her husband (Frank 1986: 100).

13. By July 1898 the Thomas Cook agency had already escorted a tourist party to the Congo interior. Cook's *Traveller Gazette* in 1902 advertised the voyage as 'a unique tour to West Africa and the Congo', priced at £120. Kingsley can be seen as fighting against this incursion into Africa by casual tourists, using climate to cordon off Africa from those whom she perceives as unprepared or unsuitable for travel.

14. For more on the advocacy of positive thinking in contemporary medicine and culture, see Holland (2000), Ehrenreich (2009) and Fitzgerald (1994).

15. *Travels in West Africa* was first published in January 1897 and Ross

discovered the malarial parasite in mosquitoes in August of the same year.

16. British Library, Additional Manuscripts 68892E 26 v+r.
17. For further discussion of travel literature meant to discourage travel, see studies on the 'Wish You Weren't Here' tradition, by Claire Lindsay (2003) and others.
18. British Library, Additional Manuscripts 68892E 38.

Chapter 5

'Self rather seedy':
Conrad's Colonial Pathographies

Alphonse Daudet, a nineteenth-century French writer, died of neuro-syphilis in 1897. He wrote a series of notes for a narrative of his own illness, titled *La Doulou*, which he never had a chance to complete. Daudet was seen as a 'sunny humorist and clear stylist' during his own time. He wrote novels, plays and articles, and was not only 'highly successful (and very rich)' in his day but also 'ate at the top literary table'. Dickens called Daudet 'my little brother in France' and Henry James called him 'a great little novelist' (Barnes 2002: vi). Only his notes to *La Doulou* were ever published – the original version in 1930, and the first English translation, *In the Land of Pain*, in 2002.

As his disease advanced, Daudet's mobility was impaired. During this time, he was attracted to books about adventure in far-off lands, likening such travel narratives to the progression of his own illness. Daudet particularly enjoyed stories of African exploration by David Livingstone and Henry Morton Stanley. In one of the earliest entries, Daudet says,

> At present I'm spending time with good old Livingstone in darkest Africa. The monotony of his endless and virtually pointless journey, the constant obsession with barometric pressure . . . and the silent, calm unfolding of the landscape – all this makes for truly wonderful reading . . . I would have made a fine explorer in Central Africa: I've got the sunken ribs, the eternally tightened belt, the rifts of pain. . . (2002: 9)

Daudet's disease creates a new landscape; navigating pain is as arduous for him as navigating the tropics is for an African explorer. He makes the comparison explicit: 'To reach that distant chair, to cross that waxed corridor, requires as much effort and ingenuity as Stanley deploys in the African jungle' (47). However, this passage also undercuts the traditional association of imperial adventure with progress. Livingstone, the idol of African exploration, Daudet refers to as 'good old Livingstone'; he terms Livingstone's journeys monotonous, 'endless' and 'virtually pointless'. The 'constant obsession with barometric pressure' is also an obsession with environmental pathology, and Daudet here seems to imply that though such an obsession may give comfort to the traveller by creating an illusion of control, the 'barometer' provides no real answers.

As his condition worsens, Daudet addresses his pain directly: 'Pain, you must be everything for me. Let me find in you all those foreign lands you will not let me visit. Be my philosophy, be my science' (42). The late stages of neurosyphilis, during which the bacterium infects the brain and spinal cord, can cause blindness, weakness, numbness and seizures. As Daudet's body twitches and spasms, it both becomes foreign to him and simultaneously demands his all-encompassing attention. My analysis draws upon this double association of disease with environment: whether actually moving or not, the sick subjects feel they are on a journey through an external geography (like Livingstone's monotonous journey through a 'silent, calm, unfolding ... landscape'); simultaneously, they are obsessed with the environment's effect on their body's internal ecology ('the constant obsession with barometric pressure'). One of Daudet's notes illustrates this beautifully:

> Outside there's a storm, hail, thunder – inside, I relax at last. Am briefly humiliated by thinking of myself as a mere barometer, glassed-in and marked-off. Then I console myself by realizing that the atmospheric pressure within this particular barometer governs more than just a column of mercury. (17)

The novelist Joseph Conrad owned and read several books by Alphonse Daudet. He says in an 1895 letter, 'You know my Daudet worship. Do you think it would be foolish of me to send him my book, I who have read all of his, in all weathers?' (qtd in Tutein 1990: 24). While it is unlikely that Conrad had access to the notes for *La Doulou*, I suggest that both authors are of a late nineteenth-century literary moment that was characterised by a concern with the symbolic registers of 'barometric pressure'. In Conrad's African writing, external environments influence characters' internal balance and therefore their health.

The exact aetiology of many tropical diseases was still unknown during the time when Conrad travelled. A late nineteenth-century, white traveller to Africa was likely to have the eerie experience of suffering physical symptoms such as nausea, fever, headache and blurred vision without being able to pinpoint the cause with scientific certainty (parasitic or viral infection, dehydration, heat exhaustion). Understandably, he or she might develop the habit of analysing possible correlations between his or her internal health state and the external environment. The resulting patterns of analysis might appear compulsive or even superstitious to those removed from the traveller's circumstance, but it does not follow that the diseases were psychosomatic.

Heart of Darkness (1899) provides many rich examples of the ominous representation of climate. For example, on his journey to 'rescue' Kurtz, Marlow finds the African climate oppressive: 'Going up that river ... The air was warm, thick, heavy, sluggish. There was no joy in the brilliance of sunshine' (Conrad 1988: 35). As the steamship nears Kurtz's camp, Marlow is advised by the Manager to set anchor for one last night before proceeding up the final part of the river. The crew spends the night onboard. Marlow describes the dawn thus:

> When the sun rose there was a white fog, very warm and clammy, and more blinding than the night. It did not shift or drive, it was just there standing around you like something solid. At eight or nine perhaps, it lifted, as a shutter lifts. We had a glimpse of a towering multitude of trees, of the immense matted jungle, with the blazing little ball of the sun hanging over it – all perfectly still – and then the white shutter came down again smoothly as if gliding into greased grooves. (41)

The mist seems to protect the African landscape from the prying gaze of the white traveller. The 'blazing little ball of the sun' is powerful out of proportion to its size and gives 'no joy' when it beats down on the heads of subjects who think it dangerous. Because normally vigorous whites could degenerate into languor in 'warm, thick, heavy, sluggish air', both air and sun present risks that whites must actively resist in order to survive.

The frequency with which critics employ atmospheric imagery in analysing Conrad's work is remarkable. E. M. Forster's mixed metaphors provide the most famous example: 'Misty in the middle as well as at the edges, the secret cask of his genius contains a vapour rather than a jewel' (1996: 132). As Robert Haugh explains, some of Conrad's contemporaries objected to *Heart of Darkness* because they perceived it as 'bogged down' in gloomy 'atmospherics', so that 'any action' is obscured by 'an elaboration of imagery and extreme emotion' (1957: 35–40). These critics' language suggests that Conrad's descriptions of climate have determined the way in which his work is discussed.

In *Conrad in the Nineteenth Century*, Ian Watt links the 'persistent image' of 'mist or haze' in Conrad's work to his impressionistic writing style. As evidence, he cites Conrad's own warning that 'Marlow's tale will not be centered on, but surrounded by, its meaning; and this meaning will be only as fitfully and tenuously visible as a hitherto unnoticed presence of dust particles and water vapour' (1979: 169). However, there is another key reason why 'mist' is linked with Conrad's characters turning inward. If tropical mist and miasma were associated with disease, even by late Victorian travellers, then the omnipresence of thick and stifling mist in *Heart of Darkness* is not only a stylistic strategy but also indicates individuals' perception of danger. The presence of 'clammy fog' may inspire them to become more watchful for signs of illness in their own bodies. Watt argues that Conrad uses a process of 'delayed decoding' in order to immerse readers in the characters' experience of both sensing and making sense of the world around them.[1] The effects of tropical environments are felt through one's physical 'impressions'; therefore, I suggest that these stories' 'impressionism' also functions to narrate the process of becoming ill. Conrad's narrators find the African environment threatening at least in part because of the risk it poses to their precarious state of health. The mist that surrounds them is not only symbolically but also scientifically and materially significant to our reading of the text.

Conrad's white characters display historically explicable illness phobias in response to the African environment. Kayerts and Carlier in 'An Outpost of Progress' (1897), and Kurtz in *Heart of Darkness* (1899), are unaware that they have contracted a disease until and even after they have begun to manifest symptoms, while Marlow is on constant watch against the real threat of disease, monitoring his body for the first signs of illness. Marlow's goal, to maintain mental fortitude and calm, is just one of his many defensive measures against dis-equilibrium caused by the tropical climate. Other measures might include avoiding exposure to heat, noxious vapours and putrefaction. Conrad's narrators are afraid of becoming ill, but unsure of the exact aetiology of disease. They react to this fear by portraying the tropical environment as threatening to their humoral equilibrium, using ominous climatic imagery.[2] This chapter offers a reading of *Heart of Darkness* and 'Outpost of Progress' as belonging to a specific sub-genre of pathography, or illness narrative, which developed in the context of travel to the tropics, characterised by climatic disease worry and racial constitutionalism. Such an approach provides new historical insights when reading these texts. It may also somewhat disarm the criticism levelled at Conrad that he uses Africa as merely an exotic backdrop for his stories.

Conrad critiques African colonial expansion by invoking the constitutional connotations of climatism. As previously explained, the nineteenth-century rhetoric of climate implied that a certain environment was or was not appropriate not only for one racialised body but for all members of that race, by drawing upon the common belief that each race shares a definable mental and physical nature, or constitution. The main white characters in Conrad's fiction are highly susceptible to environmental influences, demonstrate poor judgement and also may have vulnerable underlying constitutions. Most are afraid of tropical illness and concerned to avoid it; nevertheless, all become seriously ill. In the cases of Kayerts and Carlier, too much fear for one's own well-being leads to madness and death; for Kurtz, however, too little fear turns out to have the same result. Conrad implies that no measure can fully protect white travellers from the malignant quality of African heat and mist. By emphasising the omnipresence of these challenges, Conrad's novella and short story throw the colonial project's basic feasibility into doubt.

There are important distinctions between Conrad and the authors under scrutiny in previous chapters. Seacole perceives herself as of strong constitution and resistant to disease; Burton knows he is vulnerable to disease but hopes he can control his vulnerability by controlling his environment; Horton acknowledges his own illness, but uses it as the source of medical authority; and Kingsley portrays herself as healthful and in synch with Africa's climate, in contrast to most whites. Of the five, only Conrad creates a first-person narrator who is defined by his susceptibility to emotional distress and to disease and who is unable to mitigate this vulnerability by controlling his circumstances. This book has suggested that authors' perceptions of their own vulnerability to tropical disease affects how they relate to others. Seacole portrays as inferior those not blessed with her iron hybrid constitution, whereas Burton employs over-compensatory racism when comparing himself to local subjects. While Africans' disease resistance intimidates Conrad's white characters, when they react violently these actions are portrayed as illogical or ridiculous.

During his trip to the Congo, Conrad did not want to become ill, was afraid of becoming ill, expected to become ill and became ill repeatedly. He travelled thirty years after Burton, when germ theory was gaining a strong foothold in medical science but did not yet offer conclusive preventative and curative measures for tropical disease. Conrad was not convinced that hygienic medical science held any failsafe measures to protect him from African fever. Further, unlike Burton and Kingsley, he could not believe that whites or blacks were suffering as part of a larger cause. Instead, his narratives of illness in Africa reflect pessimism, disillusionment, anger and fear. In writing fiction, Conrad may have had less need than the others to cultivate in readers respect for an autobiographical persona. His characters are deeply fallible and sometimes quite unlikeable. Ideally, this might free readers to evaluate for themselves each one's reaction to circumstance, forming their own opinions regarding the poor behaviour of bigoted, physically weak white subjects in the colonial context.

Many contemporary pathographies begin with an already sick author who knows what disease she or he has and may be able to predict its course (see, for example, Lorde 1980; Picardie 1998). In contrast, nineteenth-century travellers to Africa and certain other colonies where the disease environments did not favour whites generally began their journeys in good health, knowingly exposing themselves to illness but unsure of the exact source of health threats. Therefore, the texts that I call 'colonial pathographies' often demonstrate a heightened vigilance on the part of the narrator to any new, possibly significant symptoms which allow him or her to infer when he or she has been exposed to disease-causing factors in the environment. This chapter will first outline the conventions of pathography and how they apply in a nineteenth-century context, using Conrad's own *Congo Diary* as a model. Then Marlow's visit to the Company doctor will be examined for its foreshadowing of the slippage between mental and physical imbalance in the colonial context. 'Outpost of Progress' treats the interlocking themes of illness and racism more transparently than does *Heart of Darkness*, and thereby provides a reader with important points of entry into the later story. Finally, I analyse *Heart of Darkness* as a colonial pathography, focusing on the narratives of Marlow's and Kurtz's illness in order to demonstrate how Conrad's ominous characterisation of the African climate undermines imperial discourse.

Conrad and Colonial Pathography: The *Congo Diary*

Psychological and symbolic readings of the 'darkness' into which Marlow travels may not only have been inspired by the book's allusive quality but also by early psychobiographies of Conrad himself. Joseph Conrad died from a heart attack on the morning of 3 August 1924 at the age of sixty-six. In her 1926 memoir *Joseph Conrad as I Knew Him*, Conrad's widow Jessie wrote, 'Looking back over the years that stretch behind me, years we spent together, his sudden death seems to have been inevitable; indeed, taking into consideration his indifferent health and nervous temperament, I marvel that he lived so long' (Conrad 1926: ix). Within the same book, Mrs Conrad asserts that her husband was 'extremely indolent . . . He shrank with an almost morbid sensitiveness from the sight of pain and distress' (13). Upon the publication of her second Conrad memoir, *Joseph Conrad and his Circle* (1935), Conrad's friend Edward Garnett accused Jessie of 'belittling the great writer and betraying her husband's trust' (Knowles and Moore 2000: 76). Perhaps informed by the earliest interpretations of Conrad's life, many critics have identified his illnesses as psychosomatic, and have superimposed a 'nervous' temperament on to his fictional work.[3]

However, Conrad was plagued by verifiable health conditions his whole life. At different times he suffered from pneumonia, German measles, gout, rheumatism, malaria and dysentery. He was especially ill during and after his 1890 journey through the Belgian Congo. In order to revise the earliest assumption that Conrad's relationship with disease was psychological and symbolic, let us assume that he had good reason for perceiving the African environment as threatening, especially in his historical context. Then perhaps the same treatment should be given to his narrators, whose experiences unfold in the same setting and under some of the same conditions. Marlow is not Conrad's mouthpiece, nor is Marlow's story simply Conrad's. It has been well established that the author distances himself from Marlow through a succession of different narrative registers and linguistic markers, as well as by applying to Marlow a certain amount of irony (see Hampson 2002; Miller 2002; Najder 2004; Paris 2006). However, the fact remains that Marlow narrates his African journey knowing the devastating effects of tropical disease. He brings this knowledge to bear in crafting his tale aboard the *Nellie*, just as Conrad brought his foreknowledge to bear in writing his book.[4] Both Conrad's diary and fiction contribute to a particular historical moment in which the terms for understanding how people related to territory were changing.

Some of the earliest narratives identified as pathographies were Sigmund Freud's case histories. He specifically uses the term in *Leonardo Da Vinci and a Memory of His Childhood* (1910). According to Freud, pathography is 'a biographical study that focuses on the way pathological elements in a person's life can illumine other facets of that life' (1963: 130). This chapter mobilises both 'old' and 'new' meanings of pathography: a study that traces the predisposing factors of individual pathology and, as defined by Anne Hunsaker Hawkins in *Reconstructing Illness*, 'a form of autobiography or biography that describes personal experience of illness, treatment, and sometimes death' (1993: 1). Hawkins argues that pathography as a genre 'is remarkable in that it seems to have to emerged *ex nihilo*' after the early 1900s, and theorises that this is because 'in earlier times illness seems to have been considered an integral and inseparable part of living (and dying)' (3). She suggests that 'only in the twentieth century' has 'serious illness . . . become a phenomenon that can be isolated from an individual's life', perhaps because 'we now consider health the norm and illness as a condition to be corrected' (11). If one productively inverts Hawkins' historical claim, one might assume that illness and physical disequilibrium was a dominant lens through which many earlier authors saw the world. In this case, one would look for characteristic elements of pathography as constitutive of and emerging from other genres, such as nineteenth-century fiction or journals, rather than emerging *ex nihilo*.

For the purposes of this analysis, pathography will include first-person and omniscient third-person narrations of characters' illness. Not all 'sick characters' or even 'sick narrators' can be termed pathographical subjects, however, and not all narratives focused on illness can be termed pathographies. As defined here, subjects of pathography demonstrate focused interiority – they observe, analyse and interpret their own sensations. Although they may often relate symptoms to a changing external environment, the larger world around them often fades; pain makes them myopic, and they focus mainly on the factors they perceive as relevant to their disease. These patients often apply some kind of scientific or methodical approach in presenting their own symptoms. They are aware that they are sick or are becoming sick. First-person narrators of pathography often feel empathy with other ill individuals while feeling alienated from well people and normal, everyday life. Also, their illnesses are not imagined.[5]

The single-minded focus of *Heart of Darkness* and 'Outpost of Progress' on the main characters' disease progression qualifies them for investigation as illness narratives. Reading tales of travel as colonial pathographies assumes that the author experienced actual illness when gathering evidence for the stories' composition – that he or she underwent real, visceral, corporeal pain and discomfort, and that these experiences affected the way he or she viewed and portrayed the colonial landscape. Therefore, it is not an anomaly that Joseph Conrad's *Congo Diary* is as single-mindedly focused on Conrad's state of health as his fiction is focused on the state of health of his characters. Conrad spent six months of a three-year contract in the Belgian Congo being trained to replace a riverboat captain for the Société Anonyme Belge pour le Commerce du Haut-Congo. His journey involved a three-week overland trek, and upriver and downriver steamboat journeys (Knowles and Moore 2000: 72). He recorded his immediate impressions in *The Congo Diary*, which he used later to refresh his memory in writing both 'Outpost of Progress' and *Heart of Darkness*. Ray Stevens argues that in the *Diary* Conrad both 'second guesses his wisdom' in coming to the Congo and 'records with increasing awareness the interaction of landscape, mood, sensory observations, impressions, and health, combined with sketches of the overland terrain' (2002: 68).

Stevens further notes that Conrad's commentary 'becomes increasingly figurative and occasionally impressionistic, especially in recording atmospheric conditions' (2002: 77). If one assumes that Conrad worried that the tropical climate's effects could make him ill, then it becomes significant when his entries emphasise the interrelationship between climatic conditions and his health. In the entry for 3 July, he says 'Health good', 'Bird notes charming', 'Gentle breeze', 'Water effects, very beautiful this morning'. The next day, after he has 'passed a bad night', he depicts the environment as more challenging: the hills become a 'chain' or a 'maze'. During the trek on the fifth day, which was 'without sunshine', he falls into a muddy puddle and says he is becoming 'jolly well sick of this fun' (1978: 9–10). As Conrad feels less and less well, the environment is portrayed as increasingly sinister. When he is 'wretched' the sun is 'heavy'. Seeing the Mission of Sutili, he states longingly 'fine buildings. Position on a hill. Rather breezy', but must move on (11–12). Near the end of his trek, Conrad feels 'rather seedy' and describes the sun rising 'red', creating an 'infernally hot day' (14). By this penultimate entry on 31 July, Africa's environment has become hellish.

Present-day pathographies are popular because they give readers hope – written by a cancer survivor or an AIDS patient, these narratives often provide the message that there is insight, awareness and appreciation of life to be gained by travelling through the 'kingdom of the sick' (Sontag 1979: 3). Conrad's African stories, in contrast, imply that there is little to be gained by taking a journey through lands of tropical disease or by wrestling with tropical illness. In letters written to his aunt from the Congo, he communicates regret: 'No use deluding oneself! Decidedly I regret having come here. I even regret it bitterly . . . My health is far from good' (1988: 188–9).

'A visit to the doctor'

The interaction between Marlow and the Company doctor has received curiously little critical attention, whereas the symbolism of other Company representatives with whom Marlow comes into contact has been mined extensively. Readers may have been unconsciously following the example Marlow appears to set, discounting the doctor because he is so out-of-date. But does the narrator truly de-authorise him? The doctor is certainly ridiculous in aspect. He is 'shabby and careless, with ink-stains on the sleeves of his jacket' and a 'chin shaped like the toe of an old boot' (Conrad 1988: 14). After taking Marlow's pulse, the doctor eagerly asks permission to gather data for his pet project of skull measurement: 'He produced a thing like calipers and got the dimensions back and front and every way, taking notes carefully.' The doctor explains his actions by saying 'I always ask leave, in the interests of science, to measure the crania of those going out there.' When Marlow asks the doctor if he measures men's skulls upon return, he smiles 'as if at some quiet joke' and says 'Oh, I never see them . . . and moreover the changes take place inside, you know.' The doctor's goal is to prove a 'little theory' of his own by examining the skull sizes of white men travelling to Africa. He is particularly excited to add Marlow to his study, as he is 'the first Englishman coming under [the doctor's] observation' (15).

The contrast between the impressions of the younger Marlow and the knowledge of the older Marlow, who narrates the story, lends the doctor and his ideas more weight than might be immediately apparent. The younger Marlow naively expresses surprise that the doctor has not travelled to Africa himself, given his evident enthusiasm for 'the Company's business'. Because the younger Marlow has not yet experienced the full danger presented by Africa to white travellers, he cannot be expected to understand why the doctor responds to his suggestion by becoming 'very cool and collected all at once' and saying 'I am not such a fool as I look' (14–15). However, the older Marlow includes this information in his narrative as a premonition of harrowing experiences to come. The very thought of going to Africa leaves this otherwise jovial doctor cold, a fact to which Marlow may wish he had paid more attention. The doctor also is imbued with prescience, smiling 'as if at some quiet joke' at Marlow's question whether he examines men's crania 'when they come back too'. The double meaning of 'Oh, I never see them' (15) is evident to our narrator, who now knows how few of the Company's men return from Africa.

All the 'gatekeepers' to Africa in this section are portrayed as menacing and powerful, including the two women knitting in the office, because they 'guard the door of Darkness', scrutinising the 'foolish and cheery countenances' of the young men being sent by the Company to almost certain death (14).[6] The doctor differs from these other gatekeepers, however, in that his exchange with Marlow implicates specific scientific theories, which have direct relevance to the younger Marlow's coming journey. It appears that the doctor is something of an amateur racial anthropologist.[7] As he both measures Marlow's skull and remarks 'you are the first Englishman coming under my observation', one may assume that he records the skull dimensions of white representatives of different nationalities.[8] When the doctor asks Marlow 'Ever any madness in your family?', it seems that he wishes to compare men's head measurements with data documenting who goes insane or dies in Africa, in order to prove that there is a correlation (15). Racial anthropology, drawing heavily upon the principles of phrenology, assumed that the skull proportions of subjects from different races could help predict their personality, intellectual capacity and mental soundness. Phrenology 'was still widespread through the 1840s', but 'was on the wane by 1850' (Van Wyhe 2004: 96). Rather than disappearing entirely, 'many of its elements were absorbed piecemeal into other practices – but without the name "phrenology"' (96). The doctor's assertion that 'the changes take place inside' demonstrates his belief that though cranial proportions indicate individual tendencies, external stressors in Africa may trip internal predispositions. The doctor's focus on madness proves well placed, as so many of the men with whom Marlow is about to have contact become mentally as well as physically ill.

When parting from Marlow, the doctor gives a final piece of advice: 'Avoid irritation more than exposure to the sun ... in the tropics one must before everything keep calm ... *Du calme, du calme. Adieu*' (Conrad 1988: 15). This admonition engages with multiple theories of tropical medicine, which deserve to be sketched briefly. The idea that over-reacting to one's environment can cause one to become ill is reminiscent of humoral theory, which insists that any climatic factor that causes an internal imbalance can bring on disease. This theory is manifest in the works examined thus far in this book. Usually authors such as Seacole and Kingsley pinpoint fear as the emotion that leaves one open to disease, but within this system irritation will work just as well. Irritation often occurs in response to a subject's perceived lack of control over his or her surroundings – 'all is not as it should be, and I cannot rectify it'. The unique challenges that Africa poses to a traveller's internal equilibrium are often related to climate – downpours, obscuring mists, moist heat and glaring sun. The doctor implies that a subject's reaction to these challenges determines whether or not he or she will succeed in Africa. It is no easy task to avoid becoming irritated by such factors of climate, just as avoiding fear of fever would be nearly impossible for Kingsley's readers.

Conrad's work mirrors the common late Victorian jumbling of mental and physical pathology, especially within the realm of tropical medicine. Conrad explicitly invokes insanity in his text by identifying the doctor as a bit of an 'alienist' who is concerned with why men go mad in the African wilderness, yet none of Conrad's characters die from insanity per se. Death comes from gunshots, hanging or the ubiquitous 'fever'. Their interior state and their grip on reality, however, have everything to do with why these men die. The illness commonly termed neurasthenia, made popular in medical discourse during the late 1880s and 1890s, provides a germane example of the late nineteenth- and early twentieth-century slippage between mental and physical illness. All of the main characters in Conrad's African fiction could be said to be suffering from this nebulous disorder. The hallucinatory and atmospheric qualities of the text mimic the symptoms of tropical neurasthenia, attributed by contemporary medical sources to sun exposure. The mental effects of physical illness are highly significant in examining Conrad's characters, in that men suffering from tropical disease were thought to 'not be themselves'.

Dane Kennedy, in his 1990 article 'The Perils of the Midday Sun: Climatic Anxieties in the Colonial Tropics', explains the 'actinic' theory of Dr Charles Woodruff as proof that climatic disease theories did not fade quickly with the advent of germ theory. Neurasthenia predates Woodruff's analysis, having been introduced by American neurologist George M. Beard in the 1870s. Woodruff simply 'impose[d] the authority and prestige of medical terminology' on to a 'condition long familiar to residents in the tropics', which had previously been called 'tropical inertia, tropical amnesia, Punjab head, and Burmah head' (Kennedy 1990: 123). However, Woodruff's 1905 book *The Effects of Tropical Light on White Men* ushered 'tropical neurasthenia' into the 'medical lexicon' as a 'clinical diagnosis' (Kennedy 1990: 123). Woodruff theorised that the 'presence in the tropics' of 'intense *actinic* radiation (by which Woodruff meant the photochemical effect of the ultraviolet band of the spectrum) undermined the health of whites, particularly pale-skinned "Aryans," who lacked sufficient pigmentation to protect their "nerve protoplasm"' (qtd in Kennedy 1990: 121).

Kennedy uses Woodruff's text to demonstrate that climatic theorists merely adopted the lexicon of contemporary science in order to bolster their pre-existing ideas. His article shows that climate remained a key factor in explanations of tropical illness until the Second World War. As will be demonstrated in the Conclusion, climatism also has an afterlife in postcolonial literature. It was certainly influential in Conrad's time, even to the extent that Marlow is 'told to wear flannel', traditionally adopted by travellers to protect themselves from exposure to tropical sun, by his affectionate aunt (Conrad 1988: 181). Travellers to the tropics also wore broad-brimmed hats, which protected the backs of their necks, or 'havelocks' – cloths designed to prevent the sun's rays from striking the neck and the brain stem, causing heatstroke.

Sun exposure not only produced heatstroke, sunstroke or physical exhaustion, according to Woodruff – it also caused 'neurasthenia'. The symptoms of 'tropical neurasthenia' were as various as 'insomnia, loss of memory, lethargy, *irritability*, and, in the most extreme cases, insanity and suicide' (Kennedy 1990: 123, my emphasis). There is a spectrum, therefore, within theories of climatic disease causation. One must avoid climatic factors such as miasma and sun as well as emotional stress (Kingsley); avoid emotional stress because it leaves one open to disease-causing factors (Conrad's doctor); or avoid all those factors, especially the sun, as it can bring on mental illness (Woodruff and other proponents of tropical neurasthenia).

Kennedy points out that tropical neurasthenia was simply the newest in a series of 'convenient repositor[ies]' for 'whatever bundle of obscure and often value-laden complaints otherwise eluded classification and explanation' (1990: 123). When critics of environmental medicine contended that the tropics could be less warm than other, supposedly 'healthy' climates, proponents of neurasthenia countered that the sunshine's quality, not just its heat, was detrimental. For example, theorist Andrew Balfour asserts that 'tropical *light* and heat . . . tend to affect deleteriously the nervous system of northern European races constantly exposed to them' (qtd in Kennedy 1990: 134, my emphasis). In Burton's work, the sun gives off 'sickly African heat' at lower elevations: it is the nature, not the degree, of the warmth and light that is detrimental. In the passage quoted at the outset of this chapter, Marlow calls the sun a 'blazing little ball', depicting it as powerful out of proportion to its size.

Marlow's visit to the doctor indicates how mental and physical illness overlap in Conrad's African fiction. It also foreshadows the main characters' dominant struggle: to maintain internal equilibrium in the face of Africa's environmental challenges. If Conrad's African stories function as colonial pathographies – narrations of characters resisting, descending into and (sometimes) returning from the state of being ill as they travel through the tropics – then the focus is on the character's internal reactions to his external environment.

Kayerts and Carlier

The importance of reading Conrad's short story 'An Outpost of Progress' in conjunction with *Heart of Darkness* should not be underestimated. As Gene M. Moore explains, Conrad's 'bitterly ironic exposé' of the 'demoralizing effects of isolation on a pair of ordinary time servers' presents 'a preliminary sketch of what the same conditions might do to a remarkable genius like Kurtz' (2004: 8). 'An Outpost of Progress' narrates the months during which two British Company officers, Kayerts and Carlier, man an African riverside ivory trading station. They come to replace the previous officer who died of 'fever'. When they arrive, they find ten station men and a station manager named Makola living there. Makola despises his white supervisors. The narrator of the story treats Kayerts and Carlier with similar disdain, providing the reader with the necessary distance to see both men's fatal errors in judgement and values. Here, the third-person narration allows an alternative 'frame of reference' (Achebe 1977: 10) through which to understand Conrad's colonial critiques, which one may only infer from *Heart of Darkness*.

This story draws upon climatic imagery to invoke illness and disease; however, in 'Outpost' Conrad portrays the effects of the African sunshine and miasma as less acute and more wearing than in *Heart of Darkness*. If Conrad's novella demonstrates to the reader the challenges of fighting climate while on the move, 'Outpost' shows the effects of the tropical environment on the static white subject. Although they arrive with benign if unenlightened intentions, Kayerts and Carlier's physical and mental health deteriorate during their stay. The breaking point comes when Makola trades, on his bosses' behalf, the ten station men to slave dealers in return for ivory. Kayerts and Carlier condemn Makola's actions, insisting that they did not know that slave trafficking was his intention. As they eventually become complicit with the exchange, however, their more serious illness begins. Eventually, in a fit of paranoia, Kayerts kills the increasingly volatile Carlier and then hangs himself at the grave of the former station chief.

The African landscape is inscrutable in both the short story and the novella, but the impenetrable wilderness in 'Outpost' pens in the station officers, rather than showing its closed face to a passing steamboat. When he arrives, Carlier 'trail[s] a sulky glance over the river, the forests, the impenetrable bush that seemed to cut off the station from the rest of the world' (Conrad 1977: 84). The men spend their time reminiscing about their lives back in England and reading the books left behind by their predecessor. Alone in their thatched house, they

> lived like blind men in a large room, aware only of what came in contact with them (and of that only imperfectly), but unable to see the general aspect of things. The river, the forest, all the great land throbbing with life, were like a great emptiness. Even the brilliant sunshine disclosed nothing intelligible. (88)

Kayerts and Carlier are unable to decode, and unwilling to learn to decode, that which they see, and this makes the African environment appear ominous to them. Conrad uses some of the same environmental elements as in *Heart of Darkness* to create this sense of foreboding, including an uncontrollably fecund jungle, or 'great land throbbing with life', along with blinding mist and sunshine that threatens rather than illuminates.

One of the main reasons these two white men stay indoors, cut off from the life that surrounds them, is because they believe that exposure to the tropical sun causes illness. When they first arrive and observe the gravesite of the former station chief, Kayerts (the superior officer) says to Carlier, 'I've been told that the fellow exposed himself recklessly to the sun. The climate here, everybody says, is not at all worse than at home, as long as you keep out of the sun … I am chief here, and my orders are that you should not expose yourself to the sun!' (86). Kayerts invokes climatism, with its roots in humoral theory, when he assumes that disease can be the fault of the victim, who weakens himself by exposure to the sun. Monitoring and maintaining one's physical equilibrium becomes a nearly obsessive state for practitioners of climatism, who believe that the over-exertion brought on by work in the tropical sun leaves them open to disease. So too does Kayerts' order assume the tone of a mantra: 'exposed himself … to the sun; keep out of the sun; [don't] expose yourself to the sun!' However, the two men make one of the mistakes against which the authors of *Tropical Trials* (1883) warn their female readers: rather than taking regular exercise in the cooler morning hours, Kayerts and Carlier barely venture out of doors at all, gradually becoming indolent and paranoid.

'Outpost' introduces a dynamic that *Heart of Darkness* will further develop: whites demonstrate racist hostility when they compare their own illness to the healthy natives; however, the narrator of 'Outpost' mocks such hostility as ineffectual and self-destructive. For example, Carlier and Kayerts waste away while waiting for the steamship to come, because they 'dare not stroll far away from the station to shoot', for fear of missing the ship's arrival or for fear of the wilderness. Carlier shoots a hippopotamus from the riverbank, but due to his own incompetence he cannot retrieve it. The carcass floats down to Chief Gobila's village, where the natives celebrate their good fortune. In a racist fit of rage, Carlier 'talked about the necessity of exterminating all the niggers before the country could be made habitable' (102).

These two racially bigoted subjects are also made ridiculous in a scene with Chief Gobila. Conrad cleverly reverses the common stereotype deployed by traditional travel narratives, with African natives overawed by symbols of modern technology and foreign advancements such as watches, beads and matches. Gobila transfers the affection he felt for the former station manager to Kayerts and Carlier, and the narrator says the white men 'returned it in a way'. Carlier 'slapped him on the back, and recklessly struck off matches for his amusement'. Kayerts 'was always ready to let him have a sniff at the ammonia bottle. In short, they behaved just like that other white creature. . .' (91). Here, it is the whites who behave stereotypically, assuming that Gobila must want to see matches lit or to smell ammonia. Common gestures of British society, such as backslapping between men, seem absurd when tolerated by this kind 'old image', as Kayerts calls him. The whites are only able to return Gobila's affection in 'a way', just as blacks have historically been stereotyped as only capable of feelings that resemble true love or devotion. The white men could ask Makola to translate for them, in order to inquire of Gobila what he really needs. However, they stay within superficial, delimited roles and are mocked for it by the narrator.

The narrator also ridicules Carlier's racially objectifying behaviour. Unable to communicate with those Africans who come to the station to trade ivory for dry goods, the white men are content to watch Makola barter on their behalf. Carlier 'swagger[s] up twirling his moustaches' during the bartering session and 'surveys the warriors with haughty indulgence'. He comments:

> 'Fine animals. Brought any bone? Yes? It's not any too soon. Look at the muscles of that fellow – third from the end. I wouldn't care to get a punch on the nose from him. Fine arms, but legs no good below the knee. . .' And after glancing down complacently at his own shanks, he always concluded: 'Pah! Don't they stink!' (89)

Although Carlier should be saying 'fine animals' or 'fine specimens' in reference to the ivory being traded, here he evaluates the human beings who bring the ivory: 'Fine animals. Brought any bone?' He analyses their physical structure and comments on their smell as if they were so many cattle. 'Outpost' calls this bigotry into question by attributing it to one of the men earlier identified as 'perfectly insignificant and incapable individuals, whose existence is only rendered possible through the high organisation of civilised crowds' (85).

When Kayerts and Carlier feel threatened by native Africans, it is often because these Africans are perceived as being at home in a hostile climate. Kayerts sees Makola as complicit with the threatening African environment. When Kayerts becomes angry and calls Makola to task for his role in the slave trading, Makola 'pronounce[s] impressively', 'You very red, Mr. Kayerts. If you are so irritable in the sun, you will get fever and die – like the first chief!' The two men lock eyes, and Kayerts shivers. Makola's words seem to him 'full of ominous menace' (98). It seems to Kayerts that Makola has power over the white man's health, or at least can predict with deadly accuracy how the African climate will affect him. Able to 'pronounce' and inspire superstitious fear in his supervisor, Makola here takes on the supernatural associations of African illness.

In 'An Outpost of Progress', it is evident that neither of the Britons is suited for Africa. Both men's health is progressively undermined the longer they are at the station, though they do not seem to notice:

> Now and then one of them had a bout with fever, and the other nursed him with gentle devotion. They did not think much of it. It left them weaker, and their appearance changed for the worse. Carlier was hollow-eyed and irritable. Kayerts showed a drawn, flabby face above the rotundity of his stomach, which gave him a weird aspect. But being constantly together, they did not notice the change that took place gradually in their appearance, and also in their dispositions. (92)

As time goes on, Kayerts and Carlier's individual conditions worsen. Carlier, 'undermined by fever, could not swagger any more, but kept tottering about'. Kayerts 'mooned about silently . . . His legs were much swollen, and he could hardly walk' (102).

In the final scenes of the story, the men become paranoid, fighting over a few remaining cubes of sugar. Kayerts shoots Carlier, thinking Carlier himself is armed. The morning after Kayerts kills Carlier, he wakes to find the house wrapped in a mist as impenetrable as that which surrounds Marlow's steamship in *Heart of Darkness*. Whereas Marlow has yet to encounter 'the horror' of Kurtz's mental decay, Kayerts has already experienced it within himself. The mist around Marlow's steamship is disturbing as it keeps him from looking outward and from progressing along a trajectory he still believes might be worthwhile (to find and recover Kurtz). However, the mist surrounding Kayert's station house keeps him trapped, alone with the reminder of his own madness in the form of Carlier's body; it is deeply terrifying to him. Conrad describes the scene thus:

> The day had come, and a heavy mist had descended upon the land: the mist penetrating, enveloping and silent; the mist that clings and kills; the mist white and deadly, immaculate and poisonous. He stood up, saw the body, and threw his arms above his head like a man who, waking from a trance, finds himself immured forever in a tomb. '*Help! . . . My God!*' (108)

When Makola arrives on the scene, sees Carlier's body and deduces what happened, he tellingly asserts, 'He died of fever.' '"Yes," repeated Makola thoughtfully, stepping over the corpse, "I think he died of fever. Bury him tomorrow"' (107). Makola means to imply that he will hide the murder for Kayerts. He thereby gains control of the situation and asserts his dominance over his white 'master'. However, Kayerts would not have killed Carlier had they not been abandoned by the Company, had they not become desperately ill and had the events not led them both to become delusional. Thus, Makola asserts a complicated truth when he says Carlier 'died of fever'.

Marlow

Conrad wrote *Heart of Darkness* upon returning to England with shattered health. Like the narrator of *The Congo Diary*, Marlow knows how sick Africa can (and did) make him from the outset of his story. In *Heart of Darkness*, the older Marlow relates the younger Marlow's experiences, imbuing even early invocations of the African environment with foreboding. The passages analysed in the following section, where Marlow links foul water, insidious mist and 'blazing sun' with illness, occur intermittently throughout the book, but when considered together, they establish a coherent experience of climatic illness threat.

Marlow's first impressions of Africa are dominated by ominous images of climate. As the steamer on which he is a passenger drops 'soldiers and custom house officers' along the coast of Africa, he says

> The edge of a colossal jungle so dark green as to be almost black, fringed with white surf, ran straight, like a ruled line, far far away along a blue sea whose glitter was blurred by a creeping mist. The sun was fierce, the land seemed to glisten and drip with steam. (Conrad 1988: 16)

The ominous landscape of Africa here reaches out towards the viewer. That element which is most familiar to the erstwhile sailor Marlow – the 'glittering' blue sea – is obscured by a 'creeping' mist. The connotations of the word 'creeping' lend the mist an insidious and invasive quality that echoes Kingsley's characterisation, discussed in Chapter 4. Although the 'colossal jungle' is a straight 'ruled line', it cannot be contained. The white surf does not delimit the jungle but 'fringes' it, and the mist extends the jungle's climatic influence outward towards the ocean. Even on the edge, the jungle is so dark green as 'to be almost black'. As Marlow prepares to travel to the heart of this dark and mysterious landscape, he sees for the first time its outermost reaches, stretching 'far far' away into the distance. The jungle is all-consuming and its dimensions defy the imagination. Marlow personifies the tropical sun, which is a source of such health worries for white explorers, as 'fierce'. The hot sun, shining on land that 'glistens and drips with steam', creates a sensual image of abundant fecundity. Warm and humid environments are ideal for the creation and support of life, and in this passage the plenty of Africa's environment strains at its bounds.

An excess of fecundity often leads to rot, and theorists of climate tell us that rot, filth and putrefaction give off disease-causing stench. As Marlow's ship gets closer to the African landscape, he portrays the land's excessive fecundity as producing excessive filth, a fact which fills him with apprehension. He says the steamboat wound 'in and out of rivers, streams of death in life, whose banks were rotting into mud, whose waters, thickened into slime, invaded the contorted mangroves that seemed to writhe at us. . .' (17). The river's 'death in life' consists of rotting vegetative and animal matter, which Marlow perceives as too putrid even for the native mangroves; the 'slime' 'invades' the mangroves, and the trees appear to 'writhe' as if they are being poisoned. As the ship pulls into the river and farther away from the sea, Marlow encounters more and more unhealthy water that contrasts with the healthy, open ocean that he loves. Watching this sludgy water, 'a sense of vague and oppressive wonder' steals over him (17). The still and fetid rivers lend to Marlow's African journey a sense of unreality.

Many postcolonial critics, including Michael Hardt and Antonio Negri in their book *Empire*, have discussed the ways in which white writers depict the 'monstrous, unbounded overabundance of life' of the colonial setting (2000: 135). Colonisers often perceived their influence as 'hygienic', counteracting the diseased, 'contagious' and uncivilised colony. Many whites also believed that 'Europeans [were] always at risk' of 'physical contamination' from the 'darkness of colonial territories and populations'. Specifically with regard to *Heart of Darkness*, Hardt and Negri say, 'Contagion is the constant and present danger, the dark underside of the civilizing mission' (135). This chapter argues that though illness is indeed a danger for whites in *Heart of Darkness*, the threat is located not in the native bodies but in the pernicious effects of the tropical environment. White subjects react with fear to the African environment; however, as one can see in the following examples, when such subjects use their fear as a catalyst for racist violence, they are unsuccessful and become objects of mockery.

In addition to their fear of foul water and insidious mist, the third main climatic factor that Marlow and his fellow travellers find threatening is the tropical heat. As the ship progresses, they encounter a French man-of-war shelling the jungle. Marlow explains:

> We came upon a man-of-war anchored off the coast. There wasn't even a shed there and she was shelling the bush . . . In the empty immensity of earth, sky and water, there she was, incomprehensible, firing into a continent . . . Nothing happened. Nothing could happen. There was a touch of insanity in the proceeding . . . and it was not dissipated by somebody on board assuring me earnestly there was a camp of natives – he called them, enemies – hidden out of sight somewhere. We gave her her letters (I heard the men in that lonely ship were dying of fever at the rate of three a day) and went on. (Conrad 1988: 17)

The parenthetical comment informing readers of the ship's fatality rate in fact illuminates the whole scene. So many men dying of fever lends the ship's population an aura of desperation. As they are suffering from 'fever', so are they behaving 'feverishly'. Such a term implies both restless action (such as compulsively shelling the bush) and mental agitation (in other words, seeing enemies where there may be none). Further, the mysterious source of tropical fever causes these men an additional sense of fear: they are sure Africa must be killing them somehow, but cannot be sure how. Is it the sun? The humid air?

The men on the ship make 'enemies' out of the natives, whom they feel must be complicit with the threatening African environment, 'hidden out of sight somewhere'. Imagined African bodies are masked by the undergrowth. Conflated with their environment, both natives and landscape become targets for illness- and fear-driven racist violence. To view the environment as complicit with and protective of indigenous peoples is an established tradition in African literature of exploration. However, when the Frenchmen in *Heart of Darkness* use their fear as catalyst for violence, their actions are depicted as frighteningly illogical.

Pathographical narrators often feel affinity with the sick and alienation from the well, and Marlow is no exception. He relates to his fellow characters according to their state of health as much as to their racial and cultural identities. The natives in *Heart of Darkness* usually remain as inscrutable as the landscape. When characterised ambivalently, it is often because they seem so at home in the environment that white characters perceive as hostile. However, as a pathographical narrator, Marlow feels sympathy with natives when they are ill, injured or displaced, even though he lacks the understanding necessary for true empathy. In the frequently cited scene in which Marlow passes a mining operation, he sees labourers dying in the shadows:

> Black shapes crouched, lay, sat between the trees, leaning against the trunks, clinging to the earth, half coming out, half effaced within the dim light, in all the attitudes of pain, abandonment and despair . . . They were dying slowly – it was very clear. They were not enemies, they were not criminals, they were nothing earthly now, nothing but black shadows of disease and starvation lying confusedly in the greenish gloom. Brought from all the recesses of the coast in all the legality of time contracts, lost in uncongenial surroundings, fed on unfamiliar food, they sickened, became inefficient, and were allowed to crawl away and rest. (20)[9]

Critics have been right to point out that Marlow creates a tableau with black bodies similar to those he creates with trees and jungle.[10] However, while he cannot understand or communicate with the natives, Marlow has an emotional connection to them based on a mutual experience of illness. The natives in the scene share a bond with Marlow: he too is 'lost in uncongenial surroundings' and 'fed on unfamiliar food'; he also 'sickens' when taken too far from home. Marlow seems to feel that, if only the mine workers had been allowed to stay in their villages and if he had had the sense to stay home, both he and they could have avoided much pain. When Marlow stumbles upon the dying men, he feels sympathy with them based on their shared identities as sick subjects, and simultaneously feels horrified, faced with illness worse than his own.

In contrast, Marlow feels disgusted by whites such as the manager, who can survive in a tropical environment. The manager is described as having 'no genius for organising, for initiative, or for order even . . . no learning, and no intelligence. His position had come to him . . . perhaps because he was never ill.' The men who 'conquer' Africa are there by default, as 'triumphant health in the general rout of constitutions is a kind of power in itself' (25). Their only skill is staying alive. The manager's uncle commends him on this. He says, 'You stand the climate – you outlast them all' (34). On the trip upriver, when faced with an obstacle, while Marlow 'frets and fumes' the manager displays calm 'resignation' (40). The type of man who is suited to serve in Africa has no 'vision', and thus helps neither the natives nor his country by being there.

Marlow believes strongly that environmental factors are linked to disease, though he is not sure exactly how. Before leaving for his journey upriver, he overhears a private conversation between the manager and the manager's uncle regarding the state of health of those posted to the station. Marlow is disturbed when the uncle makes a careless comment implying that his nephew should trust the wilderness to kill only those whites who deserve to die. Marlow describes the uncle's gesticulation:

> I saw him extend his short flipper of an arm for a gesture that took in the forest, the creek, the mud, the river – seemed to beckon with a dishonouring flourish before the sunlit face of the land a treacherous appeal to the lurking death, to the hidden evil, to the profound darkness of its heart. It was so startling that I leaped to my feet and looked back at the edge of the forest, as though I expected an answer of some sort to that black display of confidence. (35)

Marlow voices awe for the jungle that approaches superstition. The manager and his uncle are comfortable in saying that 'the climate may do away with [the] difficulty' of Kurtz for them, in an eerie echo of Mary Kingsley quoting Wordworth's sonnet ('the air and all nature will fight for you'). To Marlow, however, invoking the jungle's power for one's own ends is akin to inviting the wrath of a god, in this case the god of death (33). When the uncle gestures to 'the sunlit face of the land', Marlow feels that he makes 'a treacherous appeal to the lurking death'. What might otherwise be a bucolic image becomes threatening, in no small measure because the sunshine brings on illness. The structure of this sentence posits death as 'the hidden evil', 'the profound darkness of [the land's] heart'. In this sense, a journey to the 'heart of darkness' leads to death.

One may find further evidence that Marlow lends credence to the environmental causation of disease by examining a philosophical aside, inserted into the narration of the upriver journey. As Marlow the traveller approaches Kurtz's station, Marlow the narrator outlines what he believes are the three levels of human awareness. Some people are unaware of their surroundings because they are fools; some because they are exalted. However, Marlow says that the vast majority of us 'are neither one nor the other. The earth for us is a place to live in, where we must put up with sights, with sounds, with smells too, by Jove! – breathe dead hippo so to speak and not be contaminated' (50). In this schema, humans are aware of their surroundings through sensory perception; specifically, through the perception of unpleasant environmental realities. These stimuli must be 'put up with' as part of our lot. Not only does the human experience require perceiving and tolerating unpleasant environmental stimuli, according to Marlow, it is defined by how well we resist the corrupting influence of these stimuli. Marlow makes this process into the central metaphor for human existence.

The climax of Marlow's quest – finding and recovering Kurtz – signals the climax of his pathographical narrative as well. Kurtz's eventual death disheartens Marlow, as he feels his journey is now pointless. Within the trajectory of Marlow's pathography, rescuing Kurtz motivates his journey into the realm of death. Kurtz's own death undermines the importance of Marlow's survival: he has nothing to 'bring back' except his own bleak narrative. Within one paragraph of being informed 'Mistah Kurtz – he dead', Marlow states 'And then they very nearly buried me' (69). Instead of glorifying his battle with death, as do many narrators of pathography, Marlow emphasises that his survival is random and his resulting existence is 'futile':

> I have wrestled with death. It is the most unexciting contest you can imagine. It takes place in an impalpable greyness with nothing underfoot, with nothing around, without spectators, without clamour, without glory, without the great desire of victory . . . I was within a hair's-breadth of the last opportunity for pronouncement, and I found with humiliation that probably I would have nothing to say . . . there is a period of time which I remember mistily, with a shuddering wonder, like a passage through some inconceivable world . . . (69–70)

In startling contrast to other nineteenth-century writers' glorified struggles against tropical disease, such as in Stanley's *Autobiography*, Conrad emphasises illness's dreariness. Survivors of tropical disease can continue to battle for the cause of Empire, which may be a worthy goal in others' eyes. However, Marlow's colonial pathography reveals that he has seen corruption up close and doubts that Empire is worth fighting for. He feels ambivalent about his own survival. In this sense, he has not 'much belief in [his] own right' (69) to live, just as he does not believe in whites' right to exploit African resources.

Marlow feels keenly his own failure as a narrator of pathography: if a narrator is destined not to survive, the least he must do is to say something meaningful on his deathbed, but Marlow 'was within a hair's-breadth of the last opportunity for pronouncement', and 'found with humiliation that probably [he] would have nothing to say' (69). Further, the image of Marlow's passage through the realm of death, like a 'passage through some inconceivable world' of 'impalpable greyness' mirrors the imagery of his upriver journey: his 'misty' journey through Africa becomes a journey through the land of death.

Kurtz

Throughout Marlow's upriver narrative, both he and the reader become accustomed to thinking of Kurtz as ill. When spoken of by his colleagues and competitors within the Company's ranks, Kurtz's name becomes synonymous with both brilliance and disease. He is very smart; he is very sick. Upon his arrival at Kurtz's station, Marlow converses with the Russian man who has been caring for Kurtz. This man gives Marlow a more detailed sense of Kurtz than Marlow has been able to glean from Company authorities. The Russian sets the stage for Kurtz. He reveals that Kurtz has been raiding nearby villages rather than trading for ivory, disappearing for weeks into the back country with natives, and generally 'forgetting himself'. Marlow responds, 'Why! he's mad', an assertion which the Russian challenges hotly (56). Instead, the Russian places emphasis on Kurtz's physical state, informing Marlow 'proudly' that he 'managed to nurse Kurtz through two illnesses' (55). When Marlow seems sceptical, his companion 'breaks down'. '"I don't understand," he groaned. "I've been doing my best to keep him alive and that's enough . . . There hasn't been a drop of medicine or a mouthful of invalid food for months here"' (58). The Russian says Kurtz's current state of health is 'bad, very bad' (57).

Although Marlow, the manager and others are quick to assume that his own emotional 'excesses' led to Kurtz's illness, the Russian presents an alternative view. He implies that it is Kurtz's repeated bouts of illness that have led to his erratic behaviour; further, Kurtz would not have been so badly ill if he had been supported by the Company as expected and sent the medicine necessary to hold off the physical effects of Africa's climate. The reader is encouraged by the narrative to follow Marlow in initially discounting the Russian's opinion. He is an outlandish figure: variable, impressionable and naive. He is awed by Kurtz's grandiloquence, so Marlow thinks him to be an unreliable judge of the situation. When Marlow meets and talks with Kurtz, however, and observes the Company representatives' reactions to him, he begins to amend his initial conclusion that Kurtz is simply 'mad'.

At their first meeting, Marlow sees a man quite obviously sick. Carried on a stretcher, Kurtz raises his arm to address his followers, who will follow his proclamation whether the newcomers may live or die. Through his binoculars, Marlow sees

> the thin arm extended commandingly, the lower jaw moving, the eyes of that apparition shining darkly far in its bony head that nodded with grotesque jerks. His covering had fallen off and his body emerged from it pitiful and appalling as from a winding-sheet. I could see the cage of his ribs all astir, the bones of his arm waving . . . as though an animated image of death. I saw him open his mouth wide – it gave a weirdly voracious aspect as though he wanted to swallow all the air, all the earth, all the men before him. (59)

The descriptions of Kurtz in the passage above symbolise his inner 'nature': the 'weirdly voracious aspect' of his face, which seems to want to swallow everything around him, certainly reflects his rapacious personality. However, Kurtz's experience of illness might well have influenced the evolution of this nature. If one is to read Kurtz as a subject of colonial pathography, then his disease symptoms become significant to the analysis.

One of the men upon whom the character Kurtz is thought to have been modelled was Georges Antoine Klein, 'the chief of the "Inner Station' at Stanley Falls', who was 'ill when Conrad arrived and died on the return trip downriver' (Knowles and Moore 2000: 194). Klein died of amoebic dysentery. If ill with dysentery, Kurtz might have suffered from 'abdominal cramps, fatigue, unintentional weight loss, bloody stools, fever and vomiting'. If the parasite that causes dysentery spreads through the blood to the liver, lungs, brain, or other organs it can cause sepsis, seizure, liver abscesses and kidney failure. Victims of dysentery near death can even become delirious as the parasite enters their brains.

A visitor to Africa in Conrad's time would know the symptoms of advanced illness, especially recognising weight loss, dehydration and fever. He or she would also recognise that a victim in the last stages of disease could be subject to mental imbalance. Kurtz wastes away much as Kayerts and Carlier do, without realising how ill he has become. When being taken away in the steamboat, Kurtz says to his supervisors, 'You are interrupting my plans now. Sick, Sick. Not so sick as you would like to believe. Never mind. I will carry my ideas out yet' (61). There is little doubt, as Marlow describes him, that Kurtz is near death – he is a mere 'apparition' whose skeletal frame is wrapped in the equivalent of grave clothes. If this were not clear enough, Marlow tells the reader that Kurtz appears 'an animated image of death'. His diseased state does not negate the fact that Kurtz has been practising 'unsound methods' through a 'lack of restraint' (62, 51). However, after his initial inclination to follow the example set by the manager and pronounce Kurtz 'mad', Marlow observes Kurtz closely for himself. Once he views Kurtz's advanced state of disease, Marlow's narrative reverts back to reflecting the ambiguity of disease causation and effect. When he has a chance to compare Kurtz's primal drive for survival with the 'vile' backbiting within the Company's ranks, he says 'I turned mentally to Kurtz for relief – positively for relief' (61). At that point, he counts himself 'Kurtz's friend – in a way' (62). Marlow seems to be acknowledging that Kurtz's 'degeneration', or his trip into the 'darkness' of cruel behaviour, may have been precipitated by his journey towards the 'darkness' of death.

The Company would like to assert that Kurtz lacked the moral and mental fortitude to resist the temptations of the 'savage' land into which he ventured. Critics who follow this reading can easily reproduce a simplistic, black/white dichotomy, believing that *Heart of Darkness* merely paints Africa as a prehistoric land that serves as a backdrop for whites to play out their own repressed lusts. Small wonder that critics such as Chinua Achebe have found this critical tradition, and the text it analyses, distasteful. On the other hand, what if Kurtz's real madness was in repeatedly exposing himself to disease? As Dane Kennedy observes, 'When Noel Coward quipped that only "mad dogs and Englishmen go out in the mid-day sun," the humour hinged on his audience's understanding that it *was* mad to go out in the midday sun, at least in the tropics' (1990: 118). There were scientific explanations for this dynamic established by the psychological theorists of the time, such as Theodule Ribot, with whose work Conrad was familiar (Tutein 1990: 84). Such theorists claimed that physiological pathology could lead to 'diseases of the will', including lack of impulse control and homicidal urges (Ribot 1896). If Kurtz's abuses of power could have stemmed in part from physiological disease, then Conrad may be portraying a more nuanced effect upon the white traveller to Africa than historically he has been given credit for.

In other words, one of this colonial pathography's effects may be to suggest that even men who hold in their hearts some semblance of the 'true' colonial ideal cannot avoid becoming physically ill in Africa, and the illness perverts both their intentions and their actions. One sees the degenerative effects of illness upon Carlier when he advises 'exterminating all the niggers' during the latter stages of his African journey. Kurtz expresses this same sentiment in 'a kind of note at the foot of the last page' of his philosophical pamphlet. The note was 'scrawled evidently much later, in an unsteady hand ... at the end of that moving appeal to every altruistic sentiment it blazed at you, luminous and terrifying, like a flash of lightning in a serene sky: "Exterminate all the brutes!"' (Conrad 1988: 66). Kurtz may first have felt inspired by altruism and the 'pure' sentiments of the civilising mission, but by the end of his journey, shaking with disease, he has transformed lofty, if misguided, intentions into anger towards the Africans around him, who resist the very disease that is killing him. Thus, in Conrad's colonial pathographies, disease process, the environment and colonial politics become so involved that each one leads to and implicates the others.

Kurtz, Kayerts, Carlier and Marlow are not great men – to varying degrees, they are all fallible, prejudiced and short-sighted. However, by transcribing pain and its aftermath into pathography, Conrad makes the roles of climate, illness and disease in his colonial period significant to the readers, either reminding them of what they themselves may already have undergone, or warning them of what they may encounter should they travel into their own hearts of darkness. The interiority of his characters, their absorption in their own bodies' 'barometers', combined with the inevitability of their devastating illnesses, may therefore be one of the most lasting and compelling appeals against Imperial exploitation that Conrad could have made.

Notes

1. See Watt (1979: 175–6). Watt calls Conrad's impressionist method 'delayed decoding', whereby the reader is able to make sense of events only as their significance dawns on the fictional character experiencing them.
2. As Gene M. Moore argues in his introduction to *Conrad's Heart of Darkness: A Casebook*, '[early critical] approaches all shared a silent assumption that the meaning of *Heart of Darkness* had nothing to do with the reality of Africa'. This essay establishes that both of Conrad's African

stories have everything to do with 'the reality of Africa', as their main characters are defined significantly by how they resist the effects of Africa's unique disease environment (Moore 2004: 15).

3. Another popular reading glorifies Conrad's ill health, arguing that his life was an 'intermittent martyrdom' which forced him to turn to writing for income (Aubry quoted by Kimbrough in Conrad 1988: 73).

4. *Heart of Darkness* was originally to be even more centrally concerned with Marlow's health – Edward Garnett, Conrad's 'unofficially literary agent' and lifelong friend, expressed regret that a scene in which 'the hero [was] lying sick to death' was cut between the stages of synopsis and execution (qtd in Watt 1979: 137–8).

5. For the purposes of this chapter, disqualified from inclusion in the genre of pathography are those texts which use a sick character as a plot mechanism or which document the illness of someone who does not know she is sick (such as Bertha Mason in *Jane Eyre* or the narrator of 'The Yellow Wallpaper', for example).

6. For a measured treatment of this scene, see Watt (1979). He simultaneously summarises the possible symbolic meanings of the knitters and other figures present and explains the limitations of applying to the text a too literal, 'closed' symbolic reading (180–200). He cites Lillian Feder (1955) and Robert O. Evans (1956) as examples of critical readings which 'have made the two knitters a primary basis for a large-scale symbolic interpretation of *Heart of Darkness* in which Marlow's whole journey becomes a version of the traditional descent into hell, such as that in the sixth book of Virgil's *Aeneid*, and in Dante's *Inferno*' (190–1).

7. Griffith (1995) offers a thorough analysis of the anthropology of degeneration and primitivism in *Heart of Darkness*, but only spends two pages on the doctor scene. He sees the interaction as a straightforward parody or satire 'of the craniological theories of pseudo-scientists such as Lombroso' (160; Lombroso 1891, 1911). Griffith identifies Conrad's doctor as 'a composite of many of the scientific interests of his day: craniology, incipient alienism, phrenology, and physical anthropology'. Although he states that 'one element in the scene seems to be the anthropological concern with the impact of climate upon physiognomy', Griffith does not explore the topic further (160). He infers from Conrad's letters that he was 'skeptical' about craniology, but did not dismiss it 'as merely the province of cranks' (160–1).

8. Early pathographies also draw heavily upon cranial measurement and analysis. See Cesare Lombroso's *Criminal Man* (1911) and *The Man of Genius* (1891).

9. For more analyses of Conrad's treatment of the Matadi chain gang, see Najder (2004: 131–2), Parry (2005: 43) and Watt (1979: 220).

10. 'Blacks are not functional protagonists but figures in a landscape who do not constitute a human presence' (Parry 2005: 33).

Conclusion:
The Afterlife of Climate

This book began with a puzzle – why did the climatic paradigm of disease hold sway for so long within the colonial imagination, even as germ theory was gaining a strong foothold? Why did writers travelling to the West Indies and Africa continue to blame the interaction between bodies and the environment for illness? Undoubtedly, the links between climate and racial science made the concept of 'environmental pathology' an especially incisive political tool, allowing those who wielded it to label entire regions as fatal to subjects of a specific race or 'constitution' and thereby to delimit groups of people within specific climate 'zones'. However, as Mark Harrison observes, political reasons alone do not fully explain the 'longevity' of this conceptual system (1999: 206).

Analysis of five Victorian writers – Mary Seacole, Richard Burton, Africanus Horton, Mary Kingsley and Joseph Conrad – has shown how images of climate morphed and changed through the latter half of the nineteenth century. Authors such as Kingsley, Burton and Conrad create foreboding visions of clammy mist, rotting vegetation, dirty pools and 'sickly' sun, while writers of colour such as Seacole and Horton stress their familiarity with the secrets of their native landscapes. I have suggested that these authors continue to depict the subtle and shifting balance of heat and cold, wet and dry, long after these factors were no longer widely considered scientifically conclusive, in order to enhance their own writerly authority. Narratives of illness from the environment give credence to the speaker's own experience in ways that narratives of infection cannot. The 'longevity' of climate in the literature of Empire, therefore, shows that Victorian authors were not only concerned with containing risk, but also with unbinding it, allowing disease to float in the air or travel on the tides. To do so allowed them an expertise of 'place' that trumped any laboratory test. The lives and livelihoods of these individuals were embroiled with the continuing colonial project, which may help to explain why elements of germ theory were merely assimilated to meteorological explanations for disease during the *fin de siècle*.

However, authors continued to revisit and revise the colonial association of tropical environments with illness well into the twentieth century. For example, narratives of imperial nostalgia, such as W. Somerset Maugham's novel *The Explorer*, wish that African adventure still could be a curative for the seeming degeneration of British values and physical vigour. In contrast, postcolonial authors such as Wilson Harris engage with the colonial tradition of pathologising 'the tropics' by rewriting the symbolism of climate. I conclude with a brief consideration of how texts such as *Palace of the Peacock* 'write back' to *Heart of Darkness* by remaking the quest for knowledge into a quest for heritage and cathartic healing.

W. Somerset Maugham's *The Explorer* was published as a novel in 1908 and as a play in 1912, but is set a few years earlier. The novel wistfully harkens back to the earlier models of hyper-masculine colonial discourse provided by Stanley, Burton and Charles Kingsley. Its main character, Alec Mackenzie, seeks to abolish slave raiding in Africa and to reinforce the trade routes of British East Africa. During his visits back to England, Alec meets Lucy Allerton, a noble-spirited young woman whose father Fred has been convicted of fraud. In order to restore glory to her family's name, Lucy urges her brother George to accompany Alec on his next expedition to Africa; however, George proves as weak-natured and unreliable as his father. After murdering his native mistress, as compensation George is ordered by Alec to lead a charge against the enemy slave traders, and dies in this action.

When Alec returns to England, one of his enemies publicly accuses him of negligence, claiming that he sent George Allerton on a suicide mission. Alec asks Lucy to believe unquestioningly that his behaviour was honourable, which she attempts but is unable to do. After a brief and miserable separation, she apologises and claims 'I know that whatever you did was right and just – because you did it' (Maugham 1991: 296). As may be guessed from the foregoing line, *The Explorer* is maudlin and often trite. Maugham's contemporaries thought the same: as the headline of a 1912 *New York Times* review states, '"Explorer" Blazes No Fresh Paths, Though the Maugham Teacup Style is Briefly Put Aside for Melodrama'. However, *The Explorer* is interesting as a narrative of imperial cliché and nostalgia, which recirculates concepts of climatic illness in the early twentieth century in order to (unsuccessfully) recapture a sense of 'high imperial' pride and national vigour.

The classic themes of African exploration literature are wheeled out

– the African continent is mysterious yet familiar, the hero sorely tested but triumphant, righteous and superior. Alec self-consciously locates himself within a brotherhood of 'great' explorers, including Burton, Stanley and Livingstone. The text glosses over the very different accomplishments and motivations of each man, instead describing all three as full of great strength and vitality by using words such as 'mighty', 'great', 'Napoleonic', 'ruthless' and 'admirable' (47–8). Placing himself within this earlier lineage, Alec attempts to resurrect the traits of masculine vigour most needed by a demoralised, post-Victorian England. This need is summarised explicitly by one of Lucy's friends, Mrs Crowley, when, in the 1912 play version, she says of Alec 'I don't think I like him, but he's certainly a strong man, and in England just now everyone's so weak and floppy, it's rather a relief to come across somebody who's got a will of iron and nerves of steel' (Maugham 1912: 6).

This comment echoes the mid-century concerns of Charles Kingsley and his contemporaries that the fortitude of English subjects was degenerating as a result of excess and unhealthy habits. However, in *The Explorer* these worrisome sentiments are augmented by recent memories of the second Boer War. Whereas the shortcomings of Britain's performance in the Crimea would have been fresh in Kingsley's memory, Maugham was reacting to this more recent engagement, which was perceived by his reading public as yet another fraught and ambivalent chapter of British history. As Paula Krebs explains, 'writings about the war reveal splits in opinion and serious new concerns about British imperialism' (1999: 5).

In fact, the British government, 'crippled by the Boer War', was 'disinclined to enter upon fresh enterprises' and initially did not fund Alec Mackenzie's expeditions. Government officials 'had been taught bitter lessons before now', the narrator continues, 'and could not risk, in the present state of things, even an insignificant rebuff' (Maugham 1991: 67). A crippling of national vitality is here linked with waning imperial impulse. Losing imperial drive becomes a metaphorical emasculation: citizens are 'weak and floppy' instead of possessing a 'will of iron and nerves of steel'. If men like Burton and Stanley had let their actions be dominated by fear of failure, the narrator implies, Britain would never have reached its widespread influence and power.

Alec's power is tested and found sufficient through the trials of African travel, specifically his encounters with colonial disease. Maugham uses the African environment as a testing ground for white men's emotional and physical constitutions: only the worthy survive illness. During his first trip, Alec falls seriously ill 'and it was thought at the mission to which his bearers brought him that he could not live'. Alec 'insisted in the end on being taken back to the coast, and here, as if by a personal effort of will, he recovered'. He 'personified in a way that deadly climate and would not allow himself to be beaten by it' (48). Such a description hearkens back to constitutional theories of disease invoked by Mary Seacole and Mary Kingsley, for example, who both believe that strong will and a sensible attitude can help counteract illness.

As earlier explorers acquired a superficial knowledge of science and medicine in order to assist them in their travels, Alec returns to England and acquires 'a smattering of medical knowledge, and some acquaintance with the sciences which were wanted by a traveller . . . botany and geology, and the elements of surveying . . . and enough surgery to set a broken limb or conduct a simple operation' (48). Afterwards, he returns and makes inroads towards subduing slave trading in the region in order to make it hospitable to British intervention and trade. Exact echoes of earlier exploration rhetoric somehow fall flat, as in the following list of Mackenzie's accomplishments:

> He achieved the object of his expedition, discovered a new species of antelope of which he was able to bring back to the Natural History Museum a complete skeleton and two hides; took some geographical observations which corrected current errors, and made a careful examination of the country. (65)

These accomplishments are patently unspecific – 'some geographical observations . . . made a careful examination' – and when taken together as a list, each of these 'triumphs' seems to lose its meaning.

Maugham employs similar rhetoric regarding African travel challenges as Henry Morton Stanley in his *Autobiography* (1909), but his prose lacks the immediacy of Stanley's. Alec overcomes 'common vicissitudes of African travel': 'illness and hunger, incredible difficulties of transit through swamps that seemed never ending', and 'tropical forest through which it was impossible to advance at the rate of more than one mile a day; desertion of his bearers and perfidy of native tribes' (64). Stanley's *Autobiography* rolls the challenges posed by the African environment together with those posed by native populations. However, Maugham's list includes no sensory details and lacks emotional import – surmounting these challenges is merely a requirement for the classic storyline of African exploration.

However, Alec almost loses the progress he has made through George's perfidy and bad judgement. Maugham clearly links climate with illness: Alec writes home to Lucy that 'hitherto everything had gone well with him, and the white men, but for fever occasionally, were bearing the climate well' (128). These incidents of fever prove significant. As the narrator observes, 'people changed in Africa', not just in terms of their priorities but in their characters and behaviour as well. For example, George attempts to excuse killing his mistress by citing the negative effects of the tropical environment. Alec outlines to George his shortcomings and reminds him of a time when George flogged an African servant, even before the murder. George replies petulantly 'I did it in a moment of temper. A man's not responsible for what he does when he's got fever' (164). Such explanations recall the scenes from *Heart of Darkness*, which suggest that whites behave irrationally during their struggle with climate and illness, but that only the weakest respond through violence.

Maugham sentimentalises the era of African 'high imperialism' as a time when colonial dominantion was more noble and less craven than during the Boer War. His novel enacts a wishful fantasy that the African climate could still offer an untamed backdrop for British hero-making, but the narrative is devoid of sensory engagement with that climate. In contrast, postcolonial authors both seek to lay to rest colonial portrayals of threatening tropical landscapes and to reinvigorate these landscapes with their own associations. For example, in an autobiographical essay, Wilson Harris explains the influence of his relationship with landscape on his fiction:

> landscape/skyscape/riverscape/seascape (and their intermingled bearing on each other which transcends locality) have been a living text – if I may so put it – in the way I read and reread the elements (as if the elements were a book) when I lived in South America and travelled from the Atlantic coastland into the heartlands of the Guyanas. (2003: viii)

Harris served as a government surveyor before becoming a writer. Familiarity with savannas and rainforests permeates his work, such as *Palace of the Peacock* (1960). In this novel, a mixed-race, multicultural crew navigates a river through the jungle of Guyana. They are trying to reach an Amerindian settlement called Mariella, which they eventually find to be deserted. Instead, they discover an elderly woman, who they capture and enlist as a guide. As they continue to track the folk from 'the Mission', one after another of the crew perish; finally, the boat reaches the source of the river, only to be destroyed by an enormous waterfall (Adler 2003: 7–8).

The plot is complicated by magical and fantastical circumstances, digressions and slippages between dreaming and waking states. The unnamed 'I' narrator is partially blind and seems to dream the story. His brother Donne, the captain of the ship, is a mad visionary who relentlessly pursues his quest without giving clear explanations. Part way through the novel, the reader discovers that the crew 'is a replica of a famous crew that had been drowned on a similar exploiting mission some time before, and shuttle between life and death at their author's arbitrary demands' (Adler 2003: 9). In this light, the journey serves as a process of absolution or redemption. Depictions of the Guyanese environment are highly symbolic and function at multiple levels of meaning.

As Harris states, 'My grandmother on my mother's side was half-Arawak, half-European. My grandfather (my mother's father) was Scot and African. Such a family tree is not unusual in the South Americas. I perceive my antecedents within dimensions of dual and multiple theatre' (2003: xv). The *Peacock* crew members share a variety of bonds as well, through blood as well as memory. For instance Donne, a 'type of Elizabethan adventurer and conquistador', is 'made up of the descendents and mixtures of peoples – Europeans, Africans, Portuguese, Indians – belonging historically to different centuries and to successive waves of migrants to the Caribbean' (Adler 2003: 9). As the narrator states, 'The whole crew was one spiritual family living and dying together in a common grave out of which they had sprung again from the same soul and womb as it were' (Harris 1960: 40). The characters are able to put to rest the legacies of colonial disease and environment because they embody both coloniser and colonised.

If Donne represents Kurtz in *Palace of the Peacock*, then his brother may stand in for Marlow, the observer and recorder of events. He demonstrates the same emotionalism as Marlow, but inverted: he feels 'illogical disappointment and regret', not when the crew encounter obstacles, but instead when they are 'temporarily out of danger' (Harris 1960: 22). Although Marlow and Kurtz may have initially believed in the righteousness of the colonial impulse, which allowed them to trust in such basic narrative structures as progress towards an achievable goal, annihilation is the apotheosis of this crew's quest.

Palace of the Peacock echoes but then revises ominous representations of the tropical environment. In this novel, the prophetic figure, Donne, is present on the ship, unlike Kurtz, who waits deep in the jungle. Donne admonishes his brother, '"Rule the land, while you still have a ghost of a chance. And you rule the world. Look at the sun." His dead eye blinded mine. "Look at the sun," he cried in a stamping terrible voice' (19). Fractured legacies of colonial exploitation are embedded in this command. Donne feels a sense of urgency, perhaps because colonial control is vanishing – quick, he says, 'rule the land, while you still have a ghost of a chance'.

However, the novel follows Conrad's implication that urgency is futile: in *Heart of Darkness*, the manager has 'no entrails' and the visionary is mad; in *Palace of the Peacock*, the conquistador is dead and the listener is blind. 'Look at the sun!' may also be an encouragement to 'face down' the influences of tropical climate, which both texts show to be a futile goal. The narrator says, 'The sun was high in the heavens and the river burned and flamed' (24). Within this setting, the crew undertakes a 'Hot and mad pursuit in the midst of imprisoning land and water and ambushing forest and wood' (24). It is a 'mad' pursuit because the goals are illusory and their guide, Donne, is goaded by an invisible force. The quest also seems doomed by the resistance of the tropical environment, which 'imprisons' and 'ambushes' the ship.

The jungle also offers semantic meaning and the possibility of redemption. *Peacock*'s blind and dreaming speaker can 'see' more clearly than his comrades and is more attentive to his surroundings, which seem pulsing with life. The following scene is rich with semantic density:

> The sun glowed upon a mass of vegetation that swarmed in crevices of rocky nature until the stone yielded and turned a green spongy carpet out of which emerged enormous trunks and trees from the hidden dark earth beneath and beyond the sun. The solid wall of trees was filled with ancient blocks of shadow and with gleaming hinges of light. Wind rustled the leafy curtains through which masks of living beard dangled as low as the water and the sun. My living eye was stunned by inversions of the brilliancy and the gloom of the forest in a deception and hollow and socket. (26)

The landscape's mystery, indicated by words such as 'enormous', 'hidden', 'ancient' and 'gloom', is balanced by its exquisite beauty, suggested by 'green spongy carpet', 'gleaming hinges of light', 'leafy curtains', 'masks of living beard'. The reader can see into the crevices and hinges of nature in this scene, rather than being warded off by its incomprehensibility. The jungle is defined by brilliant contrasts rather than unremitting gloom, and nurtures life rather than death.

However, the jungle's own wild beauty does not make it necessarily hospitable for the travellers. In fact, the crew has died by natural forces once, soon to be twice. The fatal end to their journey is foreshadowed as one of the shipmates, Cameron, 'trembles a little with a sense of cruel unwanted cold'. This cold is described as 'the meaningless engagement with and stab of death that he – with the entire crew – had not yet shaken off'. Death is associated with the tropical climate, as 'a wind blowing on the water, a knife and chill they recognized like tropical fever that blew out of the Mission in an ague of fears, shaking the leaves of the dreaming forest' (44). The chill wind that Cameron feels foretells the crew's death, just as fever-carrying winds foretell disease. However, this death is both inevitable and expected, feared and welcomed.

The foregoing passage inverts the relationship between wind and fever typical within colonial climatism. First, 'tropical fever' blows 'out of the

Mission': rather than the source of civilisation and health, as in pro-imperial discourse, here the Mission is the source of disease – the crew needs to get past the influences of civilisation to the unbounded natural force of the waterfall. Secondly, the metaphor 'an ague of fears' suggests a complicated relationship between emotion and disease. Although the literal meaning of ague is 'malarial fever', its figurative meaning is 'any fit of shaking or shivering, like the cold stage of ague; quaking' (*OED* online). Therefore, the crew feel both a 'mal-aria' or 'bad air' of fear, as well as seeing the shaking from fever embodied in the form of rustling leaves. Although illness is located in the Caribbean environment, it is also linked with the characters' own agency – the crew are implicated in the creation of the Mission, and also responsible for their own emotions. The tropical environment only brings out characteristics that are already latent. Therefore, an illuminating 'shaft from the forest and the heaven of leaves' shows Donne to be 'aged' and to look 'like the devil himself' (54).

This crew are finally absolved of the legacy of colonial exploitation in which they and their ancestors took part. After the ship passes the mission of Mariella and they decide to carry on their journey, the crew members begin to die one by one in a symbolically redemptive manner. At the source of the river, the remaining party perishes under an enormous waterfall. In addition to its religious overtones, this image also recalls the power of tropical nature, which here effects retribution for colonial abuse. The crew members' ghosts, spirits or reincarnated selves then mount two ladders alongside the waterfall, having 'visions of the divine creator and healer' (Adler 2003: 11). The narrator declares,

> I had started to walk at last – after a long infancy and dreaming death – in the midst of mutilation and chaos that had no real power to overcome me. Rather I felt it was the unique window through which I now looked that supported the life of nature and gave it a full and invisible meaning and perfection in a way I know my hands and feet were formed and supported at this instant. (Harris 1960: 145)

Nature's force and violence, through the power of the waterfall, becomes the 'window' for the narrator to experience perfection and wholeness. Helplessness in the face of the tropical environment is liberating rather than threatening. At the end of *Palace of the Peacock*, the reader is told that each of the crew members 'now held at last in his arms what he had been for ever seeking and what he had eternally possessed' (152). The crew can achieve unity, both as colonisers who let go of their fear of death in the tropics and as colonised subjects who reclaim their heritage.

Exploring Victorian Travel Literature has suggested that the literature of Empire uses metaphors of health and disease in order to engage with the tropics, but in a more complex manner than has commonly been acknowledged. Victorian authors of colour, such as Mary Seacole and Africanus Horton, draw upon the imagery of threatening climates in order to protect their own independence and highlight their own familiarity with colonial environments. In addition, rather than reflecting a sense of 'imperial inevitability' (Franey 2003: 62), when explorers such as Richard Burton, Mary Kingsley and Joseph Conrad use images of rot, 'sickly' sunlight and miasma, they are suggesting the very real possibility that white bodies may not be able to survive abroad. Finally, this book has suggested that Victorian authors continued to invoke these complex systems of climatic disease in order that their narratives should be uncontestable – each becomes the only valid authority regarding his or her own experience with illness. Early twentieth-century authors such as W. Somerset Maugham can no longer draw upon the mystery of disease causation in order to create narrative suspense, so in works such as *The Explorer* one observes how climate can lose its metaphorical richness; however, this richness is reclaimed by postcolonial authors such as Wilson Harris, who reinvigorate 'climate' by rewriting the political values of a colonial tropical aesthetic.

Bibliography

'Abstract of Case of Staff Asst Surgeon Horton' (1862), Church Missionary Society Archive CMS/B/OMS/C A1 O117, Cadbury Research Library, Special Collections, University of Birmingham.

Achebe, Chinua (1977), *An Image of Africa* (Harmondsworth: Penguin).

Adeloye, Adelola (1974), 'Some Early Nigerian Doctors and their Contribution to Modern Medicine in West Africa', *Medical History*, 18(3): 275–93.

— (1992), *Doctor James Africanus Beale Horton: West African Medical Scientist of the Nineteenth Century* (Pittsburgh: Dorrance).

Adler, Joyce (2003), 'Introduction', in Joyce Adler, *Exploring the Palace of the Peacock: Essays on Wilson Harris*, ed. Irving Adler (Kingston, Jamaica: University of the West Indies Press).

Agassiz, Louis (2003), *An Essay on Classification* [1859] (Bristol: Thoemmes Press).

Alborn, Timothy (1999), 'Age and Empire in the Indian Census', *Journal of Interdisciplinary History*, 30(1): 61–89.

Allingham, Philip V. (2000), 'White Lies and Whited Sepulchres in Conrad's *Heart of Darkness*', *Victorian Web*, http://www.victorianweb.org/authors/conrad/pva52.html, accessed June 2006.

Altman, Lawrence K. (1987), *Who Goes First? The Story of Self-experimentation in Medicine* (New York: Random House).

Ambler, Charles (2011), 'African Studies: Engagement and Interdisciplinarity', *African Studies Review*, 54(1): 1–17.

Anderson, Warwick (2002), 'Review of *Climates and Constitutions: Health, Race, Environment and British Imperialism in India, 1600–1850* by Mark Harrison', *Journal of Political Ecology: Case Studies in History and Society*, 9, http://jpe.library.arizona.edu/volume_9/0602anderson.html (accessed 4 November 2013).

— (2006), *The Cultivation of Whiteness: Science, Health and Racial Destiny in Australia* (Durham, NC: Duke University Press).

Anonymous (1856), 'A Stir for Seacole', *Punch Magazine*, 31 (6 December): 221.

— (1857), 'Review of *Wonderful Adventures of Mrs. Seacole in Many Lands*', *Athenaeum Journal*, 25 July.

— (1864), 'Review of *Miscegenation, or the Theory of the Blending of Races, Applied to the American White Man and Negro*', *The Anthropological Review*, May.

— (1868a), 'Literary Notice: West African Countries and Peoples, &c., &c., and a Vindication of the African Race By James Africanus B. Horton, M.D.', *The African Times*, 23 July.

— (1868b), 'Review: *West African Countries and Peoples, &C.,&C., and a Vindication of the African Race* by James Africanus B. Horton, M.D.', *The African Times* 23 September.

— (1869), 'Review of *West African Countries and Peoples, British and Native*, by James Africanus Beale Horton', *The Anti-Slavery Reporter: Under the Sanction of the British and Foreign Anti-Slavery Society*, 1 January.

Arnold, David (1996), *Warm Climates and Western Medicine: The Emergence of Tropical Medicine, 1500–1900* (Amsterdam: Rodopi).

Arnold, David (ed.) (1988), *Imperial Medicine and Indigenous Societies: Disease, Medicine and Empire in the Nineteenth and Twentieth Centuries* (Manchester: Manchester University Press).

Barnes, Julian (2002), 'Introduction', in Alphonse Daudet, *In the Land of Pain* (London: Jonathan Cape).

Bashford, Alison (2004), *Imperial Hygiene: A Critical History of Colonialism, Nationalism and Public Health* (Basingstoke: Palgrave Macmillan).

Bashford, Alison, and Claire Hooker (2001), *Contagion: Historical and Cultural Studies* (London: Routledge).

Bernasconi, Robert, and Kristie Dotson (eds) (2005), *Race, Hybridity and Miscegenation* (New York and London: Continuum).

Bewell, Alan (1999), *Romanticism and Colonial Disease* (Baltimore and London: Johns Hopkins University Press).

Bhabha, Homi K. (1994), *The Location of Culture* (London and New York: Routledge, 2004).

Bickford-Smith, Vivian (2011), 'African Nationalist or British Loyalist? The Complicated Case of Tiyo Soga', *History Workshop Journal*, 71(1): 74–97.

Birkett, Dea (1992), *Mary Kingsley: Imperial Adventuress* (Basingstoke: Macmillan).

Blunt, Alison (1994), 'Mapping Authorship and Authority: Reading Mary Kingsley's Landscape Descriptions', in Alison Blunt and Gillian Rose (eds), *Writing Women and Space* (London: Guilford Press).

Blyden, Edward Wilmot (1901), 'The African Society and Miss Mary Kingsley' (London: J. Scott).

— (1903), 'Africa and the Africans. Proceedings on the Occasion of a Banquet, Given ... to Edward W. Blyden, LL.D., by West Africans in London' (London: C. M. Phillips).

Bock, Martin (2006), 'Joseph Conrad and Germ Theory: Why Captain Allistoun Smiles Thoughtfully', *The Conradian*, 31(2): 1–14.

Booth, William (1890), *In Darkest England and the Way Out* (London: International Headquarters of the Salvation Army).

Brantlinger, Patrick (1988), *Rule of Darkness: British Literature and Imperialism, 1830–1914* (Ithaca, NY: Cornell University Press).

— (2004), 'Victorians and Africans: The Genealogy of the Myth of the Dark Continent', in Gene M. Moore (ed.), *Joseph Conrad's Heart of Darkness: A Casebook* (Oxford: Oxford University Press).

Broca, Paul (1864), *On the Phenomenon of Hybridity in the Genus Homo* (London: Longman, Green, Longman & Roberts).

Brockway, Lucile H. (1979), *Science and Colonial Expansion: The Role of the British Royal Botanic Gardens* (London: Academic Press).

Burton, Sir Richard Francis (1857), *Personal Narrative of a Pilgrimage from El-Medina to Mecca: Down the 'Darb el Shark' on the Eastern Road (Hitherto Unvisited by Europeans) in September 1853; With a Narrative of a Trip to Harar* (London: Longman, Brown, Green, Longmans, and Roberts).

— (1860), *The Lake Regions of Central Africa* (London: Longman).

— (1863), *Wanderings in West Africa from Liverpool to Fernando Po.* 'By a F.R.G.S. With map and illustration' (London: Tinsley Bros.).

— (1901), *Wanderings in Three Continents ... Edited, with a preface, by W. H. Wilkins ... With a photogravure portrait and with illustrations by A. D. McCormick* (London: Hutchinson).

— (1991), *Goa, and the Blue Mountains, or, Six Months of Sick Leave* [1851], ed. Dane Kennedy (Berkeley: University of California Press).

Bynum, W. F. (2006), *The Western Medical Tradition: 1800 to 2000* (Cambridge: Cambridge University Press).

Caldwell, Janis McLarren (2004), *Literature and Medicine in Nineteenth-Century Britain: From Mary Shelley to George Eliot* (Cambridge: Cambridge University Press).

Carlson, Dennis G. (1984), *African Fever: A Study of British Science, Technology, and Politics in West Africa, 1787–1864* (Canton, MA: Science History Publications).

Chadwick, Edwin, and M. W. Flinn (1965), *Report on the Sanitary Condition of the Labouring Population of Great Britain* [1842] (Edinburgh: Edinburgh University Press).

Christensen, Allan Conrad (2005), *Nineteenth-century Narratives of Contagion: 'Our feverish contact'* (London and New York: Routledge).

Ciolkowski, Laura (1998), 'Travelers' Tales: Empire, Victorian Travel and the Spectacle of English Womanhood in Mary Kingsley's *Travels in West Africa*', *Victorian Literature and Culture*, 26(2): 337–66.

Clark, S. H. (ed.) (1999), *Travel Writing and Empire: Postcolonial Theory in Transit* (London and New York: Zed Books).

Conrad, Jessie (1926), *Joseph Conrad as I Knew Him. [With a portrait.]* (London: William Heinemann).

— (1935), *Joseph Conrad and his Circle* (Norwich: Jarrolds).

Conrad, Joseph (1977), 'An Outpost of Progress' [1897], in *Tales of Unrest* (Harmondsworth: Penguin).

— (1988), *Heart of Darkness* [1899], ed. Robert Kimbrough (New York: W. W. Norton).

Conrad, Joseph, and Zdzisław Najder (1978), *Congo Diary, and Other Uncollected Pieces* [1890] (Garden City, NY: Doubleday).

Corbin, Alain (1986), *The Foul and the Fragrant: Odor and the French Social Imagination* (Cambridge, MA: Harvard University Press).

Curtin, Philip D. (1989), *Death by Migration: Europe's Encounter with the Tropical World in the Nineteenth Century* (Cambridge: Cambridge University Press).

— (1998), *Disease and Empire: The Health of European Troops in the Conquest of Africa* (Cambridge: Cambridge University Press).

Dabydeen, D., and N. Wilson-Tagoe (1988). *A Reader's Guide to West Indian and Black British Literature* (London: Hansib).

Darwin, Charles (1981), *The Descent of Man and Selection in Relation to Sex* [1871] (Princeton: Princeton University Press).

Daudet, Alphonse (2002), *In the Land of Pain* [1930] (London: Jonathan Cape).

Davidson, Andrew, and David Macdonald Davidson (1893), *Hygiene & Diseases of Warm Climates*, edited [and with contributions] by A. Davidson, etc. (Edinburgh and London: Young J. Pentland).

Davidson, Roger (2001), 'Introduction', in Roger Davidson and Leslie A. Hall (eds), *Sex, Sin and Suffering: Venereal Disease and European Society since 1870* (London: Routledge).

Davidson, Roger, and Leslie A. Hall (eds) (2001), *Sex, Sin and Suffering: Venereal Disease and European Society since 1870* (London: Routledge).

Delesalle, Catherine (2000), '*Heart of Darkness* and *Under the Volcano*: The "Whited Sepulchre" and the "Churrigeresque Cathedral"', *L'epoque Conradienne* 26: 83–98.

DeLoughrey, Elizabeth M., and George B. Handley (2011), *Postcolonial Ecologies: Literatures of the Environment* (Oxford: Oxford University Press).

Dereli, C. (2003), *A War Culture in Action: A Study of the Literature of the Crimean War Period* (Oxford: Peter Lang).

Dickens, Charles (1853), *Bleak House* (London: Bradbury & Evans).

Drayton, Richard Harry (2000), *Nature's Government: Science, Imperial Britain, and the 'Improvement' of the World* (New Haven, CT: Yale University Press).

Driver, Felix (2005), 'Introduction', in Felix Driver and Luciana Martins (eds), *Tropical Visions in an Age of Empire* (Chicago: University of Chicago Press).

Early, Julie English (1997), 'The Spectacle of Science and Self: Mary Kingsley', in Barbara T. Gates and and Ann B. Shteir (eds), *Natural Eloquence: Women Reinscribe Science* (Madison and London: University of Wisconsin Press)

Edwards, Justin D., and Rune Graulund (2010), *Postcolonial Travel Writing: Critical Explorations* (Basingstoke: Palgrave Macmillan).

Ehrenreich, Barbara (2009), *Bright-sided: How the Relentless Promotion of Positive Thinking has Undermined America* (New York: Metropolitan Books).

Evans, Robert O. (1956), 'Conrad's Underworld', *Modern Fiction Studies*, 2: 56–92.

Fabian, Johannes (2000), *Out of Our Minds: Reason and Madness in the Exploration of Central Africa* (Berkeley: University of California Press).

Fanon, Franz (1967), *Black Skins, White Masks* (New York: Grove Press).

Farrall, Lyndsay Andrew (1985), *The Origins and Growth of the English Eugenics Movement: 1865–1925* (New York and London: Garland).

Farrar, F. W. (1864), 'On Hybridity', *Journal of the Anthropological Society of London*, 2: 222–9.

Feder, Lillian (1955), 'Marlow's Descent into Hell', *Nineteenth-Century Fiction*, 9(4): 280–92.

Fish, Cheryl J. (2004), *Black and White Women's Travel Narratives: Antebellum Explorations* (Gainesville: University Press of Florida).

Fitzgerald, Faith T. (1994), 'The Tyranny of Health', *New England Journal of Medicine*, 331(3): 196–8.

Flint, Kate (2012), 'Sensation', in Kate Flint (ed.), *The Cambridge History of Victorian Literature* (Cambridge: Cambridge University Press).

Fluhr, Nicole (2006), '"Their Calling Me Mother Was Not, I Think, Altogether Unmeaning": Mary Seacole's Maternal Personæ', *Victorian Literature and Culture*, 34: 95–113.

Ford, Henry A. (1856), *Observations on the Fevers of the Western Coast of Africa* (New York: Edward O. Jenkins).

Forster, E. M. (1996), *Abinger Harvest; and England's Pleasant Land* [1936], ed. Elizabeth Heine (London: André Deutsch).

Foucault, Michel (1973), *The Birth of the Clinic: An Archaeology of Medical Perception*, trans. A. M. Sheridan Smith (London: Tavistock Publications).

— (2004), *Society Must Be Defended: Lectures at the College de France, 1975–6*, trans. David Macey (Harmondsworth: Penguin).

Franey, Laura E. (2003), *Victorian Travel Writing and Imperial Violence: British Writing on Africa, 1855–1902* (Basingstoke: Palgrave Macmillan).

Frank, Arthur W. (1995), *The Wounded Storyteller: Body, Illness and Ethics* (Chicago: University of Chicago Press).

Frank, Katherine (1986), *A Voyager Out: The Life of Mary Kingsley* (London: Hamish Hamilton).

Freedgood, Elaine (2000), *Victorian Writing about Risk: Imagining a Safe England in a Dangerous World* (Cambridge: Cambridge University Press).

Fremont-Barnes, Gregory (2007), *The Indian Mutiny, 1857–58* (Oxford: Osprey).

Freud, Sigmund (1963), *Leonardo da Vinci and a Memory of his Childhood* [1910], trans. Alan Walker Tyson (Harmondsworth: Penguin).

Fyfe, Christopher (1972), *Africanus Horton, 1835–1883. West African Scientist and Patriot* (New York: Oxford University Press).

Garrison, Laurie (2011), *Science, Sexuality and Sensation Novels: Pleasures of the Senses* (Basingstoke: Palgrave Macmillan).

Gikandi, Simon (1996), *Maps of Englishness: Writing Identity in the Culture of Colonialism* (New York: Columbia University Press).

Gilbert, Pamela K. (2004), *Mapping the Victorian Social Body* (Albany, NY: State University of New York Press).

Glen, Heather (2002), *Charlotte Bronte: The Imagination in History* (Oxford: Oxford University Press).

Grant, Ben (2009), *Postcolonialism, Psychoanalysis and Burton: Power Play of Empire* (London: Routledge).

Griffith, John (1995), *Joseph Conrad and the Anthropological Dilemma: 'Bewildered Traveller'* (Oxford: Clarendon Press).

Guillemin, Jeanne (2001), 'Miasma, Malaria and Method', *Molecular Interventions*, 1: 246–9, http://molinterv.aspetjournals.org/cgi/content/full/1/5/246, accessed 1 December 2008.

Gunning, Sandra (2001), 'Traveling with Her Mother's Tastes: The Negotiation of Gender, Race, and Location in *Wonderful Adventures of Mrs. Seacole in Many Lands*', *Signs*, 26(4): 949–81.

Gwynn, Stephen (1932), *The Life of Mary Kingsley* (London: Macmillan).

Halliday, Stephen (2001), 'Looking back … Death and Miasma in Victorian

London: An Obstinate Belief', *BMJ*, 323: 1469–71, http://www.bmj.com/cgi/content/full/323/7327/1469#B4, accessed 1 December 2008.

Hampson, Robert (2002), '"An Outpost of Progress": The Case of Henry Price', in Attie De Lange and Gail Fincham (eds), *Conrad in Africa: New Essays on Heart of Darkness* (New York: Columbia University Press).

Hardt, Michael, and Antonio Negri (2000), *Empire* (Cambridge, MA: Harvard University Press).

Hardy, Thomas (1977), *The Mayor of Casterbridge* [1887] (New York: W. W. Norton).

Harris, Wilson (1960), *Palace of the Peacock* (London: Faber and Faber).

— (2003), 'An Autobiographical Essay', in Joyce Adler, *Exploring the Palace of the Peacock: Essays on Wilson Harris*, ed. Irving Adler (Kingston, Jamaica: University of the West Indies Press).

Harrison, Mark (1999), *Climates & Constitutions: Health, Race, Environment and British Imperialism in India, 1600–1850* (Oxford: Oxford University Press).

Haugh, Robert Fulton, and Joseph Conrad (1957), *Joseph Conrad: Discovery in Design* (Norman, OK: University of Oklahoma Press).

Hawkins, Anne Hunsaker (1993), *Reconstructing Illness: Studies in Pathography* (West Lafayette: Purdue University Press).

Haley, Bruce (1978), *The Healthy Body and Victorian Culture* (Cambridge, MA: Harvard University Press).

Holland, Jimmie C., and Sheldon Lewis (2000), *The Human Side of Cancer* (New York: HarperCollins).

Horne, Jackie (2004), 'Empire, Hysteria and the Healthy Girl: The Deployment of the Body in Juliana Horatio Ewing's *Six to Sixteen*', *Women's Studies*, 33(3): 249–77.

Horton, James Africanus Beale (1867), *Physical and Medical Climate, and Meteorology of the West Coast of Africa, etc.* (London: J. Churchill).

— (1868a), *Guinea Worm, or Dracunculus: its Symptoms and Progress . . . and Radical Cure* (London).

— (1868b), *West African Countries and Peoples, British and Native: and a Vindication of the African Race* (London: William John Johnson).

— (1874), *The Diseases of Tropical Climates and their Treatment. With Hints for the Preservation of Health in the Tropics* (London).

Hunt, James (1864), 'On the Negro's Place in Nature', *Journal of the Anthropological Society of London*, 2: xv–lvi.

Hunt, Shelley Leigh, and Alexander S. Kenny (1883), *Tropical Trials. A Handbook for Women in the Tropics* (London: W. H. Allen).

Hutchinson, Thomas J. (1970), *Impressions of Western Africa. With Remarks on the Diseases of the Climate and a Report on the Peculiarities of Trade up the Rivers in the Bight of Biafra* [1858] (London: Frank Cass).

Innes, C. L. (2008), *A History of Black and Asian Writing in Britain, 1700–2000* (2nd edn; Cambridge: Cambridge University Press).

Irele, Abiola (1991), 'African Letters: The Making of a Tradition', *The Yale Journal of Criticism*, 5(1): 69–100.

Jackson, John P., and Nadine M. Weidman (2006), *Race, Racism and Science: Social Impact and Interaction* (London: Rutgers University Press).

John Holt & Co. (1962), *The Early Years of an African Trader: Being an*

Account of John Holt who Sailed for West Africa on 23rd June 1862 (London: Newman Neame).

Johnson, Patrick E. (2005), 'Passing and the Problematic of Multiracial Pride (or, why one mixed girl still answers to Black)', in Harry J. Elam Jr and Kennell Jackson (eds), *Black Cultural Traffic: Crossroads in Global Performance and Popular Culture* (Ann Arbor: University of Michigan Press).

Judd, Catherine (1998), *Bedside Seductions: Nursing and the Victorian Imagination, 1830–1880* (New York: St Martin's Press).

Keller, Ulrich (2001), *The Ultimate Spectacle: A Visual History of the Crimean War* (Amsterdam: Gordon and Breach).

Kennedy, Dane (1990), 'The Perils of the Midday Sun: Climatic Anxieties in the Colonial Tropics', in John M. MacKenzie (ed.), *Imperialism and the Natural World* (Manchester: Manchester University Press).

— (1991), 'Introduction', in Richard Burton, *Goa and the Blue Mountains* (Berkeley: University of California Press).

— (1996), *The Magic Mountains: Hill Stations and the British Raj* (Berkeley: University of California Press).

— (2005), *The Highly Civilized Man: Richard Burton and the Victorian World* (Cambridge, MA: Harvard University Press).

Kenny, Judith T. (1997), 'Claiming the High Ground: Theories of Imperial Authority and the British Hill Stations of India', *Political Geography*, 16: 655–74.

Khair, Tabish (2006), *Other Routes: 1500 Years of African and Asian Travel Writing* (Oxford: Signal).

Killingray, David (2003), '*Mrs. Seacole's Wonderful Adventures in Many Lands* and the Consciousness of Transit', in Gretchen Holbrook Gerzina (ed.), *Black Victorians/Black Victoriana* (New Brunswick, NJ: Rutgers University Press).

Kimble, David (1963), *A Political History of Ghana: The Rise of Gold Coast Nationalism, 1850–1928* (Oxford: Clarendon Press).

Kinglake, Alexander William (1888), *The Invasion of the Crimea: its origin, and an account of its progress down to the death of Lord Raglan* (New York: Harper & Brothers).

Kingsley, Charles (1857), *Two Years Ago . . . Second edition* (Cambridge: Macmillan).

— (1880), *Sanitary and Social Lectures and Essays* (London: Macmillan).

Kingsley, Mary Henrietta (1897a), *Travels in West Africa, Congo Francais, Corisco and Cameroons* (London: Macmillan).

— (1897b), 'West Africa, from an Ethnologist's Point of View', *Transactions from the Liverpool Geographical Society* (Liverpool: Egerton Smith): 58–73.

Knowles, Owen, and Gene M. Moore (2000), *The Oxford Reader's Companion to Conrad* (Oxford: Oxford University Press).

Krebs, Paula M. (1999), *Gender, Race and the Writing of Empire: Public Discourse and the Boer War* (Cambridge: Cambridge University Press).

Lane, Christopher (2003), 'Fantasies of Lady Pioneers: Between Narrative and Theory', in Philip Holden et al. (eds), *Imperial Desire: Dissident Sexualities and Colonial Literature* (Minneapolis: University of Minnesota Press).

Lane, Joan (2001), *A Social History of Medicine: Health, Healing and Disease in England, 1750–1950* (London: Routledge).

Law, Jules (2003), 'Cultural Ecologies of the Coast: Space as the Edge of Cultural Practice in Mary Kingsley's Travels in West Africa', in Helena Mitchie and Ronald R. Thomas (eds), *Nineteenth-Century Geographies: The Transformation of Space from the Victorian Age to the American Century* (New Brunswick, NJ: Rutgers University Press).

Lindsay, Claire (2003), 'Wish You Weren't Here: The Politics of Travel in Albalucía Ángel's *¡Oh gloria inmarcesible!*', *Studies in Travel Writing*, 7(1): 83–98.

Livingstone, David N. (1994), 'Climate's Moral Economy: Science, Race and Place in Post-Darwinian British and American Geography', in Anne Godlewska and Neil Smith (eds), *Geography and Empire* (Oxford: Blackwell).

Livingstone, W. P. (1923), *Mary Slessor of Calabar: Pioneer Missionary* (London: Hodder & Stoughton).

Logan, Peter Melville (1997), *Nerves and Narratives: A Cultural History of Hysteria in Nineteenth-century British Prose* (Berkeley: University of California Press).

Lombroso, Cesare (1891), *The Man of Genius* (New York: C. Scribner's Sons).

— (1911), *Criminal Man* (New York: G. P. Putnam's Sons).

Lorde, Audre (1980), *The Cancer Journals* (Argyle, NY: Spinsters, Ink).

Lovell, Mary S. (1998), *A Rage to Live: A Biography of Richard and Isabel Burton* (New York: W. W. Norton).

Macleod, Roy (1988), *Introduction to Disease, Medicine, and Empire: Perspectives on Western Medicine and the Experience of European Expansion* (London: Routledge).

Martin, Sir James Ranald (1861), *Influence of Tropical Climates in Producing the Acute Endemic Diseases of Europeans on their Return from Tropical Climates* (London: John Churchill).

Matus, Jill L. (2009), *Shock, Memory and the Unconscious in Victorian Fiction* (Cambridge: Cambridge University Press).

Maugham, W. S. (1912), *The Explorer. A Melodrama in Four Acts* (London: William Heinemann).

— (1991), *The Explorer* [1908] (New York: Carroll and Graf).

McIntyre, W. David (1967), *The Imperial Frontier in the Tropics, 1865–75* (London: Macmillan).

McLaughlan, Robbie (2012), *Re-imagining the 'Dark Continent' in Fin de Siècle Literature* (Edinburgh: Edinburgh University Press).

Miller, J. Hillis (2002), 'Should We Read *Heart of Darkness?*', in Attie De Lange and Gail Fincham (eds), *Conrad in Africa: New Essays on Heart of Darkness* (New York: Columbia University Press).

Moore, Gene M. (2004), 'Introduction', in Gene M. Moore (ed.), *Joseph Conrad's Heart of Darkness: A Casebook* (Oxford: Oxford University Press).

Moore-Gilbert, B. J. (2009), *Postcolonial Life-writing: Culture, Politics and Self-representation* (London: Routledge).

Musgrove, Brian (1999), 'Travel and Unsettlement: Freud on Vacation', in S. H. Clark (ed.), *Travel Writing and Empire: Postcolonial Theory in Transit* (London and New York: Zed Books).

Najder, Zdzisław (2004), 'To the End of the Night', in Gene M. Moore (ed.), *Joseph Conrad's Heart of Darkness: A Casebook* (Oxford: Oxford University Press).

Nerlich, Michael (1987), *Ideology of Adventure: Studies in Modern Consciousness, 1100–1750*, trans. Ruth Crowley (Minneapolis: University of Minnesota Press).

Nicol, Davidson (ed.) (1969), 'Introduction' to *Africanus Horton: The Dawn of Nationalism in Modern Africa: Extracts from the Political, Educational, Scientific and Medical Writings of J.A.B. Horton, Chosen, 1835–1883* (Harlow: Longman).

Nightingale, Florence (1997), *Letters from the Crimea, 1854–1856*, ed. Sue M. Goldie (New York: Mandolin).

Nott, Josiah C. (1854), *Types of Mankind; or, Ethnological Researches, Based Upon . . .* (Philadelphia: Lippincott, Grambo).

O'Callaghan, Evelyn (2004), *Women Writing the West Indies, 1804–1939: 'A hot place, belonging to us'* (London: Routledge).

Paravisini Gebert, Lizabeth (2011), 'Deforestation and the Yearning for Lost Landscapes in Caribbean Literatures', in Elizabeth DeLoughrey and George B. Handley (eds), *Postcolonial Ecologies: Literatures of the Environment* (New York and Oxford: Oxford University Press).

Paris, Bernard J. (2006), *Conrad's Charlie Marlow: A New Approach to Heart of Darkness and Lord Jim* (New York: Palgrave Macmillan).

Parke, Thomas Heale, and Henry M. Stanley (1893), *Guide to Health in Africa, with Notes on the Country and its Inhabitants* (London: S. Low).

Parry, Benita (2005), 'The Moment and After-Life of *Heart of Darkness*', in Carola Kaplan, Peter Mallios and Andrea White (eds), *Conrad in the Twenty-First Century* (London: Routledge).

Pearce, Lynne (2004), 'Tribute to a Visionary: Interview with Elizabeth Anionwu', *Nursing Standard*, 19(4): 16–17.

Pelling, Margaret (1978), *Cholera, Fever and English Medicine, 1825–1865* (Oxford: Oxford University Press).

Persyn, Mary Kelly (2002), 'The Sublime Turn Away from Empire: Wordsworth's Encounter with Colonial Slavery, 1802', *Romanticism on the Net*, 26, http://www.erudit.org/revue/ron/2002/v/n26/005700ar.html, accessed 7 July 2013

Phillips, Anne (1989), *The Enigma of Colonialism: British Policy in West Africa* (London: James Currey).

Picardie, Ruth (1998), *Before I Say Goodbye: Recollections and Observations from One Woman's Final Year* (New York: Owl Books).

Pollack, Donald (2000), 'Physician Autobiography: Narrative and the Social History of Medicine', in Cheryl Mattingly and Linda C. Garro (eds), *Narrative and the Cultural Construction of Illness and Healing* (Berkeley: University of California Press).

Pratt, Mary Louise (1992), *Imperial Eyes: Travel Writing and Transculturation* (London: Routledge).

Prichard, James Cowles (1843), *The Natural History of Man* (Paris: H. Baillière).

— (1855), *The Natural History of Man: Comprising Inquiries into the Modifying Influence of Physical and Moral Agencies on the Different Tribes of the Human Family* (London: H. Baillière).

Reade, Winwood (1863), *Savage Africa; Being the Narrative of a Tour in Equatorial, Southwestern and Northwestern Africa* . . . (New York: Harper and Brothers).

— (1873), *The African Sketch-book*, 2 vols (London: Smith, Elder).

Ribot, Theodule (1896), *The Diseases of the Will* (Chicago: Open Court).

Robinson, Amy (1994), 'Authority and the Public Display of Identity: *Wonderful Adventures of Mrs. Seacole in Many Lands*', *Feminist Studies* 20(3): 537–57.

Robinson, Jane (2005), *Mary Seacole: The Charismatic Black Nurse Who Became a Heroine of the Crimea* (London: Constable).

Ross, Sir Ronald (1902), *Mosquito Brigades, and How to Organise Them* (London: George Philip & Son).

Royle, Trevor (1999), *Crimea: the Great Crimean War, 1854–1856* (London: Little, Brown).

Said, Edward (1978), *Orientalism* (New York: Pantheon Books).

— (1993), *Culture and Imperialism* (New York: Alfred A. Knopf).

Schama, Simon (2000), *A History of Britain*, III: *1776–2000: The Fate of Empire* (New York: Hyperion).

Seacole, Mary (1857), *Wonderful Adventures of Mrs Seacole in Many Lands* (Oxford: Oxford University Press).

Shepperson, George (1969), 'Introduction', in James Africanus Beale Horton, *West African Countries and Peoples* (Edinburgh: Edinburgh University Press).

Sims, George Robert (1883), *How the Poor Live* (London: Chatto & Windus).

Snaith, Anna (2014), *Modernist Voyages: Colonial Women Writers in London, 1890–1945* (Cambridge: Cambridge University Press)

Sontag, Susan (1979), *Illness as Metaphor* (London: Allen Lane).

Spillman, Deborah Shapple (2012), *British Colonial Realism in Africa: Inalienable Objects, Contested Domains* (New York: Palgrave Macmillan).

Spitzer, Leo (1975), *The Creoles of Sierra Leone: Responses to Colonialism, 1870–1945* (Ile-Ife: University of Ife Press).

Spurr, David (1993), *The Rhetoric of Empire: Colonial Discourse in Journalism, Travel Writing, and Imperial Administration* (Durham, NC: Duke University Press).

Stanley, Henry M. (1878), *Through the Dark Continent; or, The Sources of the Nile Around the Great Lakes of Equatorial Africa and Down the Livingstone River to the Atlantic Ocean* (London: Sampson Low, Marston, Searle & Rivington).

— (1909), *The Autobiography of Sir Henry Morton Stanley* . . . *Edited by his wife, Dorothy Stanley* [with sixteen photogravures and a map] (London: Sampson Low).

Stepan, Nancy Leys (2001), *Picturing Tropical Nature* (Ithaca, NY: Cornell University Press).

Stevens, Ray (2002), 'Three Voices of Conrad's Narrative Journey', in Attie De Lange and Gail Fincham (eds), *Conrad in Africa: New Essays on Heart of Darkness* (New York: Columbia University Press).

Stevenson, Robert L. (2006), *The Strange Case of Dr. Jekyll and Mr. Hyde* [1886], ed. Roger Luckhurst (Oxford: Oxford University Press).

Stewart, Garrett (1980), 'Lying as Dying in *Heart of Darkness*', *PMLA*, 95(3): 319–31.

Stoker, Bram (1897), *Dracula* (Westminster: A. Constable).

Thiesmeyer, Lynn (1994), 'Imperial Fictions and Nonfictions: The Subversion of Sources in Mary Kingsley and Joseph Conrad', in Nikki Lee Manos and Meri-Jane Rochelson (eds), *Transforming Genres: New Approaches to British Fiction of the 1890s* (New York: St Martin's Press), 155–72.

Thompson, Carl (2011), *Travel Writing* (London: Routledge).

Tobin, Beth Fowkes (2005), *Colonizing Nature: The Tropics in British Arts and Letters, 1760–1820* (Philadelphia: University of Pennsylvania Press).

Turner, Lynette (2000), 'Mary Kingsley: The Female Ethnographic Self in Writing', in Alison Donnell and Pauline Polkey (eds), *Representing Lives* (London: Palgrave Macmillan).

Tutein, David W. (1990), *Joseph Conrad's Reading: An Annotated Bibliography* (West Cornwall, CT: Locust Hill Press).

Van Wyhe, John (2004), *Phrenology and the Origins of Victorian Scientific Naturalism* (Aldershot: Ashgate).

Vrettos, Athena (1995), *Somatic Fictions: Imagining Illness in Victorian Culture* (Stanford: Stanford University Press).

wa Thiong'o, Ngũgĩ (2000), 'Europhonism, Universities, and the Magic Fountain: The Future of African Literature and Scholarship', *Research in African Literatures*, 31(1): 1–11.

Walkowitz, Judith R. (1992), *City of Dreadful Delight: Narratives of Sexual Danger in Late Victorian London* (London: Virago).

Ward, Candace (2007), *Desire and Disorder: Fevers, Fictions, and Feeling in English Georgian Culture* (Lewisburg, PA: Bucknell University Press).

Watt, Ian P. (1979), *Conrad in the Nineteenth Century* (Berkeley: University of California Press).

Weisse, Allen B. (2012), 'Self-Experimentation and Its Role in Medical Research', *Texas Heart Institute Journal*, 39(1): 51–4.

Wellesley, Arthur, Duke of Wellington (1973), 'Some Observations of the War in the Crimea' [1855], in *The Crimean War: Pro and Con* (New York and London: Garland Publishing).

Wellesley, Dorothy Violet Ashton, Duchess of Wellington (1977), *Sir George Goldie: Founder of Nigeria* [1934] (New York: Arno).

Wood, Jane (2001), *Passion and Pathology in Victorian Fiction* (Oxford: Oxford University Press).

Woodruff, Charles Edward, and E. W. Ulmann (1905), *The Effects of Tropical Light on White Men* (New York and London: Rebman).

Worboys, Michael (2000), *Spreading Germs: Disease Theories and Medical Practice in Britain, 1865–1900* (Cambridge: Cambridge University Press).

Young, Robert (1995), *Colonial Desire: Hybridity in Theory, Culture, and Race* (London: Routledge).

Index